# Ability
# Equity
# &
# Culture

## Sustaining Inclusive
## Urban Education Reform

*Edited by*

Elizabeth B. Kozleski
Kathleen King Thorius

Teachers College, Columbia University
New York and London

Published by Teachers College Press, 1234 Amsterdam Avenue, New York, NY 10027

*Library of Congress Cataloging-in-Publication Data*

Ability, equity, and culture : sustaining inclusive urban education reform / edited by Elizabeth B. Kozleski, Kathleen King Thorius.
  pages cm
  Includes bibliographical references and index.
  ISBN 978-0-8077-5492-4 (pbk.)—ISBN 978-0-8077-5493-1 (hardcover)—
  ISBN 978-0-8077-7246-1 (ebook)
  1. Inclusive education—United States. 2. Education, Urban—United States.
  3. Educational change—United States.  I. Kozleski, Elizabeth B.
  LC1201.A35 2013
  371.9'046—dc23
                                                                    2013034785

ISBN 978-0-8077-5492-4 (paper)
ISBN 978-0-8077-5493-1 (hardcover)
eISBN 978-0-8077-7246-1 (ebook)

Printed on acid-free paper
Manufactured in the United States of America

21  20  19  18  17  16  15  14          8  7  6  5  4  3  2  1

## DISABILITY, CULTURE, AND EQUITY SERIES

Alfredo J. Artiles and Elizabeth B. Kozleski, *Series Editors*

Ability, Equity, and Culture:
Sustaining Inclusive Urban Education Reform
Elizabeth B. Kozleski & Kathleen King Thorius, Eds.

Condition Critical—Key Principles for Equitable and Inclusive Education
Diana Lawrence-Brown & Mara Sapon-Shevin

# Contents

# Acknowledgments

To the students, teachers, and administrators who live their everyday lives in the urban schools that taught us so much about how things are, and helped us understand what is needed to create learning spaces for us all.

The National Institute for Urban School Improvement (NIUSI) had quite a band of zealots who imagined, shared, labored, and deeply cared about our work. None of what we created was possible without their commitment and dedication. We were truly fortunate to have Anne Smith, our project officer, who inspired us all to persist and sustain over 12 amazing years.

# Part I

# EXAMINING A THEORY AND FRAMEWORK FOR SYSTEMIC CHANGE

# Introduction

*Elizabeth B. Kozleski and Kathleen King Thorius*

We wrote this book for educational practitioners and change agents looking to develop their understanding of crucial areas of policy and praxis to support and expand the spread of inclusive urban education reform. Informed by cultural historical analysis, the volume shares a set of lessons learned through the work of a set of urban researchers, activists, and advocates who have been collaborating on inclusive urban school reform for more than 12 years under the aegis of the National Institute for Urban School Improvement (NIUSI). The NIUSI partnerships succeeded in forging a set of initiatives that improved some outcomes for the 13 million students in the 100 largest school systems in the United States that, at the time of the project, comprised a third of all U.S public school students. Linked or woven together by a common conceptual framework, mediated by ongoing, robust professional networks that were supported by federal funding, the experiences chronicled in this book describe how a coherent conceptualization of iterative change and a shared understanding of equity and inclusivity can move across systems from the macro to the micro while being influenced by local context.

Particularly in urban schools, where students experience marginalization in connection with racial, gender, sexual orientation, and language identities as well as ability, viable, sustainable, inclusive education reform requires an excavation of the legacies of racism, classism, and ableism that are manifested in troubling outcomes such as the overrepresentation of students of color in special education, segregated educational placements, and soaring dropout rates. While the inclusive education movement has been concerned with the access and meaningful participation in general education for students with disabilities, it has rarely critically examined and addressed the systemic barriers that exist in schools for other groups (Ferguson, Kozleski, & Smith, 2003; Kozleski, Artiles, & Lacy, 2012; Kozleski, Gibson, & Hynds, 2012). The historic underpinnings of inclusive education, particularly in the United States, have emerged from a majority White population of families and advocates who have been silent and, to some extent, color silent, as they have advanced the agenda of inclusion for children (Artiles, 2003; Smith, 2001). While this sensibility has certainly been shifting in the last few years, definitions of inclusive education have varied (Ferri & Connor, 2005). Because the authors in this book are particularly focused on inclusive education in urban settings, we offer this definition of *inclusive education* that is found in social justice theories (e.g., Fraser, 2007) to anchor our work:

> Inclusive education is a continuous struggle toward (a) the redistribution of quality opportunities to learn and participate in educational programs, (b) the recognition and value of differences as reflected in content, pedagogy, and assessment tools, and (c) the opportunities for marginalized groups to represent themselves in decision-making processes that advance and define claims of exclusion and the respective solutions that affect their children's educational futures. This notion of inclusive education as a continuous struggle reflects the notion that we exist in dynamic contexts. The margins and centers of our work are in continuous flow producing new margins and centers. (Waitoller & Kozleski, 2013, p. 35)

This book represents the work of a national team of reformers who worked over time to hone a shared understanding of their mission while balancing the demands of local and state mandates. By organizing our stories through a systemic change framework, we argue that the tensions inherent in the scale, scope, and significance of each narrative yield important and convincing evidence that systemic, thoughtful, and organic are not mutually exclusive characteristics. Rather, they are necessary to find the traction for reform that is bold enough to address the cultural contexts in which power, history, and tradition often prevail over innovation and social transformation. The journey is vital and the outcomes offer much to learn from and expand upon.

NIUSI's Systemic Change Framework (SCF) describes what reform work must look like at each systemic level (e.g., embedded district and school activity systems) of an integrated reform effort as well as the conditions and considerations necessary to organize systems around the capacity to change within and across these levels of people, policy, practice, and research (Ferguson, Kozleski, & Smith, 2003; Kozleski & Smith, 2009). The framework organizes the work of practitioners into a unified system of teaching and learning. In this framework, students are at the center of a system in which the learning contexts are organized in ways that engage students at the margins as well as those in mainstream. There are five activity systems within the framework, from classrooms (where teachers and students work together to produce learning) to the federal government that together comprise a larger educational activity system that places learning for students, practitioners, and organizations at the core of all reform efforts.

## STUDENTS

Students are at the heart of schooling. The interplay between their psychological characteristics and their cultural histories serves as the lens through which students view and interact with the world (Cole, 1996). Students expand and constrain effort as they seek to make meaning of schooling experiences. They act, from a sociocultural activity perspective, not as individual agents, but in reciprocal interaction with their fellow students and teachers, forming and reforming understanding based on the effects of their own actions and those of others. The tasks they attend to, the questions they ask, and the discourse patterns they engage are connected to the available cultural histories and practices. Further, culture mediates the ways that students understand and interpret the expectations and processes in school, the language used to make meaning (theirs, their peers', their teachers', and what is embedded in the learning materials), and the connections they and their peers have to the content and tasks. This description recognizes the dynamic nature of learning as a cultural practice that is inhibited and accelerated by individual and institutional interactions. Where students feel valued and supported, their effort expands. Conversely, where poor instruction, inadequate resources, marginalization, and lack of cultural responsiveness abound, student effort diminishes. The core of the framework represents this understanding of student learning and student effort. Chapter 3, by Kozleski and Artiles, explores these concepts in detail. In order to place equity at the center of our concerns for students' opportunities to learn and their academic outcomes, we must connect the everyday experiences of students in the educational system to their opportunities to participate within it (González, Moll, & Amanti, 2005).

In Chapter 2 Zion and Petty explore the essential element of student voice in the reform efforts of an urban district. Many of the students in urban schools, already marginalized by the unequal power distribution between teacher and student, hold memberships in multiple groups that have long histories of marginalization in the context of schooling (e.g., identified as disabled, racial minority, low income). These students are affected daily by educational decisions made by adults inside and outside of school, but their voices often go unheard in the debates about schooling and school reform. The early 2000s brought a resurgence of research on "student voice," but unlike earlier inquiry, situated it as a process of students and teachers codeveloping a frame for student participation in school reform to improve their educational outcomes, while increasing their ownership in the reform process by relying on them to define problems to be addressed by school change efforts. This chapter utilizes data gleaned from a 1-year ethnographic study of ways in which student voices were accessed and heard in school change, and presents a continuum of practices to engage youth in educational reform efforts within school systems based on the assertion that such efforts can be strengthened by deepening educators' and reformers' awareness of the multiple ways that authentic youth voice and engagement can be achieved. With this information, Zion and Petty provide educators with a framework that is a critique and improvement of school systems' efforts to respect and support students' opportunities to learn within them.

## PRACTITIONERS

The next layer of the SCF consists of professional elements that affect student effort and learning. How learning environments are established and maintained rests on the skills and creativity of teachers and other educators such as counselors, paraeducators, school psychologists, and specialized teachers for literacy, special education, and related service providers. These efforts include: learning standards, teaching design and practices, family participation in teaching and learning, group practice, and learning assessment. Chapter 4, by Santamaría Graff and Vazquez, explores the ways in which families understand and interact with teachers and schools.

In Chapter 5, Gonzalez and Mulligan explore one of a teacher's most fundamental responsibilities: designing a classroom context where all students are able to engage in deep learning. While all teachers create classroom communities in some manner, those who have shifted their desired goal from a teacher-centered classroom to a student-centered one demonstrate commitment to creating classroom communities that are inclusive. That is, all students, regardless of the categories of social groups to which they belong, and other categorical ways of being sorted (e.g., dis/ability[1]), are ensured access to and participation in learning and development.

Chapter 5 provides a discussion of the multiple forms of culture that converge in classrooms, which provide the contexts for teachers to create inclusive learning environments where all students have access to, participation in, and success with the curriculum and interactions within them. In order to consciously build a classroom culture that is inclusive and supportive for all of its students, it is important to consider how culture both constrains and affords opportunities to learn within every classroom. These forms of culture include *cultures in the classroom*, which are the cultural practices and values that students and teachers bring with them, *the classroom culture*, or the ingrained practices of the educational system and school building, and *classroom cultures*, the work and activity that students and teachers do together (Artiles & Kozleski, 2007). This chapter relies on these notions to illustrate one teacher's shift from a teacher-centered to a student-centered approach to teaching, and as a result, the creation of an inclusive classroom.

## SCHOOLS

It is within the school activity system that cultural structures and processes are established to frame and support the work of educators and students. Two chapters in this book are situated within school activity systems: one about the ways particular professional learning opportunities may be designed so that educators' learning is grounded in their own unique school and community contexts and one about the role of leadership in school-level reform efforts. Chapter 6, by Thorius and Scribner, emphasizes that teacher learning in urban schools is a critical variable in reform for equity and, in turn, equitable student achievement. The authors illustrate how and why educators must reflect on their practice not only from a technical perspective but also from a contextual and critical perspective that seeks to understand the nature of the learner from his or her potential, cultural/historical background, cognitive and socioemotional development, and the nature of the local school context and curriculum in which the student is expected to perform (Apple, 2000; Freire, 1970; McLaren & Farahmanpur, 2000).

In Chapter 7 Garrison-Wade, Gonzales, and Alexander explore the role of the urban principal in leading school-level reform. They examine what it means to prepare a school community to understand and appreciate all students, especially when most educators have very different backgrounds and experiences from their students. It is the responsibility of the principal to equip teachers with the necessary tools to develop their understanding and demonstrate their appreciation for students who are unfamiliar to them, yet principals themselves are cultural beings whose positionality (Taylor, Tisdell, & Hanley, 2000) and intersectionality (Crenshaw, 1991) shape their priorities and leadership for school reform. This chapter tells the stories of two different principals working to disrupt educational practices that became crystallized over time and no longer support the learning and development of the changing student body in their respective schools, as well as the deficit-grounded assumptions about students and families who are culturally and linguistically diverse that are used as excuses for why school reform will not work. The principals' own educational and cultural experiences and memberships serve as resources as they challenge teachers to move beyond these practices and beliefs, but also serve as sources of tension for these principals of color as they lead reform in schools where the majority of the teaching core is comprised of White teachers with normative assumptions about teaching, learning, and the purpose of schooling.

## DISTRICTS

The next level identifies the systemic reform elements at the district level. Specifically, school systems must work to close achievement gaps, improve access of minority groups to gifted and accelerated learning opportunities, reduce minority students' disproportionate representation in special education and discipline referrals, restructure and improve schools, and increase the equity effectiveness of education programs. This work is overseen by school boards who play a critical role in shaping local organizational missions and experiences. In Chapter 8 Sullivan, Abplanalp, and Jorgensen describe the work of the Madison Wisconsin Metropolitan School district over a 12-year period, which resulted in successfully restructuring a categorical, label-driven program model into one that today is nationally recognized as highly inclusive and collaborative. Concurrently, a major change effort was also occurring at one of the district's elementary schools, as an inclusive model of education was implemented in part to assure that all students were proficient at reading by 3rd grade. By illustrating the relationships across and between the district and school levels of an educational system, the authors illustrate not only the efforts engaged in at each, but also the strategies for making sure that reform efforts are distributed across them.

## STATE AND FEDERAL LEVELS

State law, regulation, and technical assistance shape the work of school systems as do the education policies of the U.S. Department of Education and the Department of Justice. These equity agendas are at the forefront of many current national and state reforms, though the definition of equity that underlies these policies may not account for all the complexities of local context (Skrla, Scheurich, Garcia, & Nolly, 2004). At the same time, school systems must have mechanisms in place to review and improve both formal policies and local practices that reproduce inequitable educational opportunities for some students in relation to weaknesses in teacher preparation and professional development. In Chapter 9 Garcia and Hart-Tervalon describe a statewide initiative to address the disproportionality of students of color in special education and, more broadly, illustrate how states can engage their local educational agencies in confronting educational equity issues.

Finally, Kozleski and Thorius's culminating Chapter 10 offers a window into making policy sticky. That is, policy can be theorized, created, and enforced, but without connecting it to people's practice and lives, it can also be rejected, worked around, subverted, and ignored. Resistance to policy is best exemplified by the ways in which No Child Left Behind (NCLB) was modified and changed at the state and local level. This chapter explores ways in which policy can emerge from a more developmental, reciprocal, and contextual process designed to create dimensionality in the ways in which policy is designed, launched, and explored.

Other key features of the SCF are the arenas of policy, practice, and research that must be engaged across each embedded activity system (e.g., district, school, classroom) of the educational system at large.

For example, across all the five activity systems, reform efforts must focus on the connections and partnerships between and across them, as well as commit to explicit inquiry on equity in schooling. On the one hand, reform includes districts' efforts to build and sustain connections and partnerships with the communities they serve, while practitioners are responsible for connecting with students and their families. On the other hand, there is a need for reform driven through identification of data to be collected and analyzed within inquiry on equity in schooling, and the development of strategies to address inequities that emerge as people, policies, practices and research converge, collide, and engage the messy everyday work of teaching and learning.

## NOTE

1. We use the term *dis/ability* or *dis/abilities* throughout this text to signal the notion that disability and ability differences are social constructions.

## REFERENCES

Apple, M. (2000). Comparing neo-liberal projects and inequity in education. *Comparative Education, 37,* 409–423.

Artiles, A. J. (2003). Special education's changing identity: Paradoxes and dilemmas in views of culture and space. *Harvard Educational Review, 73,* 164–202.

Artiles, A. J., & Kozleski, E. B. (2007). Beyond convictions: Interrogating culture, history, and power in inclusive education. *Language Arts, 84,* 357–364.

Cole, M. (1996). *Cultural psychology: A once and future discipline.* Cambridge, MA: Harvard University Press.

Crenshaw, K. W. (1991). Mapping the margins: Intersectionality, identity politics, and violence against women. *Stanford Law Review, 43*(6), 1241–1279.

Ferguson, D. L., Kozleski, E. B., & Smith, A. (2003). Transforming general and special education in urban schools. In F. Obiakor, C. Utley, & A. Rotatori (Eds.), *Advances in Special Education: Vol. 15. Effective education for learners with exceptionalities* (pp. 43–74). London, United Kingdom: JAI Press.

Ferri, B. A., & Connor, D. (2005). In the shadow of *Brown:* Special education and overrepresentation of students of color. *Remedial and Special Education, 26*(2), 93–100.

Fraser, N. (2007). Re-framing justice in a globalizing world. In T. Lovell (Ed.), *(Mis) recognition, social inequality, and social justice* (pp. 17–35). London, United Kingdom: Routledge.

Freire, P. (1970). *Pedagogy of the oppressed.* New York, NY: Seabury.

González, N , Moll, L., & Amanti, C. (2005). Introduction: Theorizing practices. In N. González, L. Moll, & C. Amati (Eds.), *Funds of knowledge: Theorizing practices in households, communities, and classrooms* (pp. 1–29). New York, NY: Routledge.

Kozleski, E. B., Artiles, A. J., & Lacy, L (2012). The dangerous politics of difference: How systems produce marginalization. In L. C. Burrello, W. Sailor, & J. Kleinhammer-Tramill (Eds.), *Unifying educational systems: Policy and leadership.* New York, NY: Routledge.

Kozleski, E. B., Gibson, D., & Hynds, A. (2012). Transforming complex educational systems: Grounding systems issues in equity and social justice. In C. Gersti-Pepin & J. Aiken (Eds.), *Defining social justice leadership in a global context* (pp. 263–286). Charlotte, NC: Information Age.

Kozleski, E. B., & Smith, A. (2009). The role of policy and systems change in creating equity for students with disabilities in urban schools. *Urban Education, 44,* 427–451.

McLaren, P., & Farahmandpur, R. (2000). Reconsidering Marx in post-Marxist times: A requiem for postmodernism? *Educational Researcher, 29,* 25–33.

Skrla, L., Scheurich, J. J., Garcia, J., & Nolly, G. (2004). Equity audits: A practical leadership tool for developing equitable and excellent schools. *Education Administration Quarterly, 40,* 133–161.

Smith, A. (2001). A faceless bureaucrat ponders special education, disability, and White privilege. *Research and Practice for Persons with Severe Disabilities, 26,* 180–188.

Taylor, E., Tisdell, E., & Hanley, M. S. (2000). *The role of positionality in teaching for critical consciousness: Implications for adult education.* Paper presented at the Adult Education Research Conference, Vancouver, Canada.

Waitoller, F., & Kozleski, E. B. (2013). Understanding and dismantling barriers for partnerships for inclusive education: A cultural historical activity theory perspective. *International Journal of Whole Schooling, 9*(1), 23–42.

# CHAPTER 1

# Theorizing Systemic Reform in Urban Schools

*Elizabeth B. Kozleski,*
*Kathleen King Thorius, and Anne Smith*

Despite more than 30 years of reform efforts, urban education systems and the schools they serve continue to struggle to provide diverse learners robust opportunities to learn (Kozleski & Smith, 2009). A number of indices continue to show grim outcomes for students, particularly students whose first languages are not English and students of color. For instance, participation in advanced placement courses, school completion rates, postgraduation education, and employment rates are lower for African Americans, Latinos, American Indians, English language learners (ELL), and students identified with disabilities than they are for students who identify as White and Asian American (Blanchett, 2006; Chapman, Laird, Ifill, & KewalRamani, 2011). Conversely, students who are African American, Latino, and American Indian experience disproportionately high rates of dis/ability identification (Artiles, Kozleski, Trent, Osher, & Ortiz, 2010). Performance gaps are wide and progress glacial (Nichols, Glass, & Berliner, 2012).

The 100 largest school districts in the United States serve more than 11 million children, almost a quarter of all the students that attended public schools in 2011. Yet those districts comprise only 2% of the more than 6,500 school districts in the nation. Whether due to the sheer size of many of these districts, or the complex bureaucracies that exist within them, or structural inequities in financial resource distribution in many urban districts, transforming urban schools and the systems that surround them is daunting business. In this chapter we argue for a specific definition of *transformation*. It has implications for the complexity of urban reform. While scaling one successful school transformation to all the schools in a district is a feat, crossing the boundaries between school districts to transform still more schools is even more challenging. Sustaining the change over time remains the holy grail. It is a goal so elusive that it seems impossible to realize. This book is about that challenge. Through a framework that accounts for the complex job of helping people design systems that work for students we

intend to trouble the notion of how to do school. Several theoretical constructs contribute to such a framework, which we detail in the subsequent
discussion. Next, we detail the key features of a sociocultural framework for
engaging transformation of urban schools. Finally, in illustrating how these
theories and features intersect, we revisit the Systemic Change Framework
presented in the Introduction, which serves as the orienting structure for the
remainder of the volume.

## DIVERSITY AMONG URBAN SCHOOLS AND DISTRICTS

The National Center for Educational Statistics (NCES) reports that of
the 21 districts participating in a study of urban district performance on
the National Assessment of Educational Progress (NAEP), only three performed at the mean for all schools in the state (NCES, 2011). Thus students in urban schools are likely to fall behind their suburban peers, and
falling behind means staying behind if schools do nothing to change conditions for learning.

Describing urban schools and districts in terms of their demographic
composition has a long history in the United States. It is part of our raced
heritage (Ladson-Billings, 2012). That is, we continue to be a country where
opportunities to learn, access to material and cultural resources, and participation in challenging curriculum are differentially distributed by racial
categories (Kozol, 2005). Students from majority racial and ethnic backgrounds benefit from a heritage which mirrors that of generations of European Americans (Leonardo & Broderick, 2011). They benefit because the
school systems they enter draw from that same heritage of shared values
and perspectives, honed over time, crafted into local, regional, and national
policy, and practiced in everyday transactions. Little learning effort is ex-
pended in translating behavioral and social performance expectations. That
leaves the gateway wide open for excelling at formal learning.

It's a setup. Children from majoritarian backgrounds are coached by
their families but they also find familiar expectations inside their classrooms
(Kozleski, Artiles, & Lacy, 2012; Lareau, 2011). In other words, the cultures of their homes and schools have enough in common that students
can do the translation work with little need for interpretation from teachers. While students who do not fit the dominant culture mold attend many
schools throughout the United States, large numbers of students in urban
schools are very different from one another and from the majoritarian institutional culture embedded in these educational settings. Relatedly, Kozol
(2005) argues that urban schools polarize divisions between the cultures
of the students and the school. Watered-down curriculum and mechanistic
pedagogies are shadows of the opportunities offered in the well-financed

and artfully resourced schools of the suburbs (Darling-Hammond, 2007). The curriculum saps engagement, convincing students that school offers little in terms of fascination, invention, and discovery (Apple, 2000).

National data from NCES (2011) show that urban districts historically draw large groups of students who identify as African Americans (about 26% of the total student body), and Latinos (about 43%), while students who identify as White comprise, on the average, about 20% of the total student body and English language learners (about 11%). These percentages fluctuate widely. As an example, African American students comprise 87% of the students in the Detroit Public Schools and only 1% in Albuquerque. Conversely, a majority of students in urban southwestern districts claim Latino heritage. While some argue that class, not race, is the most important predictor of opportunities to learn because income controls what schools children attend, race continues to be a troubling boundary for opportunity (Lipman, 2011). Nowhere is this barrier more profound than in urban schools.

For all these reasons, urban schools and districts remain troubling and troubled places (Lee, 2007). We serve most of our children of color in these schools. Urban schools offer education to children of immigrant families and are most likely to teach English as an additional language. Learning should accelerate in situations where multiple languages, perspectives, cultures, and histories converge, yet these circumstances are seen as problematic because they complicate the delivery of learning in schools designed for some—but not all—students. We explore a framework for understanding learning in the next section.

## A SOCIOCULTURAL FRAMEWORK FOR ENGAGING URBAN SCHOOL TRANSFORMATION

Without a complex framework for engaging transformation, it is difficult to make substantial progress in reforming large numbers of urban schools and districts (Ferguson, Kozleski, & Smith, 2003). In chemistry, a cell is considered to be transformed when its genetic makeup is altered chemically. This chemical makeover means that the cell cannot retreat to its former self; its altered state lasts and will produce offspring that mimic its current, not its prior, form. Similarly, if schools in the United States transformed some of the fundamental assumptions that ground their structures, organization, and practices, outcomes for students would be permanently altered (Kozleski, Gibson, & Hynds, 2012). Accordingly, a framework for engaging urban education reform requires explorations of identity and historical and current sociocultural, political, and economic conditions of urban systems and schools, as well as prevailing views about difference (Thorius & Scribner, Chapter 6 of this volume).

Further, it requires understandings of the characteristics of reforms that impact entire systems rather than isolated spaces, where they are sustained over time. While there have been and continue to be powerful reform efforts that produce student effects like improved learning outcomes and postsecondary opportunities, these efforts tend to stall out over time (Hatch, 2002). We have seen wonderfully skilled teachers make a difference in the lives of students (Kozleski & Smith, 2009). They have brought hope to children through literacy, performance, the arts, science, technology, and math. We watched engaged students transform their own and others' life chances (Lee, 2007). We have seen school leaders build on the resources of school and neighborhood communities to create pockets of synergy, hope, and transformation (Skrla, Scheurich, Garcia, & Nolly, 2004). However, transforming one school is not sufficient (Kozleski & Huber, 2012).

## GROUNDING THE WORK IN THEORY

Doing the work of transforming schools and schooling requires a robust understanding of how schools work and how they serve and fail students. Data help inform the problem; theory aids in deepening understanding and developing the path forward. As Lewin (1952) reminds us, "There is nothing more practical than a good theory" (p. 169). Our work in transforming schools has benefited greatly from three theoretical lenses: (1) cultural historical activity theory (Cole, 1996); (2) complexity theory (Lemke & Sabelli, 2008); and (3) intersectionality theory (Crenshaw, 1991). In that order, we describe briefly how we have embedded these theories in our work and how their analytical tools inform the ongoing search for sustainable, scalable, socially just change and intellectual advancement in urban schools.

### Cultural Historical Activity Theory

Cultural historical activity theory (CHAT) draws from anthropology, linguistics, sociology, and psychology to develop a theory of human learning and development (Cole, 1996; Engeström, 1987). CHAT scholars draw from the work of 20th-century Russian researchers Vygotsky and Leont'ev's notions of cultural historical psychology and Leont'ev's notions of activity theory. CHAT offers a framework for multiple kinds of investigation within and across systems, yet all are concerned to some extent with humans' shared *activity* within systems (Engeström & Sannino, 2010). In particular, the concept of activity system helps to expand how we understand the interactions between sociocultural, historical, and political contexts of systems. *Discourse* within activity systems provide a target for understanding and investigating how rules, divisions of labor, and tools organize and mediate change (Engeström, 1987). Accordingly, using CHAT helps frame questions and develop strategic processes for change and renewal. It reminds change agents to consider the activities of whole communities, be mindful of the division of labor, clarify organizational outcomes, make rules for participation explicit, engage participants, and develop context-specific tools and participant structures to mediate reform and transformation. In this section, we explore how CHAT helps to clarify the murky work of schools.

Student learning, progress through school, and successful transitions to adulthood are not merely a function of the quality of interaction between teacher and students over time. Instead, teachers and students operate within activity systems that are both self-contained and connected to the other classrooms in a school. Perhaps you work in an organization that has departments. Each of your departments functions as a self-contained unit but across the business, all of those units function together. Classrooms in schools are like that. Ms. Palmer's classroom connects to Ms. Ito's classroom, and Mr. Mack's, and so on. Teachers spread ideas from their rooms through dialogue and resource sharing (Waitoller & Kozleski, 2013). Think of the teachers as boundary workers (Akkerman & Bakker, 2011; Star, 2010). They work in their own enclaves called classrooms, but they share information, resources, and materials formally and informally. The curriculum is another boundary object that crosses classrooms; special education individualized education plans are another. Through recognition of their legitimacy, school leaders privilege some classrooms and teachers over others and in doing so, they contribute to the spread and constraint of everyday classroom practices. Teachers share with one another using a common set of standards and learning goals. A single school is connected to a whole set of schools that fits within a political unit called a school district. Reformers resolve to work on improving teacher practice, or on methods for assessment, or on community engagement. They seem to forget or dismiss that all these different activities are connected to other arenas that are also producing policies, tensions, opportunities, and activities (Kozleski, Gibson, & Hynds, 2012). These forces impact all the other activity arenas. This interconnected network of activity arenas is what we mean by *systems*.

To illustrate, we consider a small nursery where the owner develops her interest in gardening into a business and then buys plants at wholesale and sells them to drop-in customers. An activity arena is born. In the beginning, it consists of the owner and her customers. She learns to do her own books, manages her business banking account, and at the end of the year hires the services of an accountant to complete her taxes. She decides to build an online catalog and hires a web designer as a consultant. Her activity arena becomes networked to the web designer's and the accountant's activity arenas and her business grows. The owner hires help for stocking and maintaining her plants and is able to widen her plant selection. She builds a greenhouse.

Her own activity system grows. The objective is still the same: sell plants and sustain her lifestyle. But to do so, she needs to continue to expand, enough to sustain both herself and her employees. She needs systems. There are systems to manage the financial side of things, systems for managing the people, and systems for managing the plants. Her activity arena becomes more complex. Perhaps she decides to hire her own accountants, develop her own human resources department, and extend her marketing strategies. If the enterprise grows, it splits into activity arenas that have their own objectives and outcomes (Barab, Evans, & Baek, 2004). This example demonstrates how systems are sets of interconnected activity arenas that traverse from local activities, like the teacher in the classroom or the nursery worker in the greenhouse, to state and federal levels, such as the U.S. Department of Education that manages federal policies in the nation's schools (Kozleski, Gibson, & Hynds, 2012).

We argue that while we can envision the system as a whole (i.e., the nursery or the school district) it grows and develops from within. Returning to the growing nursery business, the patterns of each department are crafted by the people who work in them, with feedback from the greater enterprise about what works and what doesn't. Cultures begin to develop around the kinds of tools that are used in each arena. If there are principles around being environmentally safe, the kinds of approaches to plant management will reflect those notions. Who gets hired and why becomes predicated on those values. Changing the work flow and processes in one department has implications for how activities and everyday work happens in other departments as well. In systems like these, the most likely response to unexpected or different requests is to figure out how to accommodate the request without changing the standard operating procedure. Alter the required response enough and the affected department, led by the people inside, will either shift their work or resist the change (Collins, 2001). Shifts in one or two activity arenas will have ripple effects elsewhere. These ripples will also be resisted. First order change, in which the fundamental objectives of the organization are left untouched (Fullan, 2013), can be accomplished. But once a decision is made to transform the business from a customer service operation to a plant genome project, for instance, deep change is required in all aspects of the organization. While CHAT helps us with a vocabulary for understanding some of this complexity, complexity theory helps us map the dynamics *between* activity arenas.

## Complexity Theory

Some unique themes and narratives that emerged from work in National Institute for Urban School Improvement (NIUSI) schools and educational agencies offer insights for policymakers and education leaders alike. By and large, we learned that without a complex understanding of the ways people learn; the importance of cultural mediation; the ways that contexts afford and constrain student competence, ability, and the development of cultural capital; and the role that personal and community histories play in schools, the transformation of urban schools will remain beyond our collective grasp (Kozleski & Smith, 2009). Transforming schools is a systems problem. For schools to transform fundamentally from a cultural transmission model that brings to mind an assembly line analogy to a knowledge creation enterprise is a profound shift (Sands, Kozleski, & French, 2000). Providing students with a map of accumulated knowledge, organized into discipline-specific taxonomies, ignores the reality of ongoing revisions to what and how we understand the world around us. The mental tools that students need include the indexes to how knowledge is mapped (i.e., sorted, categorized, and sequenced) from multiple perspectives. One index is the Western civilization knowledge map replete with the advances of the scientific, industrial, and postindustrial revolutions, the political shifts from feudal to nation-state status, and the accompanying shifts in philosophy, the social sciences, and the arts. Delving into various parts of the Western knowledge map to build conceptual and discipline-specific skills helps learners use the tools of the past and also helps them understand that tools for understanding the rapidly shifting knowledge system of the information age are being built (e.g., robotic systems, digitized surgery, new analytic approaches for mining social network data). Transforming schools to meet the demands for knowledge creation challenges many of the fundamental assumptions about what schools are for, how learning progresses, who leads the learning process, and what counts as measures of learning. Transforming educational systems to produce a new knowledge outcome is only part of the complexity.

Consider the complexity of that shift. Classrooms are one kind of activity arena in school systems. For example, Ms. Vazquez's 1st-grade classroom has its own particular culture as does every other classroom in a school. The school overall also has an activity system anchored by specific cultural dynamics, the district another. The everyday activities of individuals within departments inside the state education agency have their own cultural contexts and the federal department of education another. At each of these levels are multiple activity arenas in which people with specific roles and responsibilities—CHAT theorists might say specific divisions of labor—exist. However, the opportunities for participation and the kinds of products or outcomes produced are very different because of the varied nature of cultural exchange within each arena. The notion of boundaries discussed earlier between and among *levels* of systems and *types* of activity arenas is critical because tools like curriculum, policy, and individualized educational plans transcend boundaries and yet are transformed themselves by the ways they are appropriated in particular activity arenas (Kozleski

& Huber, 2010). For example, in the latter part of the first decade of the 21st century, states joined in an effort to develop a new, common core of standards for what is to be taught in science, mathematics, and English language arts. These standards transcend activity arenas called states and also school districts and schools. Each of these activity systems grapples with understanding, use, and diffusion of the standards. *People* within their practice arenas make their own sense of the standards. Complexity theory asks that we attend to how this activity unfolds not as a single lever of change but in its complex interaction with the specific contexts of each activity arena. Skeptics, cynics, early adopters, and resisters are all operating. Timelines, economics, political agendas, and justice dialogues are in play as well. Communities engage and disengage because of the complexity of local demands. *Systemic* change, therefore, requires transcending borders among these networked activity arenas in powerful ways that cause internal and external disturbances that reset the entire enterprise. This is the challenge urban school transformation faces.

In this book we argue for transforming educational systems to ensure that all students are included. What is to be learned is part of that agenda around inclusivity. Our current system marginalizes large groups of students not only because the affordances for learning are distributed inequitably but also because the maps for what is to be learned advantage some children and have little utility for others. In shifting to a new knowledge paradigm, we risk continuing to leave groups of students behind without transforming the social constructs that undergird how we sort and categorize students. Complexity theory gives us a way of conceptualizing these multiple aspects of educational systems. It reminds us that changes in one part of the system require changes elsewhere. And when we want shift to occur and persist over time, we have to plan for and make change, often simultaneously. CHAT reminds us that this change is local and personal. Complexity theory reminds us that it is multifaceted and happens at different levels, although for different purposes.

## Intersectionality Theory

Intersectionality theory (Crenshaw, 1991) is concerned with accounting for the complexity of oppressions experienced by marginalized groups. More specifically, intersectionality theory asserts that one's social experiences and outcomes, including access to power and privilege (Andersen, 1996), are determined by the intersection of multiple, simultaneous dimensions of identity (e.g., race, class, gender, dis/ability). In sum, this theory accounts for the collisions of "sociohistorical factors and power structures, political forces, personal interactions, and other external factors that influence meaning-making, behavior, experiences, and opportunities of marginalized groups and individuals (Murphy et al., 2009)" (Sullivan & Thorius, 2010, p. 103).

Power and privilege infuse the dynamics of all activity systems interacting with the dynamics of active cultural construction. Marginalization and oppression operate not because of a single factor but in response to the multiple accumulations of microaggressions: internalized inadequacies that are messaged by the social contexts that individuals inhabit, as well as generational histories (Sue, 2010). Gender and color are one such intersection (Crenshaw, 1991). Women's work outside of households, even in 2014, is more frequent in the helping professions like nursing, secretarial support, and teaching where the numbers of women in these and similar professions range from 84% to more than 96% of the total work force (United States Department of Labor, 2010). Conversely, men populate the building professions like engineering and construction in similar majorities (United States Department of Labor, 2010). Further, movies and other media portray women in particular kinds of roles. Storm, one of the superheroes in Marvel's X-Men comics, is a Black woman with super powers. Yet her role among the other superheros is tangential and supporting, rather than a core of the continuing narrative thread (DeBerry, 2012). Intersectionality offers insight into how the cumulative effect of these representations of who young girls might grow up to be, the opportunities afforded them in school, and the specific messages they receive about their identities conspire to funnel children into particular life choices.

Power and its exercise results in privileging some aspects of a system while marginalizing others, just as some individuals and groups may be marginalized while others form the core where power is typically concentrated (Artiles & Kozleski, 2007). Disrupting the core disrupts the distribution of power and privilege and destabilizes the system, creating opportunities for new learning and its installation in daily practice. To design for transformation means addressing these key levers. Disturbing them disturbs the balance of power. Urban school transformation requires renegotiating what counts and for whom. No tinkering at the margins will reform how gender, race, ability, language, and other socially constructed notions of difference are sorted. The kind of urban reform that we discuss in this book is designed to take on the deeper, embedded forms of exclusion and marginalization that urban schools have reproduced for generations. Through CHAT, complexity theory, and intersectionality, districts and schools are able to explore ways in which marginalization and counter-marginalization narratives evolve and develop, as well as areas of research, policy, and practice necessary for addressing these marginalizations, thus contributing to inclusive, culturally responsive reform.

## KEY FEATURES OF TRANSFORMATIONAL FRAMEWORKS

The design problem for scalable, sustainable change is complex. Most school-reform initiatives focus on one aspect of improving schools. For instance, consider efforts to improve teacher quality through honing teacher assessment processes or focusing on science knowledge through partnerships with museums. These propositions have possibilities to change something, but by themselves they are not robust enough to make the vast schooling enterprise—the system—change sufficiently to maintain these efforts over time. The question is how shall education communities *design* for transformation?

The outcomes are critical. Schools must ensure that improvements in access, participation, and opportunities to learn for *all* students gain traction, build momentum, and disrupt the status quo sufficiently to transform activity, experience, and outcomes. The school systems that surround and support schools must advance processes, tools, and opportunities that change the system in which schools practice. This next section offers insight into this challenge: scaling and spreading *systems change*. To make systems change possible, it must be framed as an expansive learning endeavor in which inclusivity and cultural responsivity are core principles against which success is measured.

### Framing Reform as an Expansive Learning Endeavor

Despite over 20 years of comprehensive school reform efforts, there have been few general or special education reforms that have altered the core functions of schools in ways that have allowed for shifts in practice to occur. An important reason for this failure is that systems and the people in them are not organized in ways that promote distributed learning. Rather, most systemic reform is grounded in specific assumptions about individualized student learning and mandates necessary to ensure teacher learning for specific kinds of practice that may or may not fit well within a particular community or classroom. A top-down, authoritarian, expert-driven, compliance focused accountability reform recipe has been the mainstay of many of the comprehensive reform packages of the last 3 decades. However, this approach to change ignores how learning may be mediated in or by local contexts in partnership with community organizations, local universities, families, and nongovernment agencies. Framing reform as a collective, organizational learning endeavor in which the best research, evidence-based practices, and ongoing inquiry become the way forward offers the opportunity for marginalized communities and families to participate in remediating how schools, classrooms, and learning might look. In this book we explore the ways in which systems that we have worked with and whose stories we share in subsequent chapters have used learning as a core principle for negotiating the intersections among organizational and political structures. Because we have conceptualized and designed change activities as opportunities to learn, rather than opportunities to conform, we have created space for individuals to reconceptualize their own identities and functions within organizations that learn to face complexity, intersectionality, and inequities produced systemically. Work with schools and school districts that disproportionately identify students who are African American for special education offers a case in point.

We have described this process in much more detail in other work (e.g., Kozleski & Artiles, in press; Kozleski, Artiles, & Lacy, 2012); here we outline the notion of systems transformation as a learning activity. Using data from the districts and schools that we work with, we build geospatial maps that demonstrate where disproportionality is occurring. We depict the intensity of the disproportionality, using heat displays (red depicting more concerning ratios of disproportionality in comparison with other racial groups in a school). And, we indicate neighborhood blocks according to their family income levels. In one map, learners (district and school personnel) can see three things: (1) where disproportionality is happening; (2) the intensity of that disproportionality; and (3) where poverty overlaps—or doesn't—with disproportionate identification. Using small-group discussion, district and school personnel follow a learning protocol to examine the data and develop working hunches about what might contribute to the displays that they see. Sometimes groups want to see additional information like the experience and credentials of the teaching staff, the number of instructional assistants, the coaching and supervision models used in the school, the student scores, and the percent of students who participate in state and national assessments of educational progress. We are prepared to overlay these data on the spatial representation. These data often challenge prevailing explanations for what happens within a district. This kind of analysis is the beginning of a learning process. Evidence spurs reflection and the development of hunches. Hunches are verified or troubled. This process disturbs the core—the way that people who live in the system understand and explain how it works. Disturbances require adjustment. Adjustments mean that learning needs to occur. An opportunity exists to remediate how the people in the system understand it and their work. Personal and institutional histories can be revised in these moments. Because individuals are learning together, boundaries between roles are blurred. Authority shifts, even if only in this context. And new possibilities emerge. The work of transformation is slow, strategic, and requires skilled intervention. One group of people in one place is not sufficient for change to happen. Such activities need to happen at multiple levels of the system in order to change the activity system. Decisions to refer for special education eligibility assessment are made in schools by teachers and other practitioners. Decisions to review and ask questions about special education disproportionality are made at leadership levels. Understanding about how the system is set up to propel teachers and other practitioners to make a referral is the work of senior district leaders who lead the design of curriculum, the configuration of schools into grades, the modes of teacher coaching that are used, and the distribution of highly skilled teachers. Each activity system needs learning opportunities that fit the cycle of activity they engage. In doing this complex learning work, we are able to trace in this book the trajectories of transformation over time.

## Centering Inclusivity and Cultural Responsivity

Urban schools comprise a diverse student body including historically marginalized populations within the United States and new migrants from around the world who participate in the global diaspora. In urban schools, minority–majority racial distinctions are turned on their ends; in many of the nation's largest systems, the majority populations may be Latino or African American with strong representation from Asian, Pacific Islander, and Native American populations. Changing perceptions of race and racial groups, and majority and minority populations are in part fueled by increasing numbers of students and families whose biracial, multilingual, and global connections challenge long-held binaries embedded in identity politics. This does not mean that ideologies about race have receded from schools (Lipman, 2011). Rather, schools are sites where understandings of ability, competence, intelligence, and potential are bound by such ideologies (Ladson-Billings, 2012). When the sediments of stereotyping racial, linguistic, and ability ideologies are ignored in a rush to embrace a mythical postracial era in which racism has been eradicated, educators, scholars, and policymakers risk failing to address fundamental shortfalls in how children are viewed and supported. Wallpapering over our histories of racism has particular consequences in urban schools. To wit, urban schools are often portrayed in deficit ways that ignore the wealth of cultural traditions, ways of knowing, and languages that converge in our great cities. Further, within these complex mélanges, urban students' experiences are subjugated in conventional, White-centered approaches to curriculum, teaching, and learning in the United States (Leonardo & Broderick, 2011).

Scholars point to inequities in student access, participation, and outcomes that result from schools' narrow preferences for particular modes of communication, cognitive schemas, affect, behavior, and knowledge (Blanchett, 2006). As a result, some argue that the basic tenets of special education are steeped in identifying and treating perceived student deficits and have led to separate programs and services that promote and support the overrepresentation of culturally and linguistically diverse students in special education. As we presented in our discussion on intersectionality theory, focus on individuals ignores the intersectionality of political, economic, historic, and curricular affordances and constraints that operate to advantage some children while disadvantaging others (Artiles & Kozleski, 2007). Paris (2012) notes as well that differences add to the intellectual and social capital of a learning community. The arc from difference as a deficit to difference as an asset owes its growing traction as an idea to the work of scholars in multiple disciplines who have transformed notions of learning from individual agency to a networked social endeavor embedded in practice, language, and thought (Barab et al., 2004; Greeno, Collins, & Resnick, 1996). Such a sociocultural understanding of learning requires that practitioners, families, and researchers engage in building new understandings that explicitly attend to the sociocultural construction of inclusivity, marginalization, learning, and development (Artiles & Kozleski, 2007). The joining of these often disconnected but intersecting conversations will help to create a coherent vision for transforming urban schools with an explicit focus on inclusivity.

We propose that culturally responsive pedagogy and leadership serve to inform and enhance the ways in which inclusive education is realized. With regard to pedagogy, consideration of local urban contexts and communities requires that teachers not only shift their practice, but also adapt prescribed curricula to the learning histories and needs of their students. Classroom cultures are negotiated spaces where teachers and students create relationships that acknowledge their personal histories while acknowledging the institutional culture and expectations that stem from being within a school and system. Culturally responsive classrooms create opportunities for students and teachers to examine and contest the status quo as well as find ways to improve social and intellectual outcomes for every student. In this book we describe what such classrooms look like and how practitioners design for learning in ways that blur the boundaries between schools and communities. With culture playing a mediating role in how teaching and learning occurs, this approach offers possibilities for helping students and teachers address learning differences through equitable access opportunities and participation. As current and former special and general educators, several chapter authors describe efforts to center inclusive, culturally responsive pedagogies in their urban classrooms.

Leaders in culturally responsive, inclusive systems focus not only on what happens in classrooms, but also on the convergence of institutional and individual cultures in educational settings. By creating opportunities for dialogue, leadership, and continued critique of what is accepted as "common sense," culturally responsive leaders empower students, teachers, and families to build shared understanding of themselves and how school communities make sense of learning expectations, as well as to shape the direction and focus of systemic reform. Chapter authors in this book hold positions in schools, districts, and states, providing an authentic voice in the conceptualization of culturally responsive leadership.

*Critical examination and disruption of structures of power and privilege.* While in some areas local leadership has expanded to include the voices of teachers, students, and families in determining the direction of curriculum and instruction in local school contexts, the very nature of bureaucratic systems is that command and control strategies permeate districts whether the district is as small as 6,000 students or as large as New York City's. In command and control structures, policy and regulation are created to contain drift and unanticipated innovation in order to manage risk and exposure and arrive at specific outcomes. Yet, in doing so, the capacity to address local and specific contexts and needs is suppressed. As a result, even when democratic reform is espoused, the system cannot deal with the degrees of variation that may be needed when the emphasis is on standardization and unit replication. One of the reasons that the charter school movement seems so attractive to the current administration may be that it seems to promote innovation. In this book we examine the ways in which attention to the local voices of families, students, and teachers can produce inventive and electric curriculum that engages students and transforms student outcomes while building systems of innovation and improvement.

District and state education departments are often the chief impediment to genuine reform in urban schools. Often, these bureaucracies have longstanding cultures in which formal structures represent not only ways of separating and categorizing what people do, as in we serve children who are English language learners or students who have disabilities, but they also separate what adults do within the system. Layered on top of the functional bureaucratic categories lies the distribution of power and privilege, and bureaucracies become a gridlock of services, people, policies, and practices that are difficult to streamline, navigate, and change. While organization and systems are necessary to funnel administrative functions away from the action of teaching and learning, how they are organized, the assumptions embedded in what is valued, and the processes used to make decisions and create and distribute leadership for policies can support or strangle nimble changes in classrooms and schools.

*Dismantling structural barriers to reform.* At the macro level, the very nature of U.S. structural approaches for funding schools has disadvantaged urban school systems ever since the Great Depression (Anyon, 2005); in 2002 the United States General Accountability Office reported that 80% of our nation's urban schools are funded at a lower rate than their suburban counterparts, in spite of the recent influx of state and federal funds to shore up failing urban systems. The lack of equitable funding over an extended period of time has led to increased class sizes, lack of sufficient books and materials, shortages of certified teachers, and the deterioration of school buildings (Kozol, 2005). Researchers suggest that such structural limitations are locally manifested in overrepresentation patterns in urban schools where resources are spread so thinly that the problems of the overrepresentation of students of color and English language learners in special education are visible (Ferri & Connor, 2005). To illustrate, African American, American Indian, and Latino students are disproportionately identified for special education in some states. Some disability categories range from more than one and a half times to more than four times as likely to be identified than all other student population groups (Artiles, 2011; Losen & Skiba, 2010).

Since the early 1990s, federal investments in education have emphasized the development of approaches to comprehensive school reform that foreground organizational capacity building (Hatch, 2002). NIUSI was established during this time to merge general and special education reform efforts, particularly around the need to support learning for students with dis/abilities in general education contexts. Attempts to understand how to redesign schools peaked at the turn of the 21st century, when the reauthorization of the Elementary and Secondary Education Act produced a far-reaching federal policy, No Child Left Behind (NCLB). Vested in the use of quality management strategies similar to those used in business to propel redesign (e.g., *Six Sigma* (Harry & Schroeder, 1999); *Good to Great* (Collins, 2001), the law required schools receiving NCLB funding to measure progress based on student performance on curriculum-referenced standardized assessments. In some states these assessments had high stakes, that is, students were required to pass the assessments in order to graduate from high school. In all states the assessments brought intensive pressure to schools that failed to produce annual gains in student performances (i.e., adequate yearly progress [AYP]). NIUSI continued its work during this tumultuous time and had a front row seat in the struggles that many districts faced as they sought to create unified general and special education systems. It is this "on-the-ground" perspective that will help educators, researchers, and policymakers deepen their understanding of how to work systemically.

Without delving into all of the rules governing the playing field, the theory behind NCLB was that measurement would lead local districts to reinvest resources and effort in ways that would improve outcomes for poorly performing schools. In some districts, reinvestment and reorganization helped struggling schools. In other contexts, local politics, historical legacies, lack of resources, and unprepared leaders conflated to maintain and even exacerbate existing disparities among schools (Kozleski & Smith, 2009). Further, students who attended these schools continued to be sorted by ability, behavior, culture, economic circumstances, experience, language, and academic performance, relegating some students to limited and others to limitless opportunities (Darling-Hammond, 2007).

**Critical policy work.** Policy should teach, liberate, and drive reform. It can teach by setting a vision for what education should be. It can liberate by naming the oppressive structural barriers that require dismantling, as well as identifying local needs and agendas. However, most policy is prescriptive and designed to prevent mishaps rather than mediate agendas for transformation and local empowerment. Chapter 10 deals with these ideas and their implementation in detail, but the notion that policy drives reform is central to setting the conditions for fundamental, justice-minded, urban school transformation. Other chapter authors include researchers and parents of children with dis/abilities teams who describe the potential of participatory action research in driving and informing policy.

## A THEORETICAL FRAMEWORK FOR SYSTEMIC CHANGE

Achieving inclusive, equitable urban education reform requires connecting the work of districts, schools, and communities through the people they serve, the students and families. These connections are necessary to organize change efforts into meaningful and effective elements across the layers of activity embedded within educational systems. These connections must take into account that many reform agendas ignore the importance of understanding how current conditions maintain the educational status quo. Leadership for reform must challenge the group of dominant normative beliefs that push back against change that challenges its privilege and power. The preceding discussions about theory and features of a framework for urban reform ground NIUSI's deep and careful construction of an urban systemic change framework. In subsequent chapters, we demonstrate the notion that multiple change initiatives at different levels of the education system are necessary for transformation. This kind of change vision accounts for nested, yet boundary-crossing, activity systems (i.e., federal, state, district, school, practitioner, and student activity), as well as disruptions that are necessary across these systemic levels in order for the system to move forward on multiple equity-driven fronts. The work of disrupting these activity systems, and as a result the system as a whole, was the central project of NIUSI through its engagement with educational stakeholders around inclusive educational reform in urban contexts.

While we introduced the Systemic Change Framework in the Introduction, and explained the levels of the system in which change efforts must be focused concomitantly, we only alluded to the six goals of each activity system included in the framework as necessary to address through policy, practice, and research. While these goals differ to some degree, they are similar in function and purpose (i.e., aligned) across activity arenas. Whether within the federal, the practitioner, or the district activity arena, or the state department of education or the local school building, urban education reform efforts must consider the ways in which resources are equitably developed and distributed, and the ways in which governance and decision making are shared and center marginalized perspectives. Further, while equitable resource development and distribution is about the creation of new assets, goals toward examining and improving infrastructure (e.g., ways in which space and time are used) are also vital desired outcomes in order to level the urban education playing field for all students, their families, and communities. Further, forging and strengthening relationships in which strengths and resources of surrounding communities are valued and inform policy, practice, and research is a crucial goal across each systemic activity level. This goal refers to relationships with families and district residents for those at the practitioner, school, and district level; and at the federal and state level, relationships with constituents who include those served directly by the system.

We assert, as well, that policy, practice, and research across these levels cultivate a culture of renewal and improvement. That is, efforts are never complete, and improvement is always viewed as an opportunity for the system to grow. These efforts at the practitioner level may include critical reflection on one's assessment practices with the purpose of expanding classroom activities that offer choices for students' demonstration of what they've learned.

The final goal to engage within and across activity arenas of urban education systems is the centering of concerns with equity, and, relatedly, inquiry that only *begins* with quantitative measurement. This kind of inquiry asks, Who benefits and who does not from the ways things are? (Kozleski, Gibson, & Hynds, 2012).

## CONCLUSION

While there has been ample attention to the multiple ways in which issues of power, race, and class afford and constrain urban school reform efforts, some unique themes and narratives that emerged from work in NIUSI schools offer insights for policymakers and education leaders alike. This book represents the work of a national team of reformers who worked over time to hone a shared understanding of their mission while balancing the demands of local and state mandates. By organizing each chapter's story within a theoretical framework for systemic change (Kozleski, Gibson, & Hynds, 2012), the tensions inherent in the scale, scope, and significance of each narrative provide important and convincing evidence that systemic, thoughtful, and organic are not mutually exclusive but necessary to find traction for reform bold enough to address the cultural contexts in which power, history, and tradition often prevail over innovation and social transformation. It is our hope that the stories detailed in the subsequent chapters make the case for the vitality of this journey and that the outcomes experienced as a result of the NIUSI work offer much to learn and expand upon.

## REFERENCES

Akkerman, S. F., & Bakker, A. (2011). Boundary crossing and boundary objects. *Review of Educational Research, 81*(2), 132–169. doi:10.3102/0034654311404435

Andersen, M. L. (1996). Foreword. In E.N.L. Chow, D. Wilkinson, & M. Baca Zinn (Eds.), *Race, class, and gender: Common bonds, different voices* (pp. ix–xii). Thousand Oaks, CA: Sage.

Anyon, J. (2005). *Radical possibilities: Public policy, urban education, and a new social movement.* New York, NY: Routledge.

Apple, M. (2000). Comparing neo-liberal projects and inequity in education. *Comparative Education, 37,* 409–423.

Artiles, A. J. (2003). Special education's changing identity: Paradoxes and dilemmas in views of culture and space. *Harvard Educational Review, 73,* 164–202.

Artiles, A. J. (2011). Toward an interdisciplinary understanding of educational equity and difference: The case of the racialization of ability. *Educational Researcher, 40,* 431–445.

Artiles, A. J., & Kozleski, E. (2007). Beyond convictions: Interrogating culture, history, and power in inclusive education. *Language Arts, 84,* 357–364.

Artiles, A. J., Kozleski, E., Trent, S., Osher, D., & Ortiz, A. (2010). Justifying and explaining disproportionality, 1968–2008: A critique of underlying views of culture. *Exceptional Children, 76,* 279–299.

Barab, S. A., Evans, M. A., & Baek, E. (2004). Activity theory as a lens for characterizing the participatory unit. In D. H. Jonassen (Ed.), *Handbook of Research for Educational Communications and Technology* (2nd ed., pp. 199–214). Mahwah, NJ: Lawrence Erlbaum.

Blanchett, W. J. (2006). Disproportionate representation of African American students in special education: Acknowledging the role of White privilege and racism. *Educational Researcher, 35,* 24–28.

Chapman, C., Laird, J., Ifill, N., & KewalRamani, A. (2011). Trends in high school dropout and completion rates in the United States: 1972–2009 (NCES 2012-006). U.S. Department of Education. Washington, DC: National Center for Education Statistics. Retrieved from http://nces.ed.gov/pubsearch

Cole, M. (1996). *Cultural psychology: A once and future discipline.* Cambridge, MA: Harvard University Press.

Collins, J. (2001). *Good to great: Why some companies make the leap . . . and others don't.* New York, NY: Harper Collins.

Crenshaw, K. W. (1991). Mapping the margins: Intersectionality, identity politics, and violence against women. *Stanford Law Review, 43*(6), 1241–1279.

Darling-Hammond, L. (2007). Race, inequality and educational accountability: The irony of 'No Child Left Behind.' *Race Ethnicity and Education, 10*(3), 245–260.

DeBerry, D. (2012). *Storm and the X-Men as racial projects.* Tempe, AZ: Arizona State University.

Engeström, Y. (1987). *Learning by expanding: An activity-theoretical approach to developmental research.* Helsinki, Finland: Orienta-Konsultit.

Engeström, Y., & Sannino, A. (2010). Studies of expansive learning: Foundations, findings and future challenges. *Educational Research Review, 5*, 1–24.

Ferguson, D. L., Kozleski, E. B., & Smith, A. (2003). Transforming general and special education in urban schools. In F. Obiakor, C. Utley, & A. Rotatori (Eds.), *Advances in Special Education: Vol. 15. Effective education for learners with exceptionalities* (pp. 43–74). London, United Kingdom: JAI Press.

Ferri, B. A., & Connor, D. (2005). In the shadow of *Brown*: Special education and overrepresentation of students of color. *Remedial and Special Education, 26*(2), 93–100.

Fullan, M. (2013). *The new learning of educational change.* New York, NY: Routledge.

Greeno, J. G., Collins, A. M., & Resnick, L. B. (1996). Cognition and learning. In D. Berliner & R. Calfee (Eds.), *Handbook of Educational Psychology* (pp. 15–45). New York, NY: Macmillan.

Harry, M. J., & Schroeder, R. (1999). *Six sigma: The breakthrough management strategy revolutionizing the world's top corporations.* New York, NY: Doubleday.

Hatch, T. (2002). When improvement programs collide. *Phi Delta Kappan, 83*(8), 626–634.

Kozleski, E. B. (2011). Dialectical practices in education: Creating third spaces in the education of teachers. *Teacher Education and Special Education, 34,* 250–259.

Kozleski, E. B., & Artiles, A. J. (in press). Mediating systemic change in educational systems through sociocultural methods. In P. Smeyers, K. U. Leuven, D. Bridges, N. Burbules, & M. Griffiths (Eds.), *International handbook of interpretation in educational research methods.* New York, NY: Springer.

Kozleski, E. B., Artiles, A. J., & Lacy, L (2012). The dangerous politics of difference: How systems produce marginalization. In L. C. Burrello, W. Sailor, & J. Kleinhammer-Tramill (Eds.), *Unifying educational systems: Policy and leadership* (pp. 217–229). New York, NY: Routledge.

Kozleski, E. B., Gibson, D., & Hynds, A. (2012). Transforming complex educational systems: Grounding systems issues in equity and social justice. In C. Gersti-Pepin & J. Aiken (Eds.), *Defining social justice leadership in a global context* (pp. 263–286). Charlotte, NC: Information Age.

Kozleski, E. B., & Huber, J. J. (2010). Systemic change for RTI: Key shifts for practice. *Theory into Practice, 49,* 1–7.

Kozleski, E. B., & Huber, J. J. (2012). System-wide leadership for culturally responsive education. In J. Crockett, B. Billingsley, & M. L. Boscardin (Eds.), *Handbook of leadership and administration for special education.* London, United Kingdom: Routledge.

Kozleski, E. B., & Smith, A. (2009). The role of policy and systems change in creating equity for students with disabilities in urban schools. *Urban Education, 44,* 427–451.

Kozol, J. (2005). *The shame of the nation: The restoration of apartheid schooling in America.* New York, NY: Crown.

Ladson-Billings, G. (2012). Through a glass darkly: The persistence of race in education research and scholarship. *Educational Researcher, 41,* 115–120.

Lareau, A. (2011). *Unequal childhoods: Class, race, and family life.* Berkeley, CA: University of California Press.

Lee, C. D. (2007). *Culture, literacy, and learning: Taking bloom in the midst of the whirlwind.* New York, NY: Teachers College Press.

Lemke, J., & Sabelli, N. (2008). Complex systems and educational change: Towards a new research agenda. *Educational Philosophy and Theory, 40*(1), 118–129.

Leonardo, Z., & Broderick, A. A. (2011). Smartness as property: A critical exploration of intersections between Whiteness and disability studies. *Teachers College Record, 113,* 2206–2232.

Lewin, K. (1952). *Field theory in social science: Selected theoretical papers by Kurt Lewin.* London, United Kingdom: Tavistock.

Lipman, P. (2011). *The new political economy of urban education: Neoliberalism, race, and the right to the city. Critical social thought.* New York, NY: Routledge.

Losen, D., & Skiba, R. (2010). *Suspended education: Urban middle schools in crisis.* Los Angeles, CA: UCLA Civil Rights Project.

Murphy, Y., Hunt, V., Zajicek, A. M., Norris, A. N., & Hamilton, L. (2009). *Incorporating intersectionality in social work practice, research, policy, and education.* Washington, DC: NASW Press.

National Center for Education Statistics (NCES). (2011). *The nation's report card: Trial urban district assessment mathematics 2011* (NCES 2012-452). Washington, DC: Institute of Education Sciences, U.S. Department of Education.

Nichols, S. L., Glass, G. V, & Berliner, D. C. (2012). High-stakes testing and student achievement: Updated analyses with NAEP data. *Education Policy Analysis Archives, 20*(20). Retrieved from epaa.asu.edu/ojs/article/view/1048

Paris, D. (2012). Culturally sustaining pedagogy: A needed change in stance, terminology, and practice. *Educational Researcher, 41,* 93–97.

Sands, D. J., Kozleski, E. B., & French, N. (2000). *Inclusive education for the 21st century: A new introduction to special education.* Belmont, CA: Wadsworths.

Skrla, L., Scheurich, J. J., Garcia, J., & Nolly, G. (2004). Equity audits: A practical leadership tool for developing equitable and excellent schools. *Education Administration Quarterly, 40,* 133–161.

Smith, A. (2001). A faceless bureaucrat ponders special education, disability, and White privilege. *Research and Practice for Persons with Severe Disabilities, 26,* 180–188.

Star, S. L. (2010). This is not a boundary object: Reflections on the origin of a concept. *Science, Technology & Human Values, 35*(5), 601–617. doi: 10.1177/0162243910377624.

Sue, D. W. (2010). *Microaggressions in everyday life: Race, gender, and sexual orientation.* Hoboken, NJ: Wiley.

Sullivan, A. L., & Thorius, K.A.K. (2010). Considering the intersections of difference among students identified as disabled and expanding conceptualizations of multicultural education. *Race, Gender & Class, 17*, 93–109.

United States Department of Labor. (2010). *Twenty leading occupations of employed women: 2010 annual averages.* Retrieved fromwww.dol.gov/wb/factsheets/20lead2010.htm#.UJvvUtePzWI

United States General Accountability Office. (2002). *School finance: Per-pupil spending differences between selected inner city and suburban schools varied by metropolitan area.* Washington, DC: Author.

Waitoller, F., & Kozleski, E. B. (2013). Understanding and dismantling barriers for partnerships for inclusive education: A cultural historical activity theory perspective. *International Journal of Whole Schooling, 9*(1), 23–42.

Wolbring, G. (2008). The politics of ableism. *Development, 51*, 252–258.

# Part II

# CENTERING STUDENTS AND FAMILIES IN URBAN SCHOOL REFORM

# CHAPTER 2

# Student Voices in Urban School and District Improvement

## Creating Youth–Adult Partnerships for Student Success and Social Justice

*Shelley Zion and Sheryl Petty*

Mountainview School District (a pseudonym), one of 13 public school systems serving a metropolitan area of almost a million and a half people, has engaged in an earnest effort to reform its three middle schools and two high schools. The adults are excited about the potential of many of their reform ideas, but students indicate they have a different perspective as they talk with an outside adult about their perception of their roles in school reform:

> "The teachers never ask us how we feel about anything."
> "You're just not significant enough for them to give a crap about you or what you think."
> "Yeah, it's always about their [teachers'] perceptions and never about yours [students'] really in this school."
> "I dunno. It doesn't matter what we think because they're a higher authority, so whatever they say goes, even if it's unfair to us, it doesn't matter what we think."
> "They [teachers] don't listen to us, even if we do talk and if they [teachers] give us enough time to supposedly listen, they still don't listen."
> "I don't think kids can really change much in the school."
> "We have no say in anything." (Zion, 2009)

Although the interests of students are at the heart of many school improvement efforts, they are infrequently consulted and only engaged in limited fashion as adults develop improvement strategies. While students are affected daily by educational decisions made by adults inside and outside of school, their voices often go unheard in the debates about schooling and school reform (Glendon, 1991; Lincoln, 1995; O'Hair, McLaughlin, & Reitzug, 2000). National policy, empirical research, and the discourse about practices in education often fail to include the subjective experience of students and their perceptions about schools and learning in any central way (Bechtel & Reed, 1998; Erickson & Schultz, 1992; O'Hair et al., 2000). Rather than begin efforts to reform by understanding how schooling is experienced by students themselves, most reform efforts are conceptualized, organized, and implemented by professional educators, sometimes in collaborative efforts with community leaders, researchers, and policy analysts. Levin (2000) notes that "education reform cannot succeed and should not proceed without much more direct involvement of students in all its aspects" including providing a "sustained and meaningful role for students in defining, shaping, managing and implementing reform" (p. 155). Ultimately, it is the students' experiences of schooling that provide the gauge against which we can judge our success or failure in reform work.

Further, many educational reform programs are grounded in the belief that schools exist to prepare students for participation as citizens in a democratic society (Davies, 2002; Gay, 1997; Novak, 2002; Smith & Fenstermacher, 1999). From this perspective, the ideal of equal opportunity for all students to achieve and improve their array of life choices is paramount. Thus these educational reforms focus on ensuring that all students are afforded the highest-quality educational opportunities, regardless of their socioeconomic, cultural, or linguistic backgrounds. In spite of these democracy-related educational goals, notions of democracy often do not extend to authentic opportunities for participation in decision-making processes or real leadership experiences during the time that students spend in the K–12 educational system (O'Hair et al., 2000). This chapter synthesizes literature around student engagement in school reform, provides a theoretical framework for this engagement that accounts for the ways in which students might participate in active ways in school reform efforts, and describes a transformative process for educators, researchers, and policymakers to engage, foreground, and sustain student voice as a critical link in reforming schools and education systems. This discourse is key to conceptualizing a systemic change framework for educational transformation in which the students are not merely recipients but active, engaged contributors to the design and development of their own educational experiences.

There are numerous efforts around the country to engage youth in the process of school reform. Some of these efforts are *internal* to school systems and include surveying students about their opinions on schools and teaching, having youth panels on specific topics, student councils, student representatives on school improvement teams or district advisory boards, and other structures much like some of the efforts of the National Institute for Urban School Improvement (NIUSI) or All-City Council in Oakland, CA (www.facebook.com/pages/All-City-Council/274383329615). For instance, NIUSI facilitated student participation in focus groups that examined classroom climate. Data from these focus groups were used to inform changes that schools made their schoolwide positive behavior support agendas. Other efforts are *external* to school systems and include the involvement of youth-focused and youth-led nonprofit organizations and groups, and the prolific field of youth education organizing. See, for example, the Funders' Collaborative on Youth Organizing (www.fcyo.org) and the Annenberg Institute for School Reform's writing on "Youth Voice and Educational Justice" (annenberginstitute.org/commentary/2010/07/youth-voice-and-educational-justice). Many of these community-based organizations, groups, and organizing efforts target and engage the most disenfranchised youth in school systems, namely students of color, low-income students, and English language learners.

What is needed is well-grounded theory building that examines how and for what purposes student voice might be engaged (Robinson & Taylor, 2007). Further, the meaning of voice itself and how it is connected to identity, personality, relationship, and belonging needs to be explored and theorized. In this chapter, we describe a continuum of practices to engage youth in educational reform. The rationale for a continuum of such practices is grounded in the following assertions:

1. Often educators and adults have limited knowledge of the most powerful ways to partner with and engage youth in educational reform.
2. Though there is enormous theory and practice in the youth development field and the work of community-based organizations and groups *external* to school systems related to youth voice, engagement, advocacy, and empowerment, many of those involved in systemic education reform work *within* school systems are unaware of or unconnected to these efforts (Hosang, 2003; Joselowsky, Thomases, & Yohalem, 2004; Pittman & Tolman, 2002; and What Kids Can Do & MetLife Foundation, 2004).
3. Efforts within school systems can be strengthened by deepening educators' and reformers' awareness about the multiple ways that authentic youth voice and engagement might be enacted (Cammarota & Fine, 2008; the *Funders' Collaborative on Youth Organizing*, www.fcyo.org/toolsandresources; and the *Forum for Youth Investment*, http://forumfyi.org/pubs).
4. Authentic youth voice and engagement are resources for educators to critique their own efforts within school systems and deepen partnerships with students to improve systems.

In the next sections, we discuss approaches to and some of the existing theoretical frameworks for the integration of student voice in educational reform efforts.

## EXISTING FRAMEWORKS FOR THE INTEGRATION OF STUDENT VOICE IN EDUCATIONAL REFORM EFFORTS

Charles Reigeluth (1994) identifies *process* as a key aspect of systems change theory, focusing on how change happens and in what steps it is implemented. He proposes four process elements that can achieve transformative change: (1) The needs of the people served by the system drive reform; (2) people's beliefs and values anchor all reform; (3) reform incorporates a shared vision; and (4) reform requires an evolution of mindsets about the system. Some educational reformers have applied these proposed elements of change processes in ways that emphasize ensuring the sustainability of change by including all parts of the school system in the process and understanding the interrelationships between components within school systems (Ferguson, Kozleski, & Smith, 2003; Fullan, 2000; Klingner et al., 2005; Squire & Reigeluth, 2000). Yet, while these models tend to focus on outcomes of school reform for the benefit of students, they do not include students as core participants in the change process.

Levin (2000) names three arguments for including students in education reform that parallel Reigeluth's recommendations: (1) Participation and investment happens when everyone gets involved; (2) the unique perspectives that students bring to school reform can strengthen improvement efforts; and (3) families and staff are influenced by the voices of students. Levin also suggests that the shift from teaching to learning reflected in sociocultural ways of constructing knowledge means that students must be engaged in creating the world of school. Finally, he also reminds his readers that school outcomes are created by students, so their investment in designing school is essential to its ultimate success.

While many reformers and educators espouse the term *systemic change,* ideas about who is contained within a system differ. Several groups of people are served by education systems: students, families, community members, practitioners, policymakers, and society at large. Students and families are immediate consumers of what is offered locally. Yet community members and society at large benefit from the results of an education system. These results are as varied as skilled workers prepared to take on the complex needs of a modern community from health care to technology infrastructure, from service careers to technical expertise, from community services to national policymaking. And beyond skills to contribute to economic well-being, there are also intangibles that may result from a strong educational foundation such as the capacity to understand and participate in improving the democratic process locally as well as at the state, national, and international levels. Because so much rests on how a community rears the next generations and because there are such significant outcomes for so many kinds of stakeholders, reform efforts must incorporate or build on the beliefs, values, vision, and needs of each of these stakeholders. Most reform efforts include only some stakeholders—typically, school-level administrators, practitioners, and policymakers. This limits the effectiveness of the change processes since changes are implemented after responding to the needs of some of the people, using the reformers' beliefs and values to determine what should be valued and addressed. Overwhelmingly, this approach creates a shared vision among only the school professionals and ignores the need for challenging basic assumptions held by the reform leaders that are rarely surfaced and examined. An important avenue to examining these hidden assumptions is engaging groups currently marginalized in the system. In urban schools this often includes low-income families and communities of color. Many school systems minimally engage these families and community members via approaches that do not create ongoing, powerful structures for cocreating educational reform agendas. All-too-common practices include inviting families who are hourly wage earners to school during work hours and then being surprised when families are unable to participate or using email as a form of communication for families who have no access to computers at home. When families and community members fail to show up at their designated time, they may be dismissed as noncontributors. But dismissing these families and communities begs the question of how aware schools are of the life circumstances of the families of students they serve, whose voices schools value, what beliefs schools have about the desire and ability of certain groups of people to participate powerfully in change efforts, and what supports (or barriers) are established so that families and communities participate in and lead transformative school work.

As central stakeholders and beneficiaries of the educational system, students (and their families and community members) should be considered essential participants to any effort to reform educational systems. The research literature reveals that students can participate in research and documenting, school restructuring, classroom management, and community action (Bechtel & Reed, 1998; Cammarota & Fine, 2008; Finn & Checkoway, 1998; Lee & Zimmerman, n.d.; Metzger, 2004). Studies demonstrate that, when students are included in planning and decision-making processes, substantive and transformative change happens. Meaningfully partnering with youth and students on education reform work requires unearthing what are often unconscious assumptions about the capacity and appropriateness of students to be engaged in reform work. As Hart (1992) notes, there are a range of ways in which young people can be "engaged," from being tokenized, assigned, informed, consulted, and sharing in decision making to leading and initiating action.

We may somewhat more readily recognize and challenge our beliefs about limited capacity and involvement in relation to people of color, women, and other *adult* marginalized groups, yet we may unconsciously hold these perspectives in relation to youth and students.

Some of this myopia about student voice comes from the historical perspectives that educators have about their profession and their work. While it is true that we may know a great deal about what has been, we are not clear about what it means to be a student in the 21st century. The world in which we live will certainly create very different adult lives than the ones that most educators aspired to in their own upbringing. To learn what it is like to be a student in this place and time, "we need to embrace more fully the work of authorizing students' perspectives in conversations about schooling and reform" (Cook-Sather, 2002, p.12).

Building on these ideas, we propose that there are five initial requirements for any endeavor that purports to *transform* schools:

1.  It must examine the assumptions and beliefs that underlie any initiative to reform and/or change schools.
2.  In order for the change to be transformative, it must involve the entire community of stakeholders.
3.  Issues of power and privilege must be transparent and open for discussion.
4.  Students must be part of the conceptualizing, data collecting and analysis, strategic planning, and evaluation of impact.
5.  Students and families must have key leadership roles.

In this chapter, we challenge the notions that only some groups of people can be meaningfully involved in deliberation and decision making about educational change and that some stakeholders (in this case, students) cannot and should not be so powerfully engaged. We hope educators surface their perspectives on what they believe are the most appropriate roles for youth (and in particular, *which* youth) to play in transformation efforts. From here, we encourage educators and others working on reform to reflect on their personal, school, and district practices around youth involvement to see if these practices align with their beliefs and perspectives about the proper role and potential for youth involvement in educational improvement efforts. By understanding these perspectives, reformers (of all ages) can become more strategic in the systems change efforts they undertake and in examining the degree of impact those changes have in creating more effective school systems. In this way, we as educational systems change agents will be better able to collectively push the envelopes of our thinking toward what is most powerful in creating improved educational systems that serve all students well and help build a society and world of reflective, compassionate, and engaged citizens.

In the following sections, we lay out a framework for educators to consider that includes several important features of change efforts:

1. potential youth roles in educational change processes;
2. the capacities needed for youth and adults to work together meaningfully toward change;
3. the supports youth and adults need to undertake this work with vigor and creativity; and
4. a focus on moving youth engagement from the school to the community in an emancipatory model that broadens the notions of the purpose of education and engagement.

We hope that educators and those working toward educational systems transformation can locate themselves, their perspectives and frameworks, and their policies and practices in this model.

## ARENAS FOR STUDENT VOICE WORK AND YOUTH–ADULT PARTNERSHIPS

In this section, we discuss three arenas for youth voice work in educational improvement efforts. These approaches and goals appear commonly in the literature on reform, though they are often labeled differently. First, we address *voice and engagement* as it requires a commitment on the part of adults to actively question their philosophy of the role of students in school reform. Next we move to the more tangible task of *skill building* for both adults and students. Finally, we discuss authentic *community involvement and change*, which is the outcome we seek for powerful student voice work. At the end of the chapter is an introductory rubric for educational reformers and activists to begin to reflect on their own practice. Our perspective is that the most powerful student voice work and youth–adult partnerships come from robust work in all of these areas combined:

1. *Student voice and engagement*: broadening our conceptualization of engagement to include not only engaging students in their own learning, but also partnering with students as coproducers of educational systems' reform agendas by engaging students in helping to conceptualize reform work and evaluate it with educators, in continuous improvement cycles

2. *Skill building*: tapping youth's existing skills and helping youth and adults to build additional skills and competencies so they can work together most powerfully in systemic education transformation efforts

3. *Community involvement and change*: creating supportive structures for youth to impact, shape, and benefit their communities as the ultimate goal in education and engagement practices

## Student Voice and Engagement

Robinson and Taylor (2007) argued that the practice of work with student voice carries with it four core values: (1) "communication as dialogue" where there is trust, openness, and collaboration; (2) including all voices, especially those who have been historically "silenced" or are considered "critical or conflicting" to dominant ways of communicating; (3) recognizing that power relations are unequal and hence attention must be paid to which students are listened to and how they are listened to; and (4) acknowledging that change is possible through acting on the contributions of students as change agents (p. 8).

Attention to these four core values not only creates the space in which adults engage with students in sharing power and thereby develop understanding that is not rooted in "the way it's always been," but also allows for emancipatory practices that radically change the way we structure schooling for the most marginalized youth. A critical first step that educators must take when beginning student voice work is to engage students, and in doing so, educators must recognize the various ways that students may make meaning of who they are, their place in schools, and whether they are engaged productively or not, actively or passively. Too often, when adults in schools think of engaged students, they only recognize those students who are compliant, who fit with school norms, and who are successful in navigating the system as it currently functions. Other students may be either actively or passively engaged in resistance to the dominant cultural norms, values, and expectations imposed by the school. They may not be viewed as successful by school standards because they have developed identities in opposition to those norms. As a result they are often discounted, excluded from student voice work, and marginalized.

Harnessing the energy and insights of marginalized students can create great benefit for school reform efforts. Given that marginalized students are very often the metric for school reform success, it seems imperative to focus our efforts at student engagement on understanding the perspectives and issues they see. By doing so, we might uncover, from the perspectives of students, the deeper purposes of school and use that information to suggest new possibilities for the ways we do public education in the United States that will allow us to live up to the promise of equitable educational opportunities and outcomes for all students (Klingner et al., 2005).

As Miramontes, Nadeau, and Commins (1997) noted, "Schools can make a positive and significant difference for students when educators account for the complex interaction of language, culture, and context, and decisions are made within a coherent theoretical framework" (p. 15). To engage in critical pedagogy that supports adults and students in challenging traditional beliefs about the ways that school works requires a commitment to the construction of knowledge by sharing power and authority between students and teachers, challenging the hegemonic or "common sense" notions of what school is and should be, and sharing control of the curriculum and pedagogy of the classroom. Sharing power with students and questioning the political and social structures of school create a space in which students and adults broaden their understandings of themselves, the assumptions that society operates by, and the ways in which the world works (Giroux, 1997; McLaren, 1989).

Some readers may feel that those who are too young, who are belligerent, who are criminal offenders, who have particular kinds of disabilities, who espouse particular beliefs, who are from particular racial/ethnic and other backgrounds, who have particular ways of communicating, or who lack particular skill sets have either not gained or have forfeited their right to fully participate in society. These are important questions to ask, for communities and society to be in conversation about and come to conclusions regarding. The key issue here is that *we ask* these and other questions, especially the questions about what we risk creating among ourselves if we *do not* fully engage all of society's members and support each other in our ability to fully participate in the cocreation of and benefit from our social systems. Social justice advocates want to prepare students to be productive citizens in a democratic society (Goodlad, 1996). We must discuss our role and responsibility in creating dependency, alienation, voids, and righteous anger in society due to dismissing the wisdom all individuals bring through their participation. This approach will also help us understand the systems we have erected that have already caused so many to become alienated and righteously angry, as the Occupy movements of 2011 in the United States and elsewhere have demonstrated.

In the case of younger children, there is a growing body of literature that indicates these students can also be engaged more powerfully than is often done in typical educational reform work (e.g., Leachman & Victor, 2003; Palmer & Wehmeyer, 2003). The question here is whether we have done a thorough job of providing the full array of supports, infrastructure, and opportunities from which everyone in society benefits. Until we do so, it may behoove us to suspend final conclusions about who does and does not deserve to participate.

Cook-Sather (2002) discusses the role of trust in education:

> Although it is rarely articulated as such, the most basic premise upon which different approaches to educational policy and practice rest is trust—whether or not adults trust young people to be good (or not), to have and use relevant knowledge (or not), and to be responsible (or not). The educational institutions and practices that have prevailed in the United States, both historically and currently, reflect a basic lack of trust in students and have evolved to keep students under control and in their place as the largely passive recipients of what others determine is education. Since the beginning of formal education students have been designated tabula rasa or worse, wild and dangerous spirits in whom educators must inspire fear and awe. (p. 4)

The "good citizen" can be framed in several ways: (1) citizenship manifested in individual acts such as volunteering; (2) citizenship involving participating in local community affairs and staying informed on local and national issues; and (3) the "justice-oriented citizen" who includes the previous levels, but has a more critical stance and is active on social, economic, and political issues (Watts & Guessous, 2006, citing Westheimer & Kahne, 2003, p. 60). This notion of *activism* is core to our ultimate student voice in educational reform aims. Activism is a key to creating a society of informed, engaged, and inspired people who are continually cocreating and reinventing the world and our social systems in more just fashions.

## Approaches to Engaging Youth

How do we acknowledge the need for social or cultural capital to engage in the ways school is set up, or who may be passively *or actively* resistant (often with good reason) to engaging in such structures? We can begin by acknowledging a fundamental need of adolescents—their need to engage in meaningful relationship with adults—and to begin to develop those relationships by improving the ways that adults and youth engage in communication with each other.

> For education to occur there must be communication, and dialogue is the cornerstone of communication. Education must involve all parties. It is not our role to speak to the people about our own view of the world, nor attempt to impose that view on them but rather to dialogue with the people about their view and ours. We must realize that their view of the world, manifested variously in their actions, reflects their situation in the world. (Freire, 1973/2005, p. 77)

The roots of the word *dialogue* are the Greek words *dia* and *logos*, which means "through words or meaning" and, as we will use it here, refers to shared inquiry, thinking, and reflecting together. The outcome of an effective dialogue is that each party has given up efforts to "make *them* understand *us*" and, instead, come to a greater understanding of the relationship between each other (Isaacs, 1999). This requires that we embrace different points of view, end dichotomous efforts at determining a right and wrong way of doing or being, and place as much value on the voices and perspectives of students as we do on those of adults. The inherent difficulty in establishing a productive and ongoing dialogue lies in the fact that our thoughts and actions are motivated by prior experiences of which we may not even be fully aware. However, all perspectives must be accepted as part of the whole, no matter how challenging or difficult (Isaacs, 1999). Geren (2001) suggests that the discourse or dialogue that leads to the improvement of a human situation does not come naturally but is a learned process, requiring individuals to give up their self-interest for the good of the common interest. Learning to communicate and create shared spaces where all voices are heard and recognized is a complex task that requires intentional efforts to build those skills and value systems. This applies for adults no less than students. In the next section, we will address ways to build the skills that both youth and adults need to engage and communicate with each other effectively.

## Youth and Adult Skill Building

In order to support the most powerful development of youth voice in educational improvement, both adult practitioners and youth must build specific skill sets. This section explores the skill and competency needs for youth and adults to be able to work together in educational reform efforts in new and powerful ways.

Tolman, Ford, and Irby (2003) note that youth can play a number of roles in reform efforts, including active learners, educators of their peers and/or adults, advocates, organizers, leaders, service providers, researchers, philanthropists, and decision- and policymakers. These authors additionally note that youth can play a role at various levels of educational reform work, including individual, classroom or program, school or organization, community or city, and national and international levels (Tolman et al., 2003). Helping youth develop the capacity to take on most, if not all, of these roles and participate at all of these levels with success will require significant skill building for both youth and adults.

A range of skills and competencies can focus youth voice work. Competencies encompass multiple areas including academic, social, moral, cultural, vocational, civic, physical, as well as organizing skills to promote community involvement and change (Pittman & Tolman, 2002; Scheie et al., 2003). These competencies form the basis of "civic skills of relationship building, issue research and strategy development, public and interpersonal communication [which are] skills for organizing and advocacy" (Scheie, 2003, p. 3). Tolman et al. (2003) note that intellectual skill building includes problem solving, social skills, and intrapersonal skills. These are closely linked to organizing skills (p. 29). Levin's (2000) list expands to "defining problems, gathering evidence, analyzing data, writing proposals, and working effectively in teams," which are also significant educational outcomes in themselves (pp. 165–166).

Additionally, supporting youth in effective partnering with adults is an important skill-building area because it allows young people to take their "intuitive and experiential sensibilities and perspectives about what needs to be done and shap[e] them into programs, action agendas, and policy recommendations" (Forum for Youth Investment, 2005, p. 3). This extends the range of 21st-century skills being discussed in many reform dialogues about student skill-building needs. While all notions of 21st-century skills include academic, vocational, and basic civic foci, fewer include the types of cultural and organizing skills these authors speak of as essential youth skills. Further, the precise meaning of each of these skill sets for students is often a point of confusion for practitioners since similar terms can mean different goals or outcomes. Adults need support in building a similar, complementary range of skills in order to effectively support and partner with youth to fully participate in reform efforts. Building such a broad range of skills requires deep, authentic dialogue and two-way communication between adults and students, as well as youth truly engaged in their own learning.

***Social, cultural, interpersonal, and academic skills*** refer to how youth and adults are supported to be able to engage with "difference" in all of its forms in healthy ways. These skill sets include fostering a sense of receptivity to learning about others and their worldviews, experiences, and perspectives, grounded in one's own views, history, and cultures, *while* maintaining and cultivating openness to listening, learning, and growing. Academic skills are the focus of existing standards and accountability systems across states in the country. These (as well as the other skill sets) are essential for participation in a democracy, and consequently for helping co-create and enact educational transformation agendas where different and often contentious perspectives are present.

***Moral skills*** include deep reflection on the consequences of the choices we make in educational systems improvement work and involve the capacity for *courage*. This is a particularly critical skill area given the well-documented disproportionate and egregious impacts reform efforts have too

often had on students of color, low-income students, students with disabilities, and other marginalized groups. Supporting skillful joint reflection with youth and adults (especially those who have been most impacted by reform or lack of reform efforts) is essential and difficult work.

*Civic and organizing skill building* offers facility with community organizing and advocacy and supports students in altering power relations and creating change in their communities. Youth organizing supports leadership development in that youth act on issues defined by them and affecting them and their communities. Organizing also involves youth in the design, implementation, and evaluation of improvement efforts. Youth organizing builds skills including political education, analysis, community research, campaign development, direct action, and membership recruitment. The skills developed in youth organizing helps young people become lifelong community leaders (Torres-Fleming, Valdes, & Pillai, 2010).

*Analytical and communication skill areas* of problem definition, data analysis, proposal writing, team work, strategy development, and public communication are generic to any institutional change effort as well as specific to carrying forward educational improvement agendas. These areas are often not taught explicitly as part of the standard K–12 curriculum for youth (and may or may not be covered in teacher and administrator credential programs for adults). Hence they become crucial for our purposes of building the capacity of youth and adults to "team" with each other in conceiving, implementing, and evaluating systems improvement work. The ability of youth and adults to build consensus around what the problems are, locate and/or collect and analyze data relevant to the identified problems (and engage in consensus-making conversations about that data, which are often controversial in what they show about the experiences of and impacts on marginalized students), jointly develop strategies to address these areas, and communicate effectively to various constituent groups about all of the preceding are all formidable skill domains for youth and adults to strengthen.

*Cultural competency skills* are embedded in all of the above areas and apply specifically to working with and between marginalized youth and adults, and all groups with various types of demographic, ideological, and other differences. These competencies include ensuring that interactions are not "color-blind" and take into consideration the specific experiences, perspectives, and ways of communicating of racial/ethnic, language, ability, gender, age, and other cultural groups, which have often been denigrated, ignored, and/or misunderstood (Lindsey, Nuri Robins, & Terrell, 2009). Ensuring cultural competency as an undergirding domain of skill building includes examining the impacts of power and cultural capital differences among cultural groups (e.g., White and affluent practitioners and youth, versus youth of color and low-income youth), and how these affect the influence that groups have upon reform efforts. Student and adult demographic representation (i.e., a range of ethnicities, genders, income levels, abilities, language backgrounds, levels of success in school, sexual orientations, and so on) is a crucial first step in creating the conditions where interpersonal, social, and cultural proficiency skills can be built. Creating this environment also sets the stage for deepening awareness of how differences in cultural capital influence communication across groups and creates relative power differentials in identifying issues and solutions, and advancing reform agendas.

Finally, these skill-building efforts (see Table 2.1) can only become sustainable when policy environments are erected within schools and school systems where their ongoing development is supported via skilled practitioners, consultants, funding, and other infrastructure, as needed. Attention to power, cultural capital, and student demographic representation in service provision, programs, opportunities, and/or pathways for growth and involvement available to youth is critical (Pittman & Tolman, 2002). We have noted the importance of ensuring the centrality of "conflicting voices, silenced voices, and critical voices" (Robinson & Taylor, 2007, p. 10) for their ability to illuminate often hidden reform issues and potentially powerful and intersecting solutions. All of these efforts and skill areas are predicated upon youth and adults developing the actual capacity to partner effectively with one another. "Partnership" here refers to the areas that practitioners can reflect on in their own experiences, namely the qualities of mutual respect and regard for the wisdom, intelligence, and capacity to contribute meaningfully to the joint work at hand, the commitment to supporting one another and being critical friends, and openness to learning and listening skills.

In sum, there are key skill and competency areas for youth and adults in order to participate effectively in educational reform agendas: (1) traditional *academic* and *vocational* skills; (2) *social, cultural,* and *interpersonal* skills including self-awareness and cultural proficiency in engaging with youth and adults from different demographic backgrounds; (3) *moral* skills, which include deep reflection about one's individual choices and consequences and how these choices are impacted by broader social and historical circumstances; (4) basic as well as more advanced *civic* and *organizing* skills; (5) skills that support *carrying educational reform agendas* such as problem definition, data analysis, proposal writing, team work, strategy development, and public communication; and (6) skills for *effective partnering* between youth and adults.

TABLE 2.1. Youth and Adult Training and Skills Needed to Promote Ongoing, Powerful Student Voice

| Adults | Youth |
|---|---|
| • Listening and partnering in an ongoing (and not one-off) basis with youth from multiple backgrounds, perspectives, and ways of communication | • Listening and partnering with adults from multiple backgrounds, perspectives, and ways of communication |
| • Learning about the nature and impacts of power and cultural capital | • Learning about the nature and impacts of power and cultural capital |
| • Developing cultural proficiency skills, or how to engage with difference in healthy, constructive ways without being color-blind | • Developing cultural proficiency skills, or how to engage with difference in healthy, constructive ways without being color-blind |
| • Meaningfully changing their practice based on what they learn from youth | • Participating in dialogue, debate, and decision-making processes |
| • Partnering with local and national youth organizations that are skilled at this work | • Building skills in problem definition, gathering evidence, data analysis, proposal writing, and working in teams |
| • Creating supportive policy environments, such as working with school boards to establish friendly, supportive policies with accountability mechanisms | • Taking leadership roles |
| • Ensuring sufficient funding as well as skilled and experienced staff resources to do a robust job at erecting and monitoring powerful structures and practices to support youth voice | • Participating in political efforts |

## Community Involvement and Change: Moving Youth Engagement from School to Community

We turn now to community involvement and change, the third area of student voice work. This area is concerned with supporting the development of youth who are informed and engaged citizens as the ultimate goal of youth voice work in education. According to the 2010 U.S. Census there are about 63 million youth between the ages of 10 and 24 (Howden & Meyer, 2011). Given the energy and potential in that age range, we believe it is critical for the benefit of our communities and the social fabric of our society to engage and support these youths' collective vision, leadership, energy, and talents toward community transformation (Miao, 2003, as cited in Hosang, 2003, series preface).

Creating supportive structures for youth to impact and benefit their communities could be viewed as the ultimate goal of education. Certainly, engaging youth as agents for self-, peer, and community development can contribute to youth development and community improvement. Community engagement contributes to the identity formation of young adults who know themselves as caring activists, committed to improving community life, who have the skills, knowledge, and relationships for lifelong community leadership and responsible citizenship (Scheie, 2003). How this kind of lifelong commitment evolves depends on the ways in which youth are mentored and supported to become informed and engaged citizens. Youth outcomes such as confidence, civic engagement, connectedness, feeling competent and useful, belonging, good mental health, optimism, and social skills are key factors in academic engagement, success, and commitment to continued learning (Pittman & Tolman, 2002; Sagor, 2004; Tolman et al., 2003).

Challenges in schools and school systems are connected to their surrounding communities. Therefore, communities and community-based organizations are critical partners in schools' and school systems' ability to support youth and create healthy communities. By being involved in their communities, neighborhoods, cities, and beyond, youth begin to understand how systemic issues intersect. By making the connections between and among community characteristics and cultures, youth learn to become or deepen their existing capacity as strategic, sophisticated, and active agents of change. Many youth may already be deeply engaged in this type of work, while others may have limited supports and resources for such engagement.

Many schools, districts, and community organizations design programs and strategies to help students become more deeply involved in their communities. Several factors seem to shape the focus of youth programs. The first is the *type of community involvement work* that might involve volunteer work, service learning, internships, community action research, or community organizing. The second factor is the *type of goals* that are set for community involvement work. For instance, the change focus might be at the individual, local, regional, national, or global level, with a desire to lead to individual change, institutional change, community change, or societal change. As the level changes, so do the strategies for communication, networking, and measuring success.

A third factor is the degree to which *youth themselves play a central role* in shaping and selecting the community involvement options. Some programs may engage youth in an activity or project that already has set goals and priorities, while others might engage youth in identifying, assessing, and selecting potential sites, issues, and types of engagement. These factors are neither mutually exclusive nor rigidly formulated. Our experience has shown us that the degree of youth voice in designing the community involvement work, goals, desired impact, and the activities that will take place in the work should be clearly spelled out and agreed upon by the youth, adults, and participating school(s), district(s), and/or agency(ies).

We argue that community involvement and change work can lead youth to deeper engagement with school, and life in general, and hence to more powerful decision making as a result of deeper investment in themselves, their neighborhoods, and belief in their capacity to positively impact their environment. These goals for youth voice work extend beyond typical engagement strategies being used in the field and the skill building discussed in the preceding section of this chapter (Scheie, 2003; Watts & Guessous, 2006).

We note that others have been deeply engaged in categorizing the types of community involvement that are possible for youth, from intervention to youth development, to empowerment, to systemic change. These possibilities have been elaborated in the *Youth Engagement Continuum*, widely used in the youth development field (LISTEN, Inc., 2003, pp. 7–10). Each level of youth engagement—*youth services, youth development, youth leadership, youth civic engagement*, and *youth organizing*—is essential to provide rich opportunities for youth to help strengthen community health (see Table 2.2).

## Redressing Power Distribution and Cultural Capital

As we have mentioned, attention to power and cultural capital continues to be essential with community involvement and change as youth voice goals. As youth are engaged in identifying issues of importance in their personal lives and communities, both locally and globally, they are confronted with harsh realities of difference in access to resources, opportunities, and outcomes in all sectors including education, health care, housing, and other economic and social conditions. The dialogue skills and other areas of skill building discussed in the previous sections come to bear more sharply when youth begin to lend their knowledge, perspectives, and efforts to improve community conditions.

In all areas, from volunteer work and internships to community action research, to organizing, youth's awareness of the significance and impact of their community involvement work can also take on a range. Understanding significance and impact can take many forms. For instance, some community involvement experiences may help students develop awareness of the institutional and community contexts in which youth are working. Other experiences may extend awareness to how institutions impact communities. As well, youth may have the opportunity to explore how and to what end community institutions intersect with each other or across different sectors such as employment, social services, mental health, juvenile justice, and

TABLE 2.2. Youth Engagement Continuum (Developed by LISTEN, Inc., 2003, p. 10, and modified by Movement Strategy Center, 2012. Used with permission.)

Intervention → Development → Collective Empowerment → Systemic Change

| | Youth Services | Youth Development | Youth Leadership | Youth Civic Engagement | Youth Organizing |
|---|---|---|---|---|---|
| **Supporting Young People** | • Clients | • Participants<br>• Youth Workers | • Participants<br>• Youth Workers<br>• Leaders<br>• Staff<br>• Board Members | • Participants<br>• Youth Workers<br>• Leaders<br>• Staff<br>• Board Members | • Leaders<br>• Staff<br>• Board Members<br>• Organizers |
| **Providing Youth with Services and Opportunities** | Provide supports to address individual problems and behavior by helping young people with basic needs (personal, health, safety, and so on) | "Youth Services" offerings plus:<br>• Access to caring adults and safe spaces<br>• Opportunities for youth/adult partnerships<br>• Age-appropriate support | "Youth Development" offerings plus:<br>• Authentic youth leadership opportunities built into programming<br>• Opportunities to participate in community projects | "Youth Leadership" offerings plus:<br>• Opportunities to engage young people in advocacy and negotiation<br>• Engaging young people in political education and awareness | "Youth Civic Engagement" offerings plus:<br>• Involves youth as part of core leadership and governing body<br>• Engages in alliances and coalitions<br>• Builds and develops a base of youth |
| **Focused Programming** | Treatment plus Prevention<br>• Meeting young people where they are | Growth plus Development<br>• Building individual competencies | Capacity plus Skill Building<br>• Supporting young people as decision-makers and problem-solvers | Capacity Building<br>• For power analysis and action, and negotiation around issues identified by young people | Capacity Building for Collective Action<br>• Engaging in recruitment, popular education, and campaign development around issues identified by young people |

TABLE 2.2. Youth Engagement Continuum, Continued.

Intervention → Development → Collective Empowerment → Systemic Change

| | Youth Services | Youth Development | Youth Leadership | Youth Civic Engagement | Youth Organizing |
|---|---|---|---|---|---|
| How It Looks with Education Reform | To ensure that students can focus on school work, school lunch programs offer free or reduced price breakfast and lunch to students who meet eligibility requirements. | Academic enrichment programs support middle or high school students with academic tutoring, college counseling, and life preparation. | Leadership programs provide eligible youth with leadership development opportunities to engage as active leaders on school campuses through student government and districtwide school councils. | Youth leaders research college readiness and access by designing and collecting 1,000 surveys from students. Based on survey findings, youth leaders develop policy recommendations to increase college readiness and access. | Youth leaders are part of a coalition with parents and teachers to reduce racial/ethnic disparities and increase college access for all students. Youth build collective power for policies that make college preparatory classes mandatory for all students and increase college counselors on campus. |

transportation. Additionally, as youth become more involved in their communities, their awareness of the *systems* dimensions of issues can deepen. In this way, their ability to help develop penetrating analyses of educational issues and solutions can become that much more potent.

For example, youth who participated in an effort to expand a West Coast school district's approach to engaging students began to partner with central office staff and school board members (personal communication, 2008). Over the course of their engagement with the district, the youth began to deepen their understanding of the political, funding, and bureaucratic challenges that educators were facing in their attempts to create more powerful structures for engaging youth, as well as in their overall district improvement efforts. In turn, the adults involved in the effort deepened their awareness of and appreciation for the contributions that youth can bring to reform work. (See the work cited in *Voices in Urban Education* http://annenberginstitute.org/sites/default/files/product/197/files/VUE30.pdf)

## Nuances of Community Involvement Approaches

It is important to be intentional about personal goals for benefiting from, building, and deepening youth awareness, understanding, voice, and action. Youth will not automatically build deeper awareness of social issues as a result of every community involvement effort. Additionally, the degree of sophisticated awareness that youth develop will depend on the kind, range, and rigor of data and research youth have access to (or build themselves) about the institutions, neighborhoods, and communities they are working to impact. Students' depth of awareness will also depend on how powerful and structured the dialogue formats are that they participate in (i.e., the curricular and pedagogical practices within school hours and/or in after-school settings to which they have access). These surrounding and supportive conditions are important so that youth can be deeply reflective about their analyses, the work they are undertaking, why they are undertaking it, to what end(s), and how their efforts might be course-corrected if need be, to become more powerful.

It is also important to remember that youth *come with* a depth of experience and knowledge about their communities. Therefore community involvement work as a critical component in school, district, and community improvement should *build on* youth's existing expertise and skills, truly capitalizing on the tremendous assets that all youth bring.

To execute the most robust community involvement efforts along these lines will require ongoing development for youth and adults of the full range of skills discussed in the last section of this chapter. Continued vigilance is necessary to reflect on which youth from which demographic categories have true access to the full range of community involvement opportunities and supports. Ensuring representation based on race/ethnicity, income levels, gender, sexuality, ability, language, and all other areas of marginalization is critically important.

Practitioners wishing to engage youth in robust strategies and approaches should ask themselves which youth have access to community involvement opportunities based on relative success in school determined via tests, grading, and other common assessments. Youth who have struggled in school can be motivated anew, and youth who have disconnected or given up on their success can be profoundly inspired to re-engage in school by being able to participate in community change work on issues and with organizations that interest them (Petty, 2008). Often, students who have struggled in school are deeply concerned about school conditions and thrive when given authentic opportunities and supports to help create meaningful change.

Additionally, it is critical to consider what kinds of experiences youth desire as well as what experiences will help deepen their ability to "care about, act for and [be] effective at improving their communities" (Scheie, 2003, p. 3). This support for engaged citizens extends from areas where youth might naturally gravitate (i.e., institutions or experiences familiar to them) to organizations and community involvement opportunities that may be unfamiliar, uncomfortable, or intimidating to them. Youth from both economically disadvantaged and more privileged backgrounds can lead lives where they have limited contact with people whom they would consider "different" from themselves. Hence a range of deep community involvement opportunities can be powerful venues to bolster youth's learning about themselves and others for youth who would otherwise have limited opportunities and supports to do so.

As with all students, participation should come with agreements about how the community involvement opportunity relates with the core academic work and can bolster success there. The relationship between community change work and traditional academics warrants deep discussion and planning by youth and adults. Ideally, collaborative decisions by youth and adults would be made about whether community change work is *core* or *peripheral* to goals for student learning and success (i.e., academic standards and building global, 21st-century skills) and, if community change work is considered core, what is considered rigorous in terms of youth voice, goals of the work, and developing and evaluating the involvement opportunities.

Ensuring the highest-quality work in community involvement and change as a youth voice goal requires creating supportive policy environments. Policy intervention might include the following: working with school boards to establish *policies with teeth* that are supportive of youth doing powerful school, district, and community involvement and change work; ensuring *skilled and experienced staff* at district, school, and community organization levels; ensuring the development of a cohesive *infrastructure* supporting ongoing authentic and powerful youth voice; ensuring sufficient *funding*; and *drawing on the expertise of local and national* youth organizations who are skilled at this work (Pittman & Tolman, 2002).

## Emancipation: Unleashing the Full Potential of Student Voice in Education Reform

Our use of the term *emancipation* for this section heading and as an ultimate aim of student voice work was inspired by Robinson and Taylor's (2007) discussion of "emancipatory education" (p. 9). We take this notion of emancipation as the ability to participate fully in the human community. This concept is similar to "sociopolitical development" or the

> evolving, critical understanding of the political, economic, cultural, and other systemic forces that shape society and one's status within it, and the associated process of growth in relevant knowledge, analytical skills, and emotional faculties. It broadens or replaces a narrow focus on adjustment, coping, resilience, and similar concepts that connote accommodation, with the more empowering notions of a collective sense of agency, commitment to action, and activism. . . . [I]t explicitly acknowledges oppression and the influence of social forces outside the individual. (Watts & Guessous, 2006, p. 60)

Voice, dialogue, sociopolitical development, and emancipation are core to participation in the human community. Lack of authentic avenues and supports for meaningful voice and engagement for all students leads to limited authentic participation in the world. This limited participation can further lead to perpetual alienation of individuals and fragmentation of society.

We are aiming for "a sustained and meaningful role for students in defining, shaping, managing, and implementing reform" (Levin, 2000, p. 155). The degree to which we help foster such conditions for voice and engagement across age (youth and adults), race, language, ability, and other demographic categories is the degree to which we will help foster individuals who are equipped to help transform our educational systems and, in turn, cocreate a more just society. The converse of this point is also true: The degree to which we inhibit authentic voice and engagement as part of education reform work is the degree to which we will inhibit our ability to cocreate a more just society. If we are not in real dialogue with one another (i.e., if some voices are valued and supported to authentically participate over others), we will not be able to develop powerful enough collaborative skills to be in constant, often tension-filled, constructive, and compassionate dialogue together across differences on a perpetual basis.

For those who may have the concern that, when students do voice their perspectives on education, they are not focused on or concerned about the same things as adults, Alyeska (1999) offers this thought:

> The students' emphasis on relationships, roles, respect, and reality does not contradict the policymakers' emphasis on rigor, rules, and required exams. Many educators affirm that these are, in fact, the means to achieving the high standards set. (p. 1)

Frequently, students raise many of the same issues and concerns adults are focused on, as well as emphasizing other critical areas often not part of adult education reform dialogues. Joselowsky and Davis (2004) make the case that, while adults may bring systems and other valuable perspectives to reform discussions, youth can also bring deep analyses of educational system challenges as well as a grounded, current, and visceral understanding of the realities in schools and districts and clarity about the real impacts of reform efforts on their experiences and readiness for life.

In this chapter we have attempted to lay out the various approaches we have seen taken in student/youth voice in education reform so that we could emphasize some of the more powerful, robust approaches and how these can impact systems change work. For urban systems engaged in this work, we encourage you to reflect on your processes and progress using the tool that we have created contained in Table 2.3. This rubric is designed to help everyone engaged in urban schools transformational work to gauge their progress in emancipatory systemic change. We hope that readers will take the information presented in this chapter and read the rest of the volume with authentic student voice in mind: specifically, how student voice *does*, *does not*, *can*, and *should* intersect with urban education reform.

## NOTE

This chapter work complements the considerable efforts of the Funders' Collaborative on Youth Organizing (www.fcyo.org), the Annenberg Institute for School Reform's work (http://annenberginstitute.org/community-organizing-engagement) on *Youth Organizing in Education Reform* (http://annenberginstitute.org/sites/default/files/product/197/files/VUE30.pdf), Cammarota and Fine (2008), and many others in raising awareness of the approaches, rigor, and power of authentic youth voice and engagement in advancing educational systems change nationally. We target this chapter to educators and change agents who may be less familiar with these bodies of literature and practice.

TABLE 2.3. Rubric for Evaluating Student Voice Approaches in Educational Systems Change Efforts

| | Participation | Power, Cultural Capital, and Diversity | Education | Infrastructures |
|---|---|---|---|---|
| **Basic Practice:** Traditional, in classroom and schools | Student opinions are solicited. Standard structures such as student councils and clubs exist. Classroom and school practices presume that adults choose and that students comply. | Student participants represent "typical" kids and only those who are successful in school. | No training or skill building provided. | Adult involvement in student voice work is limited to volunteers who lead clubs or initiate them. Resources are limited. There are no requirements for student input or involvement. |
| **Emergent Practice:** Empowering students in classrooms and schools | Students have multiple opportunities to provide feedback and to engage in activities designed to improve school. Opportunities limited to traditional focus on student engagement in preset school goals. Students may be included in determining classroom practices, but have a limited role in conceptualizing, designing, implementing, and/or evaluating reform work. | Efforts are made to ensure participation of diverse students, (i.e., those with disabilities, gender, race, ethnicity, languages, relative success in school, and so on) and to attend to the voices and perspectives of those students. | Some training is provided, but is directed at youth. | Teachers are invited to include student voices in classroom decision making. Additional resources to support that work, or to remove barriers created by curriculum or bell schedules, are not addressed. Training in how to do so is not provided. Successful inclusion of student voice is not part of the reward or evaluation structure for adults. |

TABLE 2.3. Continued

| | Participation | Power, Cultural Capital, and Diversity | Education | Infrastructures |
|---|---|---|---|---|
| **Powerful Practice:** Classroom, school, community, and district | Students are engaged in leadership roles in all decision-making groups at the school, in the district, and in the community.<br>Students participate in choosing issues to focus on. They develop data collection methods, collect and analyze data, make recommendations, and implement and evaluate changes.<br>Robust systems exist for youth to participate in ongoing ways in the conceptualization, design, implementation, and evaluation of reform efforts in the classroom, school, and community. | All students participate in a variety of decision-making forums. Representation of demographic groups, including race/ethnicity, economic status, school success, gender, ability, and language is proportional to school population.<br>Intentional efforts to include the perspectives of students whose opinions and experiences are different from (or in opposition to) the school or larger population are present. | Adults are encouraged to engage students in active learning to share decision making in the classroom, and to uncover students' funds of knowledge and use them to facilitate learning and development.<br>Adults are encouraged to develop opportunities for students to engage in extracurricular activities.<br>Funding and resource allocation, along with professional development activities, support these goals. | School policies are designed to focus attention on the inclusion of youth voice in decision making, not only at the classroom level, but also at the school and district levels.<br>All adults are expected to participate with youth and develop their own skills.<br>School actively pursues relationships with other organizations in the community that extend opportunities for engagement and emancipation. Funding and structures ensure the success of these efforts. |

59

## REFERENCES

Alyeska, A. (1999). *Motivation for learning: Youth voices for educational change: A discussion among high school students at the Council of Chief State School Officers 1999 summer institute.* Washington, DC: Forum for Youth Investment, International Youth Foundation.

Bechtel, D., & Reed, C. (1998). Students as documenters: Benefits, reflections and suggestions. *NAASP Bulletin, 82* (594), 89–95.

Cammarota, J., & Fine, M. (Eds.). (2008). *Revolutionizing education: Youth participatory action research in motion.* New York, NY: Routledge.

Cook-Sather, A. (2002). Authorizing students' perspectives: Toward trust, dialogue, and change in education. *Educational Researcher, 31*(4), 3–14.

Davies, L. (2002). Possibilities and limits for democratization in education. *Comparative Education, 38*(3), 251–266.

Erickon, F., & Shultz, J. (1992). Students' experience of the curriculum. In P. Jackson (Ed.), *Handbook of research on curriculum* (pp. 465–485). New York, NY: MacMillan.

Ferguson, D. L., Kozleski, E. B., & Smith, A. (2003). Transforming general and special education in urban schools. In F. Obiakor, C. Utley, & A. Rotatori (Eds.), *Advances in Special Education: Vol. 15. Effective education for learners with exceptionalities* (pp. 43–74). London, United Kingdom: JAI Press.

Finn, J., & Checkoway, B. (1998). Young people as competent community builders: A challenge to social work. *Social Work, 43,* 335–346.

Forum for Youth Investment. (2005).*Youth engagement in educational change: Working definition and lessons from the field.* Washington, DC: Forum for Youth Investment.

Freire, P. (2005). *Education for critical consciousness.* New York, NY: Continuum. (Original work published 1973)

Fullan, M. (2000). The three stories of education reform. *Phi Delta Kappan, 8,* 581–584.

Gay, G. (1997). The relationship between multicultural and democratic education. *The Social Studies, 88*(1), 5–-12.

Geren, P. (2001). Public discourse: Creating the conditions for dialogue concerning the common good in a postmodern heterogeneous democracy. *Studies in Philosophy and Education, 20,* 191–199.

Giles, H. C. (1998). *Parent engagement as a school reform strategy.* ERIC/CUE Digest No 135. New York, NY: ERIC Clearinghouse on Urban Education.

Giroux, H. (1997). *Pedagogy and the politics of hope: Theory, culture, and schooling.* Boulder, CO: Westview Press.

Glendon, M. (1991). *Rights talk: The impoverishment of political discourse.* New York, NY: Free Press.

Goodlad, J. I. (1996). Sustaining and extending educational renewal. *Phi Delta Kappan, 78*(3), 228–234.

Hart, R. (1992). *Innocenti Essays: No. 4. Children's participation: From tokenism to citizenship.* Florence: UNICEF International Child Development Centre. Retrieved from www.unicef-irc.org/publications/pdf/childrens_participation.pdf

Hosang, D. (2003). *Occasional Papers Series on Youth Organizing, No. 02. Youth and community organizing today.* New York, NY: Funders' Collaborative on Youth Organizing.

Howden, L., & Meyer, J. (2011). *Age and sex composition: 2010.* Washington, DC: U.S. Census Bureau. Retrieved from www.census.gov/prod/cen2010/briefs/c2010br-03.pdf

Isaacs, W. (1999). *Dialogue and the art of thinking together.* New York, NY: Random House.

Joselowsky, F., & Davis, K. (2004). *Meaningful youth roles: Engagement strategies to move young people to the center of high school reform.* Washington, DC: Forum for Youth Investment.

Joselowsky, F., Thomases, J., & Yohalem, N. (2004). *Creating "good" schools observation and discussion tool: Helping young people and adults have conversations about what makes a "good" youth-centered school.* Washington, DC: Forum for Youth Investment.

Klingner, J. K., Artiles, A. J., Kozleski, E., Harry, B., Zion, S., Tate, W., . . . Riley, D. (2005). Addressing the disproportionate representation of culturally and linguistically diverse students in special education through culturally responsive educational systems. *Education Policy Analysis Archives, 13*(38), 1–42.

Leachman, G., & Victor, D. (2003). Student-led class meetings. *Educational Leadership, 60*(6), 64–68.

Lee, L., & Zimmerman, M. (n.d.). *Passion, action and a new vision for student voice: Learnings from the Manitoba School Improvement Program.* Winnipeg, Canada: Manitoba School Improvement Program.

Levin, B. (2000). Putting students at the centre in education reform. *Journal of Educational Change, 1,* 155–172.

Lincoln, Y. (1995). In search of students' voices. *Theory into Practice, 34*(2), 88–93.

Lindsey, R., Nuri Robins, K., & Terrell, R. (2009). *Cultural proficiency: A manual for school leaders.* Thousand Oaks, CA: Corwin Press.

LISTEN, Inc. (2003). *Occasional Papers Series on Youth Organizing, No. 01. An emerging model for working with youth: Community organizing + youth development = youth organizing.* New York, NY: Funders' Collaborative on Youth Organizing. Retrieved from www.fcyo.org/media/docs/8141_Papers_no1_v4.qxd.pdf

McLaren, P. (1989). *Life in schools: An introduction to critical pedagogy in the foundation of education.* New York, NY: Longman.

Metzger, D. (2004). Rethinking classroom management: Teaching and learning with students. *Social Studies and the Young Learner, 17*(2), 13–15.

Miramontes, O., Nadeau, A., & Commins, N. L. (1997). *Restructuring schools for linguistic diversity: Linking decision-making to effective programs.* New York, NY: Teachers College Press.

The Movement Strategy Center & The Funders' Collaborative on Youth Organizing (2012). *The power of transformative youth leadership: A field analysis of youth organizing in Pittsburgh.* Pittsburgh, PA: The Heinz Endowments.

Novak, B. (2002). Humanizing democracy: Mathew Arnold's nineteenth-century call for a common, higher, educative pursuit of happiness and its relevance to twenty-first-century democratic life. *American Education Research Journal, 39*(3), 593–637.

O'Hair, M. J., McLaughlin, J., & Reitzug, U. L. (2000). *Foundations of democratic education*. Belmont, CA: Wadsworth.

Palmer, S., & Wehmeyer, M. L. (2003). Promoting self-determination in early elementary school: Teaching self-regulated problem-solving and goal setting skills. *Remedial and Special Education, 24,* 115–126.

Petty, S. (2008). *Oakland Street Academy: Alternative school lessons for mainstream education* (Unpublished doctoral dissertation). Fielding Graduate University, Santa Barbara, CA.

Pittman, K., & Tolman, J. (2002). *New directions in school reform: Youth-focused strategies versus youth-centered reform*. Washington, DC: Forum for Youth Investment.

Reigeluth, C. M. (1994). What is systemic change and is it needed? In C. M. Reigeluth & R. J. Garfinkle (Eds.), *Systemic change in education* (pp. 3–11). Englewood Cliffs, NJ: Education Technology.

Robinson, C., & Taylor, C. (2007). Theorizing student voice: Values and perspectives. *Improving Schools, 10*(1), 5–17.

Sagor, R. (2004). *The action research guidebook: A four-step process for educators and school teams*. Thousand Oaks, CA: Corwin Press.

Scheie, D. (with Robillos, M., Bischoff, M., & Langley, B.). (2003). *Organizing for youth development and school improvement: Final report from a strategic assessment*. Minneapolis, MN: Rainbow Research.

Smith, W., & Fenstermacher, G. (Eds.). (1999). *Leadership for educational renewal: Developing a cadre of leaders*. San Francisco, CA: Jossey-Bass.

Squire, K. D., & Reigeluth, C. M. (2000). The many faces of systems change. *Educational Horizons, 78,* 143–152.

Tolman, J., Ford, P., & Irby, M. (2003). *What works in education reform: Putting young people at the center*. Baltimore, MD: International Youth Foundation.

Torres-Fleming, A., Valdes, P., & Pillai, S. (2010). *2010 Youth organizing field scan*. Brooklyn, NY: Funders' Collaborative on Youth Organizing. Retrieved from www.fcyo.org/media/docs/7697_2010FCYOYouthOrganizingFieldScan_FINAL.pdf

Watts, R. J., & Guessous, O. (2006). Sociopolitical development: The missing link in research and policy on adolescents. In S. Ginwright, P. Noguera, & J. Cammarota, (Eds.), *Beyond resistance! Youth activism and community change* (pp. 59–80). New York, NY: Routledge.

What Kids Can Do & MetLife Foundation. (2004). *Students as allies in improving their schools: A report on work in progress*. Providence, RI: What Kids Can Do. Retrieved from www.whatkidscando.org/publications/pdfs/saa_finalreport.pdf

Zion, S. D. (2009). Systems, stakeholders, and students: Including students in school reform. *Improving School, 12,* 131–143.

# CHAPTER 3

# Beyond Psychological Views of Student Learning in Systemic Reform Agendas

*Elizabeth B. Kozleski and Alfredo J. Artiles*

In Eagle District, middle schools serving students ages approximately 12 through 15 (grades 6 through 9) offer classes in language arts. In one classroom, the teacher, Kris, leads a lesson on interpreting text and developing an argument. She has selected a chapter from the autobiography of the U.S. comedian, Dick Gregory. Dick Gregory achieved some degree of public recognition during the civil rights movement in the 1960s and 1970s. In his autobiography, he traces the roots of his commitment to civil rights. One anecdote is devoted to his first conscious experience of racism, an encounter in elementary school. Students in the class we observe have read the excerpt, "Not Poor, Just Broke," from Gregory's autobiography and are engaged in small groups about the room, answering a set of questions on a handout the teacher has prepared. The questions include the following: "Why did Gregory interpret this experience as racism? What evidence is provided that might have led him to make that conclusion? What do you think the teacher's intent was in this situation? What in the text makes you think that? Have you ever experienced or witnessed a similar situation? What do you think that the group could have done in this situation?"

Students in the small groups are closely reading the text, offering support from the text for their interpretation. Other students are taking notes for discussion that will occur later. There is dialogue, contention, and resolution occurring. On close observation, some students in the room are unable to locate their evidence. It seems that they cannot read the text. Their fellow students help them out. Kris coaches the small groups to organize their evidence. Periodically, she looks up from her small group discussions to check on the group as a whole. The students are engaged in the task. There is obvious intensity and focus from the students and the teacher. (Kozleski, Zion, & Hidalgo, 2006, p. 15)

Entrenched inequitable educational opportunities, resource distributions, and outcomes documented for the last several generations in the United States plague our urban schools, communities, and the national landscape (Anyon, 2005). Access to higher education and employment eludes African Americans, American Indians, and Latinos while the population of preschoolers has become majority-minority (Frey, 2013). Students who identify themselves in any of these racial/ethnic categories are more likely to struggle academically, drop out before graduation, be referred for disciplinary action, and be identified for special education services (Aud et al., 2010). Grim outcome data must change if the rising generation of urban school-aged children is to have access to the creative class of jobs touted as America's niche in the world economy (Florida, 2002), rhetoric common in the current neoliberal national education agenda.

At the core of all educational arenas is student learning. Student learning is both an object and outcome of classroom activity systems. What it looks like differs across classrooms depending on the classroom activity system and the systems with which it interacts. In this chapter we remind our readers of the complex nature of learning, informed by the interdisciplinary field of learning sciences, and how such perspectives might reframe the nature of curriculum and learning contexts in urban schools. Rather than emphasize being competitive in the global marketplace, we argue that school success is the degree to which all students are able to access, participate, and acquire robust tools for inventing, engineering, and responding to the complex problems of the 21st century. Contemporary views of learning are grounded in interdisciplinary scholarship with roots in anthropology; educational, cognitive, and cultural psychology; computer science; and applied linguistics, among others. A distinctive aspect of this scholarship is a concern with learning as it occurs in everyday life and how to stimulate it across multiple formal and informal contexts (Greeno, 2006).

We argue these contemporary theories and research about learning must inform the redesign of urban schools. Without a serious reconsideration of what constitutes learning and therefore how schools, classrooms, and curricula must be designed, the discouraging educational outcomes that disadvantage urban students will continue. It is indefensible to accept a system of education that systematically marginalizes and hinders whole segments of our communities. This book addresses that justice dilemma, acknowledging the multiple factors that contribute to the current state of urban education. Learning is at the core of the collective action needed to resolve the many inequities that result from equipping only some children to grapple with the thorny complexities of knowledge creation.

Beyond an emphasis on teaching as a set of drills and routines, which Sawyer (2006) described as "instructionism," assumptions about what learning comprises often go unchecked in setting agendas for urban education reform. Understanding the connected multifaceted nature of learning is key to transforming the design of learning. The purpose of this chapter is to outline key considerations in contemporary views of learning and discuss their implications for urban school reform. First, we define learning, contrasting it with historical views. Second, we explore where learning happens and what this means for remediating learning practices in urban schools. Third, we offer alternative ways of designing learning opportunities grounded in interdisciplinary knowledge.

## FRAMING BIG IDEAS ABOUT LEARNING

The learning sciences have come a long way in understanding how people learn and, in particular, in understanding the complexities and sophistication of the learning strategies infants, young children, and school-age children engage (Bransford, Brown, Cocking, Donovan, & Pellegrino, 1999; Greeno, 2006; Sawyer, 2006). Indeed, learning scientists concur that students do not learn more deeply simply because teachers provide better instruction. Rather, students must actively participate in their own learning. Yet many people, including educational researchers, policymakers, teachers, and parents, continue to believe that education should be based on instructionism rather than on learning (Sawyer, 2006). All too often attention to improvements in student performance conceptualizes learning as a process of receiving knowledge and reproducing skills that are transmitted from a teacher to a student or group of students (Oakes, 2009); receiving and reproducing skills and processes with increasing dexterity are at the core of instructionism.

When such a view of schooling and the role of learning is ascendant, school leaders assess teacher performance through the degree to which teachers enact certain processes and whether students retain particular slices of knowledge. This mentality trumps approaches that conceptualize learning as a design problem (Design-Based Research Collaborative, 2003). In fact, most current accountability systems for measuring educational outcomes take the instructionism tack and, in doing so, constrain the ways that learning is designed (Berliner, 2009). Instructionism assumes that learning occurs because of what teachers do with the curriculum, not because of interactions between teaching processes and how students actively make meaning, engage, resist, contest, and internalize mental schemas about the world around them and their role in it (Engeström & Sannino, 2010). Historically, the notion of learning has been theorized and studied using a psychological perspective, relying largely on behavioral and cognitive lenses. This analytic preference created key challenges that date back to the early work on learning, most prominently measurement issues since learning, by virtue of its very nature, cannot be measured directly. As Koschmann (2011) explained, "For the educational psychologist, learning is a purely operational construct—it is what the test instrument reveals" (p. 4). As we explain below, however, learning theory has broadened the unit of analysis beyond the confines of people's psyches.

In our earlier description of a lesson in an urban middle school language arts classroom, the classroom teacher, Kris, designed and supported the learning environment in multiple ways. She took the state and district literacy standards for middle school students and carefully built the classroom curriculum around those anchors. Kris engaged and sustained student effort through selection of text that resonated with students' lived experiences and provided the chance to interact around the material in ways that extended their reasoning. Finally, by enlisting all the students in discussion, she engineered the distribution of learning throughout the classroom. The notion of learning as a distributed network is well developed in the learning sciences (Rogoff, 1998). That is, thinking is distributed throughout a group of learners and their internal knowledge is mapped together to produce new knowledge that, in turn, becomes internalized (Jelinek, 2013). In this chapter's snapshot of her classroom process, Kris's role was to facilitate learning, directing students' attention to the questions and the kinds of evidence they needed to address those questions. For instance, when her students with disabilities needed support to engage the reading independently, she scaffolded instruction by working with a small group of struggling readers, building their fluency through the background knowledge they gained in this activity. Her small group, held later in the day, focused on skills and strategies specific to the literacy needs of her students. While she did this small-group intensive instruction, the rest of the class prepared for the next step in the activity by outlining their responses to the questions posed. These outlines shaped a 2-day process called "writers workshop" that occurred later in the week in which students wrote and rewrote their arguments in dyads (Morris, 2013). Consistent with contemporary learning theories, retention of information lost its centrality, and instead, student *understanding*, *representation*, and *use* gained significant currency. This brief discussion of the Kris's classroom practice helps anchor the following description of learning.

## LEARNING INSIDE THE HEAD AND OUT IN THE WORLD:
## A SITUATIVE PERSPECTIVE

We subscribe to the broad perspective on learning that Greeno, Collins, and Resnick (1996) describe as "situative/pragmatist-sociohistoric." This perspective aims to bridge the longstanding divide between psychological and social perspectives on learning, and although this approach is still being debated and refined, it represents one of the best efforts to formulate the complex and interdependent social, psychological, and contextual aspects of learning (Koschmann, 2011). This perspective conceives learning as emerging from opportunities to participate in social practices that are context bound, that is, that are relevant to communities of individuals that share background understandings and a history of collaborative activity. As individuals participate in these communities, they develop identities that are meaningfully connected to these groups. In this view, the construct of practice is crucial for, as Koschmann (2011) explained, "practices come . . . with worlds attached" (p. 6). The specific meanings of participants' words, actions, and behaviors are situated in the particular circumstances in which they are used by people who share a history of participation; thus practices "both constitute and are constituted by their context" (p. 6). A practice-based perspective on learning, therefore, imposes on researchers the requirement to produce detailed accounts of the actual practices in which learning is produced, the conditions under which they took place, and the consequences of these practices. Moreover, a situative perspective on learning aims to trace changes in social practice (Koschmann, 2011).

For communities of learners, learning increases fluidity in participation, as well as developing tools for reflexivity that enable individuals and communities to hone performance and achieve goals or outcomes. For example, a social practice might be waiting to listen while someone else explains what a math problem is asking. This social practice might entail stopping to listen as well as considering the content of what is said and the degree to which it matches or reframes what the listener understands. A third part of this process entails making a decision about which interpretation of the math problem should be used to move toward finding a solution. Notice, however, that these processes are not all shaped entirely by local circumstances. The interpretive and analytical work produced by participants in this practice is, to borrow from Gee (2005), "licensed by some theory of the domain [in this case math] and then use the procedures ('methods') of that theory's approach to answer the question" (p. 12). Indeed, the social practice is embedded in the discipline of math. Learners are engaged in a joint enterprise that will contribute to refining their understanding of a new part of the world of mathematics.

### Learning Happens Through Activity

Activity produces mental maps or schemas that help students predict, problem-solve, analyze, synthesize, and create. Mental maps are anchored by semantic networks that categorize and link concepts, and create classification systems. These systems are manifested in sorting systems that range from simple to complex. Still used today, Linnaeus's taxonomy for naming and ordering organisms is an example of the complexity of sorting systems. But learning is more than storing information; it is the ability to act, improvise, reorganize, challenge, and remediate what is known or assumed, based on new information. While cognitive psychology has been consumed with how individuals receive, order, produce, and create, sociocultural psychologists have been interested in how the world around individuals mediates and shapes what individuals attend to, the tools they use, and how they gain expertise through participation in social interaction.

This view of learning encompasses and expands the work of cognitive and behavioral psychology as it shifts the locus of learning from individual to collective activity (Greeno et al., 1996). It emphasizes the role of culture in the ways in which knowledge is developed and distributed, how particular affordances for learning in our environments are perceived and utilized, what is valued within a community, and how "tools for thinking" are transmitted and embedded within the learning tasks made available and deemed significant within particular contexts. We consider each of these elements in the following paragraphs.

*Culture.* Atkinson (2004) remarks that "it seems far more sensible to say that culture exists co-constitutively in the world and in the head, and that heads and worlds may therefore not really be such separate and isolated locations after all" (p. 284). Atkinson speaks for many contemporary scholars who argue that culture is both something that is received from the contexts that we inhabit and created internally (Cole, 1996). We negotiate the assumptions and understandings that we retain from our cultural histories with the lived reality of the here and now of our lives. Students, then, live in a constant state of cultural reproduction and production (Artiles, 2003).

In urban schools this notion of negotiating culture is particularly palpable because of the diversity of views, experiences, and practices that are part of daily life. Culture is embedded in how students approach problems and tasks, how they manifest their identities, whom they seek out, and what they understand as learning. Atkinson (2004) makes the point that multiple cultural tools and lenses intersect in educational venues across political boundaries: national, community, professional-academic, classroom culture, student culture, and youth culture. We would argue that these are just a *few* of the many cultural contributors to an education system. The notion of these simultaneously operating cultures supports the argument that culture is not fixed but a mutually constituted, dynamic understanding of any local and situated context. Conceptualize each of these spaces as having particular cultural tool sets that traverse different cultural scales, histories, and activity arenas. For example, professional-academic activity arenas cross classrooms, schools in a district, states, and national boundaries. Physics teachers share common professional questions and share some links through their discipline that afford the opportunity to exist within an international professional community around physics teaching as well. As actors move through these spaces, they interact, and appropriate and inform each other's understanding through their mental and material tools. Thus culture continues to shift and inform how learning occurs in and among classrooms, schools, and school districts.

*Learning affordances.* There was a time in Western civilization when there were no sofas (Dejean, 2009). With sofas and the development of other comfortable seating in the 18th century in France, groups of people became more likely to gather in one another's homes after the evening meal. In doing so, they began to discuss contemporary issues. These gatherings became known as *salons,* places where socially desirable, intellectually diverse individuals met and created new cultural spaces and ideas (Dejean, 2009). While sofas did not create salons, they were part of the affordances of the time that made such gatherings more comfortable and desirable. In the parlance of learning scientists, affordances are part of the ecology of learning spaces (Gibson, 1979). Affordances suggest actions. Computer tablets offer the opportunity to touch and explore. Carpet squares on the floor of a kindergarten classroom offer a place to sit or material to build a fort. But, the carpet squares and the computer tablet don't offer the same affordances. Hutchby (2001) reminds us that affordances are not only objects; they can be people, other species, and the abilities that we each possess to walk, see, hear, and so forth. Where affordances are available, like tables that are easily moved and reassembled in alternate configurations, they make it possible to group and regroup learners. As a result, teachers are more likely to design different kinds of learning processes because of access to those affordances. Where classrooms are equipped with multiple sources for gathering new information, like computer tablets, smart phones, and computers, students are more likely to search for new information.

*Affordances have cultural implications.* They signal that certain kinds of activity should occur. There are many places now in the world where sofas would be hindrances rather than affordances. For nomadic people, for whom sofas would make travel from site to site difficult; rugs perform a similar kind of affordance. That is, they signal a place to rest and engage in thinking and speaking activities rather than manual labor. Desks in a row, facing forward toward a chalkboard, signal another kind of assumption about learning. The best curriculum in a poorly designed and static learning environment with little or no access to the available array of possible learning affordances makes the work of students and teachers more complicated and less engaging.

***Embedding tools for thinking.*** The situative view of learning has particular utility for understanding the practices of groups such as classrooms of students within a developmental level, school, or discipline because it assumes a distributed, emergent, and ecological stance in relationship to cognitive processing and performance (Cole, 1996). In Kris's classroom, students with different histories, identities, capacities, interests, and practices worked together to build a body of practices that helped them learn from one another, distributing the construction of knowledge among the students, the materials, and the tools they used to problem-solve. It was messy. Learners had different skill sets. They anticipated what was to happen from their own point of view and had to renegotiate that imagined outcome with the reality of the capacities of group members, time constraints, and intellectual and material resources. To guide this learning, Kris needed tools to mediate how learning proceeded. These tools had several purposes. They had to be designed to help students respond to the learning challenge posed. They had to structure the process for learning in such a way that the group could learn together. The tools had to have some generalizability to other learning problems. Finally, they had to be accessible to the students without teacher mediation.

Kris created one tool that signaled shifts in the kind of activity each group was to make. She gave each team a set of boxes, one of which was green, indicating the place to start. Another was yellow, signaling a place to use caution, and the third was red, designed as the stopping place. Inside each of these boxes were two items. In the green box was a start-up protocol with four questions: (1) What is the problem you need to solve? (2) When does it need to be solved? (3) What are the features of a good solution? (4) What do you expect to know when you're done? The second item was an assessment, designed to be used at the end of that segment of the process. The team had to answer the following: (1) Who will lead your process? (2) Who will be your timekeeper? (3) What strategies will you use to review the text? (4) How will you catalog your evidence? In the yellow and red boxes, the learning tools were different because the activities needed for that part of the task were different. Understanding how to break down the task, how to organize it, and how to work with others to completion were all necessary elements of the problem-solving toolkit.

In accommodating one another, the students assessed, trimmed, and shifted their stances to move forward in their problem solving. The shifts helped them realize new ways of addressing the task as they became more aware of their own collective tool sets, including their limitations. And herein lies a central aspect of tool-mediated action. These learners participated in the activity as a means to master these tools, but we should note that learners first make use of new tools in ways that might imply a more sophisticated comprehension/handling of the tools. Thus teachers, as critical mediating tools, should play a consequential role in assisting learners to move from initial *mastery* to the *appropriation* of tools (Werstch, 1998). Kris's role was to point out contradictions and tensions so that they had vocabulary to name their struggles and to learn from them, thus actively mediating these learners' appropriation of math tools.

In short, tools for thinking are central to the situative learning perspective because they stress the mediated nature of human actions and learning. Tool-mediated action also reminds us of the dialogic nature of learning due to the intense meaning-making processes involved in students' engagements with tools (Werstch & Kazak, 2011). Through the use of tools, learners are inducted into the practices of a community, but beyond enculturation, learners' participation in tool-mediated action enables them to forge identities that are meaningful to a social practice and thus contribute to students' "ontological construction" (Packer, 2011).

## Learning as Participation

The scholarship on how people learn emphasizes that learning is not solely an individual or cognitive phenomenon, but it takes place in a complex system of social, emotional, and cultural arenas. Contemporary research reviews shed light on design principles for learning in rapidly changing environments (Bransford, 2007; Bransford et al., 1999), on how a generation of learners has been shaped by their digital experiences (Beck & Wade, 2004; Gee, 2004; Prensky, 2001), and on how educational institutions can begin to rethink their practices (Davidson & Goldberg, 2009). At a time of increasing complexity, teachers most often focus on single interventions that do not account for the dynamic complexity of culture as a central feature of how people learn. For instance, Sieveke-Pearson (2004) found that among a middle school team that received a week of intensive professional learning on embedding literacy skills in content areas, followed by a year of coaching and mentoring in their classrooms, content area teachers used only a few strategies to enhance their students' literacy skills. Thus, even when explicit models of professional learning are employed to help teachers know how to use a set of teaching strategies, at the end of the day, those strategies may not become part of a teacher's practice repertoire. This finding may be explained in part by overreliance on a view of teaching as something that adults perform, thus rendering a fragmented perspective on what transpires in classrooms and other places that produce teacher and student learning. In contrast, understanding that students actively participate in learning changes the nature of teacher roles and identities in teachers' own learning processes as they increasingly master their practice through experience and participation.

## The Crucial Role of Access: Inclusive/Exclusive Participation Systems

Greeno, Collins, and Resnick (1996) might point out the importance of the context in which learning takes place. In Kris's classroom the racial diversity of her students contributed to the heightened interest in the story. The reorganization of the classroom into team spaces signaled a different kind of performance would be required than that when sitting in rows in desks. Kris's focus on the relationships among students and their need to rely on one another to address the learning challenge changed the dynamics of the relationships among students. This kind of learning design emphasizes the social nature of learning activities, the material and social resources for learning, the roles that learning takes on within the broader environment, the knowledge distributed within social networks, and the practices for exchanging information. This view of learning is particularly well suited to the design and research of learning spaces when the concern is helping learners attend to their interactions with one another to deepen their understanding, see problems through multiple perspectives, and apply their accumulated knowledge to understanding new ideas. The agenda takes precedence while the role of the teacher as the portal to learning recedes. Consider a second scenario in another classroom in Kris's building.

Madeline was a veteran English teacher with a love of the classics. She wanted to introduce her class of students to *Beowulf*. She divided her class of 25 students into five small groups. She introduces a lesson on epics and distributes an article for the class to read. She explains that she wants each group to read a specific part of the article, discuss it among themselves, and then be prepared to share that part with the rest of the class, a reading activity called a "jigsaw." Her monotone voice and slow pace of delivery has a soporific effect. By the time that she has given her introduction, students are quietly glancing at one another and making hand gestures. The teacher does not seem aware of this, although she may be purposely ignoring what is going on.

In the same slow monotone, Madeline tells the first group, which she calls "Group A," to read the entire first page and approximately to the middle of the second page. After the entire direction is given, a student in another group asserts, "We're group A." Madeline looks at him and concurs that the student is right, his group is A. She then turns to that group and gives them the same instructions as slowly and deliberately as she did to the group that she first thought was Group A. She then walks to each of the other groups, assigning them a section to read. The students are quiet, showing no emotion when they look at the teacher. Several stare into space. One has his head down on his desk. Another, seated with his back to the blackboard, sits back, closes his eyes and rests his head against it. Madeline doesn't increase her energy level or change her strategy to engage the students individually or as a group. When she has finished giving the assignment to each group several students seem puzzled. One whispers to a tablemate, "What's the assignment?" (Kozleski et al., 2006, p. 16)

The teacher, not the material or the activity, served as the gateway to learning in Madeline's classroom. Madeline's students were stopped at that gateway by Madeline's need to filter or contain the approach that her students took to engaging with the materials. Her instructions, not the tools that she gave her students to discuss, trumped the opportunity for learning. In Kris's school an entire hallway of classrooms hosted teachers where the teaching was vibrant, the students engaged, and the atmosphere for learning electric. Yet, even in the same school, other classrooms like Madeline's lacked that vibrancy and sense of engagement that come from an active learning design. Learning is a central, defining function of each human being. We learn throughout each day through our daily activities and spaces. Learning emerges from what is available and valued in the environment (access), the opportunities for participation, and the scaffolds to increasingly sophisticated and skilled practices. When learning contexts are impoverished, students turn their attention and their learning tools elsewhere.

The research is clear (Anyon, 2005; Kozol, 2005; Nichols, Glass, & Berliner, 2012): Many urban schools offer impoverished education. Throughout this book we explore multiple contributions to the fundamental lack of opportunity to learn. A major contribution to the lack of improvement in what students are able to do and become as a result of their time served in urban schools is the limited understanding of learning that undergirds the daily classroom activities of urban students.

## Opportunities Required

As students move from home to community to school, they absorb different approaches to process, interpret, and make meaning of the world around them in light of their own cultural histories, daily practices, and assimilated norms (Gee, 2006). They adopt and discard practices and interests based on the people who model, influence, and lead them. As children become more and more fluent in using their cognitive tools, they are able to interpret and synthesize at increasingly more sophisticated levels.

The Systemic Change Framework (SCF) reminds us that multiple activity arenas (e.g., classrooms, schools, school districts) shape the arc of student outcomes. As these arenas interact with each other, those interactions compound the impact of any one space. For example, classrooms where superb teaching, strong peer support, and/or exciting learning challenges accelerate learning influence the activities of other classrooms where inadequate reading materials, spotty attention to individual needs, troubling peer interactions, or other confounding issues constrain learning. Conversely, the classes where learning is poorly designed, coached, or mediated influence the classrooms where powerful learning occurs. Teachers and students are boundary crossers between these activity arenas (Waitoller & Kozleski, 2013). Teachers cross these boundaries through informal conversations, grade-level meetings, and shared materials. Occasionally, they may visit each other's rooms, before, during, or after classes are in session. Similarly, students offer commentary to teachers about their experiences in other classes. Offhand comments like "Ms. Brown doesn't do it like this," intended to challenge authority, share information, or get an alternative ruling, enter teachers' consciousness. They may consider comments like this in reference to their own processes. In so many ways tiny accumulations of information begin to drift across classroom boundaries. Such information can influence their designs for learning. Also, students' activities are influenced by what they experience in different settings, with different teachers and students. These experiences change and shape activities and practices for students and teachers. The cumulative effect of weak or poorly selected readings and materials in some classrooms sets up how students are prepared or anticipate what will occur in other classrooms. Student understanding, histories, and responses shape what teachers do as well. Different results in different classrooms collide and interact, compounding successes and failures. Some of this boundary crossing emancipates teachers and students, expanding their tools for designing and participating in learning. Some boundary crossing constrains and limits how students and teachers understand their work and engage their practices.

Mental tools include the ability to think systemically, moving fluently between part-to-whole and whole-to-part analytical approaches to problem solving. Fluency in information literacy involves the use of multiple search strategies, the ability to curate multiple discourses and intellectual knowledge streams, and the ability to translate information into useful discourse. Creativity and adaptability allow individuals to shift focus and participation as context and circumstances demand. Persistence, self-regulation, teamwork and collaboration, and leadership for learning are all socioemotional aspects of a strong learning suite of tools (Ito et al., 2013).

While learning is predicated on opportunities to participate and construct meaning through interaction, it also requires engagement. As a result, teachers, schools, and districts must focus resources on providing those conditions, opportunities, tasks, role models, relationships, and information that support and nurture student learning. Further, you might want to note how these shifts in how learning is conceptualized go beyond "appreciative" notions of what counts as knowledge, which in relation to teacher learning toward working with diverse learners is usually restricted to discussions of surface connection between curriculum and background knowledge that essentializes student groups.

## Connections

Three key points anchor this section on connections. First, the term *connections* refers to the connections made between every life outside of school, the formal discipline-specific knowledge offered in schools, and the challenges that families, communities, and society face as the future becomes the present (Ito et al., 2013). Second, limited views of culture constrain how many urban teachers design learning. Therefore, connections to and through the curriculum to life challenges are oblique at best and most often are left to students to fuse. Third, teaching pedagogies often do not offer ongoing and embedded social and technical supports.

Most education initiatives targeting cultural responsivity or competence rely on a view of culture defined largely as student traits that mediate learning, such as ethnicity, social class, or language background. Although the cultural histories of students are important, using race, ethnicity, ability, or other group markers as proxies for between-group differences, ignore both within-group differences and the intersectionality of multiple cultures and sociological and psychological factors, and as a result relegate culture to a way of sorting and differentiating groups (Artiles, Kozleski, Trent, Osher, & Ortiz, 2010). This static perspective of culture stresses background markers at the expense of a more instrumental, practice-based view of culture as a core feature of learning, based on historical legacies embedded within learning structures, and tools (including instructional language) that mediate learning. Moreover, other key dimensions of culture are not taken into account, such as school and classroom cultural practices. In addition, the effective use of culture as a mediating tool in learning environments has been limited to sparse local practices in only a few classrooms, schools, and sometimes districts (Kozleski & Smith, 2009). The vignettes from Kris and Madeline's classrooms offer some idea of the different kinds of approaches that teachers take to designing their lessons.

Kris's example reminds us that connections between and among students as well as the life experiences they have had offer the possibility of sustained engagement. It has been difficult to go to scale with these practices because of the intensity, time, and human resources needed for the transformative work required to understand and engage culture as an inherent aspect of learning (Artiles & Kozleski, 2007). What is required is a support and feedback model that allows teachers to develop new understandings of the intersection of culture and learning, explore their emerging schemas in practice, and refine newly acquired practices. In this way teachers not only gain proficiency in the use of new knowledge, but also in honing their mental models for modifying and adapting knowledge schemas to the complex hybrid environments of today's schools (McLaughlin & Talbert, 2006). Teachers need to elaborate a networked view of culture that intersects with and mediates learning through tools, rules of engagement, the organization of community, and the division of labor (Barab, Evans, & Baek, 2004).

## REFRAMING LEARNING: TRANSFORMING SYSTEMS

The National Institute for Urban School Improvement (NIUSI) work happened in many urban schools across the country. One of our accomplished principals described her vision for learning:

> When you enter the school, there would be a sign that reads "Welcome. We love you. Come into this exciting place and you will learn, you will love learning, and you will always want to learn." It would be a place where everyone works together to help one another to learn and achieve. The community would feel welcome and become a part of the learning community. Activities would take place all the time. Children and staff would awaken in the morning saying, "Oh wow, I'm going to have an exciting day today." Always a lot of excitement! The school would be alive. Even without a magic wand, I can see the vision taking shape at our school. (Ferguson & Bloomberg, 2001, pp. 12–13)

This vision requires rich, complex notions of what learning is and how it might be organized and accomplished in urban schools. This chapter offered a way of conceptualizing learning for urban schools, and explored alternative and expanded ways of translating learning grounded in interdisciplinary knowledge. We described the multiple facets of the learning sciences particularly focused on what is known about how learning occurs, and how that might translate into curriculum and pedagogy in the classroom. We argue that the measure of school success is the degree to which all students access, participate in, and acquire robust mental tools for participating in the everyday practices of their lives.

# REFERENCES

Anyon, J. (2005). *Radical possibilities: Public policy, urban education, and a new social movement.* New York, NY: Routledge.

Artiles, A. J. (2003). Special education's changing identity: Paradoxes and dilemmas in views of culture and space. *Harvard Educational Review, 73,* 164–202.

Artiles, A. J., & Kozleski, E. B. (2007). Beyond convictions: Interrogating culture, history, and power in inclusive education. *Language Arts, 84,* 351–358.

Artiles, A. J., Kozleski, E. B., Trent, S., Osher, D., & Ortiz, A. (2010). Justifying and explaining disproportionality, 1968–2008: A critique of underlying views of culture. *Exceptional Children, 76,* 279–299.

Atkinson, D. (2004). Contrasting rhetorics/contrasting cultures: Why constrastive rhetoric needs a better conceptualization of culture. *Journal of English for Academic Purposes, 3,* 277–289.

Aud, S., Hussar, W., Planty, M., Snyder, T., Bianco, K., Fox, M., . . . Drake, L. (2010). *The condition of education 2010* (NCES 2010-028). Washington, DC: National Center for Education Statistics, Institute of Education Sciences, U.S. Department of Education.

Barab, S. A. Evans, M. A., & Baek, E. (2004). Activity theory as a lens for characterizing the participatory unit. In D. H. Jonassen (Ed.), *Handbook of research for educational communications and technology* (2nd ed., pp. 199–214). Mahwah, NJ: Lawrence Erlbaum.

Beck, J., & Wade, M. (2004). *Got game: How the gamer generation is reshaping business forever.* Boston, MA: Harvard Business School Press.

Berliner, D. (2009). *Poverty and potential: Out-of-school factors and school success.* Boulder, CO and Tempe, AZ: Education and the Public Interest Center and Education Policy Research Unit. Retrieved from http://epicpolicy.org/publicatio/poverty-and-potential

Bransford, J. (2007). Preparing people for rapidly changing environments. *Journal of Engineering Education, 96*(1), 1–3.

Bransford, J., Brown. A. L., Cocking, R. R., Donovan, M. S., & Pellegrino, J. W. (Eds.). [Committee on Developments in the Science of Learning, with additional material from the Committee on Learning Research and Educational Practice, National Research Council] (1999). *How people learn: Brain, mind, experience, and school.* Washington, DC: National Academy Press.

Cole, M. (1996). *Cultural psychology.* Cambridge, MA: Harvard University Press.

Davidson, C., & Goldberg, D. (2009). *The future of learning institutions in a digital age.* Chicago, IL: John D. and Catherine T. MacArthur Foundation.

Dejean, J. (2009). *The age of comfort: When Paris discovered casual—and the modern home began.* New York, NY: Bloomsbury USA.

Design-Based Research Collaborative. (2003). Design-based research: An emerging paradigm for educational inquiry. *Educational Researcher, 32*(1), 5–8.

Engeström, Y., & Sannino, A. (2010). Studies of expansive learning: Foundations, findings and future challenges. *Educational Research Review, 5,* 1–24.

Ferguson, P., & Bloomberg, R. (2001). *Schools on the move: JC Nalle Elementary School.* Denver, CO: National Institute for Urban School Improvement. Retrieved from www.urbanschools.org/publications/on_the_move.html

Florida, R. (2002). *The rise of the creative class: And how it's transforming work, leisure, community and everyday life.* New York, NY: Basic Books.

Frey, W. (2013). *Shift to a majority-minority population in the U.S. happening faster than expected.* Washington, DC: Brookings Institution. Retrieved from www.brookings.edu/blogs/up-front/posts/2013/06/19-us-majority-minority-population-census-frey

Gee, J. P. (2004). *What video games have to teach us about learning and literacy.* New York, NY: Palgrave Macmillan.

Gee, J. P. (2005). It's theories all the way down: A response to "Scientific Research in Education." *Teachers College Record, 107,* 10–18.

Gee, J. P. (2006). A sociocultural perspective on opportunities to learn. In A. A. Moss, D. C. Pullin, J. P. Gee, E. H. Haertel, & L. J. Young (Eds.), *Assessment, equity, and opportunity to learn* (pp. 76–96). Cambridge, United Kingdom: Cambridge University Press.

Gibson, J. J. (1979). *The ecological approach to perception.* London, United Kingdom: Houghton Mifflin.

Greeno, J. G. (2006). Learning in activity. In K. Sawyer (Ed.), *Handbook of the learning sciences* (pp. 79–96). Cambridge, United Kingdom: Cambridge University Press.

Greeno, J. G., Collins, A. M., & Resnick, L. B. (1996). Cognition and learning. In D. Berliner & R. Calfee (Eds.), *Handbook of Educational Psychology* (pp. 15–45). New York, NY: Macmillan.

Hutchby, I. (2001). Technologies, texts, and affordances. *Sociology, 35,* 441–456.

Ito, M., Gutiérrez, K., Livingston, S., Penuel, B., Rhodes, J., Salen, K., . . . Watkins, S. C. (2013). *Connected learning: An agenda for research and design, A research synthesis report of the Connected Learning Research Network.* Irvine, CA: Digital Media and Learning Research Hub.

Jelinek, P. (2013). The brain and constructing knowledge. In T. B. Jones (Ed.), *Education for the human brain: A roadmap to natural learning in schools* (pp. 63–80). Lanham, MD: Rowman & Littlefield Education.

Koschmann, T. (Ed.). (2011). *Theories of learning and studies of instructional practice.* New York, NY: Springer.

Kozleski, E. B., & Smith, A. (2009). The role of policy and systems change in creating equity for students with disabilities in urban schools. *Urban Education, 44,* 427–451.

Kozleski, E. B., Zion, S., & Hidalgo, T. (2006). *The Connecticut case study.* Denver, CO: The National Center for Culturally Responsive Educational Systems.

Kozol, J. (2005). *The shame of the nation: The restoration of apartheid schooling in America.* New York, NY: Crown.

McLaughlin, M. W., & Talbert, J. E. (2006). *Building school-based teacher learning communities: Professional strategies to improve student achievement.* New York, NY: Teachers College Press.

Morris, L. (2013). *RTI meets writer's workshop: Tiered strategies for all levels of wrtiers and every phase of writing.* Thousand Oaks, CA: Corwin Press.

Nichols, S. L., Glass, G. V., & Berliner, D. C. (2012). High-stakes testing and student achievement: Updated analyses with NAEP data. *Education Policy Analysis Archives, 20*(20). Retrieved from http://epaa.asu.edu/ojs/article/view/1048

Oakes, J. (2009). Commentary: Access and differentiation: Structuring equality and inequality in education policy. In G. Sykes, B. Schneider, & D. N. Plank (Eds.), *Handbook of education policy research* (pp. 973–975). New York, NY: Routledge.

Packer, M. J. (2011). Schooling: Domestication or ontological construction? In T. Koschmann (Ed.), *Theories of learning and studies of instructional practice* (pp. 166–188). New York, NY: Springer.

Prensky, M. (2001). Digital natives, digital immigrants. *On the Horizon, 9*(5), 1–6.

Rogoff, B. (1998). Cognition as a collaborative process. In D. Kuhn & R. S. Siegler (Eds.), *Handbook of child psychology: Vol. 2. Cognition, perception, and language* (5th ed., pp. 679–744). New York, NY: Wiley.

Sawyer, R. K. (2006). The new science of learning. In R. K. Sawyer, (Ed.), *The Cambridge handbook of the learning sciences* (pp. 1–16). New York, NY: Cambridge University Press.

Sieveke-Pearson, S. J. (2004). *Exploring relationships between professional development and student achievement* (Doctoral dissertation). Retrieved from ProQuest Dissertations Publishing. (UMI No. 3138721)

Waitoller, F., & Kozleski, E. B. (2013). Working in boundary practices: Identity development and learning in partnerships for inclusive education. *Teaching and Teacher Education, 31,* 35–45.

Wertsch, J. (1998). *Mind as action.* New York, NY: Oxford University Press.

Wertsch, J., & Kazak, S. (2011). Saying more than you know in instructional settings. In T. Koschmann (Ed.), *Theories of learning and studies of instructional practice* (pp. 152–166). New York, NY: Springer.

# CHAPTER 4

# Family Resistance as a Tool in Urban School Reform

*Cristina Santamaría Graff and Sandra L. Vazquez*

Beatriz and her husband arrived in the United States in 2001 from a small, rural town in Oaxaca, Mexico. Beatriz came from a farming family, attended public school, and graduated high school before moving to southern Arizona with her husband who had secured a construction job. Although Beatriz found the transition from Mexico to the United States difficult, she was excited about raising a family where she had extended family and believed economic opportunities abounded. Her hope was to acquire enough money in the United States so she and her husband could buy land in Oaxaca. By 2004, Beatriz had two daughters, Amelia and Megan, and she was certain her family would be back in Mexico in the next couple years. However, Beatriz's hopes for her family began to change when Megan turned a year old.

Megan was ill from age 1 to 3 with ear infections, and at age 3, was diagnosed with autism. Beatriz and her husband had never heard of autism and were perplexed by the diagnosis. Although both had noticed Megan was not developing communicative and interactive skills as quickly as her older sister had, they assumed Megan was *"atrasada"* and *"lenta"* (behind and slow). They committed themselves as proactive communicators with Megan's teachers to ensure Megan's success in spite of her challenges.

On the first day of Megan's kindergarten year, Beatriz was immediately aware of the language barrier between herself and Mrs. S., Megan's teacher. Beatriz knew very little English and Mrs. S. did not speak any Spanish. Beatriz told Mrs. S. about the detrimental effects dairy and sugar had on Megan's behavior and wanted Mrs. S. to monitor Megan's eating during recess and lunch. Instead of feeling heard, Beatriz felt ignored so she returned the following day with her husband whose conversational skills in English were more developed than hers. This time Beatriz sensed through Mrs. S.'s body language a deliberate resistance in responding to her husband's questions, perhaps due to prejudice against her. She shared in an interview with Cristina Santamaría Graff, *"Yo estoy segura que si yo fuera Americana, tuviera la piel [blanca] y el cabello rubio, luego me hubieran conseguido los servicios que necesitaba mi niña."* (I'm certain that if I were American, had White skin and blond hair, they [educators/special education team] would have given my daughter the services that she needed.) Out of frustration, Beatriz and her husband stopped making classroom visits. Soon afterwards, Megan got into trouble for disruptive behavior and was, according to the principal, "uncontrollable." When Beatriz picked Megan up from school, sugar covered Megan's mouth and face. Beatriz felt the educators had let her daughter down.

Beatriz sought alternative support networks, specifically from groups for parents of children with disabilities, to assist her in communicating Megan's needs. She soon heard about Cristina's Participation Action Research (PAR) group centered on creating action plans for addressing barriers to participation in schools for Mexican-origin parents of children with disabilities. After the 16-week PAR study, Beatriz reported she had begun to let go of negative feelings she felt toward Mrs. S. and was finding positive ways to communicate more effectively with her. Furthermore, as Beatriz gained confidence in her own communicative skills and knowledge, she began to see herself as a leader and sought opportunities through which she could be a resource for other Spanish-speaking parents and families of children with disabilities.

## HISTORICALLY UNDERSERVED FAMILIES AND RESISTANCE

Families like Beatriz's who are "historically underserved" (Artiles, Kozleski, Trent, Osher, & Ortiz, 2010, p. 279) desire excellent educational opportunities for their children and are willing to make significant sacrifices to support them academically. However, within the U.S. school system they find themselves at a disadvantage that can be attributed to their diverse racial, cultural, and linguistic backgrounds, as well as their limited social and economic status. Historically underserved families have been represented as limited, peripheral, or nonparticipants in their children's education by school personnel whose expectations of parents are based in U.S. mainstream definitions of parent involvement (Guldberg, 2008; Ramirez, 2003; Turney & Kao, 2009). When *parent involvement* is conceptualized as specific behaviors such as volunteering in the classroom, attending school events and conferences, and correcting a child's homework, school personnel may overlook or dismiss alternative and subtler ways that families participate in their children's education (Ramirez, 2003; Ramirez & Soto-Hinman, 2009; Valencia & Black, 2002). Historically underserved families who have children with disabilities are further marginalized if they do not possess the skills, knowledge, or language proficiency to participate as equal stakeholders in key decisions: for example, at the Individualized Educational Program (IEP) meetings where, many times, they are expected to understand educational and medical terminology and complex concepts related to diagnosis, assessment, procedural guidelines, and special educational laws (Salas, 2004; Salas, Lopez, Chinn, & Menchaca-Lopez, 2005).

Accordingly, families who are rarely included in the "critical and serious work of rethinking educational structures and practices" (Fine, 1993, p. 683) that directly impact their children have resisted systems that locate them in subordinated positions of status and power. In school systems where families are "outsiders" *family resistance*, either overt or hidden, has been construed as disinterest or as a threat (Olivos, 2004). In this context, resistance is an act against expectations and norms of what it is to be a parent and to be involved at school. For example, resistance can manifest in what is perceived by school personnel to be a lack of interest or involvement in school-related activities (e.g., nonattendance at teacher-parent conferences), a direct opposition to school rules and teacher expectations (e.g., apparent apathy if their child is late to school or misses instructional time), or a deliberate attempt to thwart teachers' efforts to improve student achievement (e.g., lack of assistance with homework).

In school systems where families are located as "insiders" but do not have equal status and power in the educational decision making about their children, family resistance may be demonstrated through subtler, less overt ways. For example, families may appear to concur with school personnel, but in actuality weigh their options carefully and choose to what degree they will cooperate.

Built on understandings of the powerful roles families must play in their children's education, this chapter explores how urban education reform efforts focused on empowerment and authentic change understand family resistance as a transformational resource to reposition historically underserved families as insiders and equal stakeholders within school systems. Elements of Beatriz's story are woven throughout the chapter to illustrate specific manifestations of resistance as a resource in urban education reform as she confronts educational systems that debilitate or empower her as a participant in her daughter's education and schooling. Understanding *why* and *how* historically underserved families resist school systems and the ways in which systems constrain or support these families is essential in reform efforts that seek to transform educational structures and practices that have excluded and marginalized this population.

## Family Resistance in Urban School Reform

Historically underserved families are generally positioned in subordinate or inferior roles within school systems whose values and traditions are reflective of the dominant society (Cardoso & Thompson, 2010; Gonzalez & Ayala-Alcantar, 2008; McKenzie & Scheurich, 2008). Because resistance literature "has been marred by its own theoretical and conceptual limitations" (Solórzano & Delgado Bernal, 2001, p. 310), historically underserved families consistently have been represented through deficit perspectives that prevent their rich cultural and historical legacies from being explored multidimensionally and dynamically. In urban school reform the purpose of understanding family resistance is to unearth and illuminate reform issues to be addressed that may have otherwise been overlooked by system insiders, as well as to recognize its manifestations so that educators, as well as other stakeholders, can proactively address challenges potentially detrimental in building authentic, collaborative relationships between families and schools. While resistant behavior can be reactionary, self-defeating, conformist, or transformational (Solórzano & Delgado Bernal, 2001), when conceptualized as a resource for transformational change in urban school reform, it becomes a force through which marginalized and disempowered populations oppose oppressive systems, overcome challenges, and become empowered. Ideally, this empowerment occurs with the support of those representing the dominant culture (i.e., school personnel and leaders).

In order to achieve these shifting understandings of resistance as a resource, transformational frameworks, such as the Systemic Change Framework (Ferguson, Kozleski, & Smith, 2003), provide educators with a multidimensional lens through which resistance among historically underserved families is examined in critical, yet positive, ways. Embedded within such frameworks are action-oriented goals that all stakeholders who are committed to authentic change must consider: (1) to excavate issues relevant to urban education reform from families' perspectives; (2) to determine which educational structures and systems are creating barriers to families' empowerment; (3) to acknowledge families' unique and creative approaches to communication and participation in their children's education and schooling; (4) to define the space in which authentic collaboration and meaningful interaction intersect for school personnel and families; (5) to document and analyze stakeholders' change efforts within school systems to determine to what degree steps toward reform have been integrated and effective in producing long-lasting and empowering transformation; and (6) to critique social oppression and to be motivated by social justice (Solórzano & Delgado Bernal, 2001).

## Understanding Family Resistance

Now, we turn to a review of literature on what we assert are problematic ways that family resistance has been theorized, providing examples from Beatriz's story where appropriate as rationale for how and why these theorizations may be reframed as transformational and contributive in urban education reform efforts.

***Theorizing resistance as family deficit.*** Through deficit-driven frameworks, people of "difference" have been systematically marginalized in our society through institutional systems that have supported the imperialistic notion that White European Americans are more intelligent and thus superior to all others (Villenas & Deyhle, 1999). Through this mindset the disenfranchisement of the "other" has been legitimized as sound practice to protect traditional "American" values (Berkhofer, 1978). As retaliation to unfair practices that place disproportionate amounts of privilege and power in the hands of those representing the dominant group, many people of "difference" have resisted, protested, or spoken out to reclaim the freedoms and protections that are rightfully theirs (Freire, 1970/2000; Tuhiwai Smith, 1999).

In the educational arena, deficit theories gained popularity during the 1950s and 1960s and have continued to influence practices and policies that detrimentally impact historically underserved students and their families. IQ and cultural deficit theories posit that limited aptitude and an inferior cultural upbringing are at the heart of poor academic performance for students who come from historically underserved families (Suzuki & Valencia, 1997; Villegas & Lucas, 2002). When traditional notions of parent involvement are framed through a deficit lens, families become the scapegoat for the significant achievement gap between White, middle-class students and their own children, as educators equate what they perceive as families' apparent disinterest and lack of involvement in their children's schooling to low test scores, high dropout rates, and school failure (Olivos, 2004; Yosso, 2005). With this logic, some educators and researchers have come to the conclusion that an education makes little difference for students who are considered intellectually or culturally inferior (Bernstein, 1975; Herrnstein & Murray, 1994; Jensen, 1973).

Families' roles and responsibilities in deficit-oriented school systems are constrained by perceived assumptions of what historically underserved families can contribute to student outcomes and by a failure of school personnel to recognize families' strengths as well as the meaningful ways they participate in their children's education. Often, parents are dismissed as important stakeholders in schools when their actions or behaviors are interpreted as insignificant or mistaken for apathy (Cummins, 1996; Olivos, 2004; Valdes,

1996). Families, however, are not always victims of the structural determinants that undervalue their importance. Their agency enables them to resist, mediate, or negotiate each situation they face and decide what makes sense for their family and circumstances (Giroux, 1983; Solórzano & Delgado Bernal, 2001).

An alternative way to understand what some perceive as lack of interest in children's schooling is illustrated by cases where Latino families have demonstrated resistance to unsupportive school systems by choosing to be absent from events or by remaining silent, often interpreted as laziness or disinterest (Valencia & Black, 2002). However, when understood as "a defense mechanism against oppression and humiliation" (Olivos, 2004, p. 30), absence becomes a conscious action and statement. Similarly, Latino families have used silence as a tool to avoid feeling exploited or inferior in conversations with dominant White group members (Ochoa & Pineda, 2008). Latino families who feel undercut and undervalued in meetings or interactions with school personnel have, many times, chosen silence to protect their dignity even if they do not agree with or understand the terminology discussed or decisions presented (Salas, 2004).

For Beatriz, maintaining a sense of pride for herself and for her family was a compelling reason for discontinuing her one-on-one conversations with Megan's teacher. Ceasing classroom visits that inevitably led her to feel ignored and rejected was an act of self-preservation, even though her action meant a continued uncertainty about whether her daughter's health and well-being were being positively addressed. Her inability to communicate effectively with Megan's teacher and her perceptions of school personnel's assumptions of Mexican parents led her to the following conclusion: *"Es muy triste porque ellos creen porque es uno mexicano o porque es uno hispano, uno nunca va a hablar, uno nunca va a investigar."* ("It is sad because they believe that because one is Mexican or because one is Hispanic, that one is not going to talk or one is not going to investigate.")

Beatriz believed that being Mexican prevented her from being taken seriously and that her expert knowledge as a parent was invalidated because of language barriers and discrimination. Consequently, she resisted exclusionary school practices by choosing absence from and silence in daily conversations with Megan's teacher.

***Theorizing resistance as cultural difference and cultural capital.***
Unlike IQ and cultural deficit theories that place the onus of a student's poor achievement in schools on his or her heredity and upbringing, the theory of cultural difference describes students' underachievement as resulting from a home–school mismatch (Lareau, 1989; O'Connor, 2001). The discrepancy existing between the traditions, values, culture, and language of the school environment versus those in the home environment has been analyzed to

document how differences can lead to misunderstandings and miscommunication between school personnel, students, and families (Delgado Gaitan, 1991; Harry, 2002; Peña, 2000; Zarate, 2007). Underlying presumptions of this theory, however, stress the need of historically underserved families to conform and assimilate to the school culture so that their children will not be significantly disadvantaged (Smart & Smart, 1995). An expectation exists that real change in attitude or action should be assumed by families; school personnel may be aware of their privileged positions, but are not urged to transform the ways in which they interact (Gonzalez & Ayala-Alcantar, 2008; Suárez-Orozco, 2000). More often than not, "schools facilitate the exclusion of students and parents by (consciously or unconsciously) establishing activities that require specific majority, culturally based, knowledge and behaviors about the school as an institution" (Delgado-Gaitan, 1991, p. 21). This exclusion is further perpetuated when school personnel continue with the status quo and rarely review and reflect critically upon the ways in which their actions perpetuate behaviors that isolate, distance, or marginalize families from diverse backgrounds.

Like cultural difference theory, social, cultural, and economic capital theories compare those with status, power, resources, and financial stability to those without. *Capital*, according to Bourdieu and Passeron (1977), is an accumulation of cultural knowledge through formal schooling and other experiences, as well as the skills and abilities one inherits. Those with extensive social networks and connections (social capital), a strong education and mastery of language (cultural capital), and significant monetary assets and resources (economic capital) are likely to have significant leverage and influence to navigate a profitable or successful trajectory within U.S. society (Yosso, 2005).

In educational literature, families who have been historically underserved are typically portrayed as entering the school system with deficiencies since their capital may not be recognized as valuable by those representing the dominant culture. Many times, school personnel, who are limited in their knowledge of families' cultural backgrounds and traditions, are unable to connect students' success in school to the *funds of knowledge* or the repositories of skills and knowledge that families transmit generationally (Moll, Amanti, Neff, & Gonzalez, 1992). When capital is positively associated with paradigms that privilege White European Americans, the attainment of it is exclusively available to a limited few. Historically underserved families, by definition, are consequently restricted to the pursuit of this capital and never have the opportunity to fully attain it.

Frameworks that analyze historically underserved families' value and worth by comparing them to members of the dominant U.S. culture are inherently biased. When school systems and other institutions that provide services to these families evaluate them by using tools or criteria based on dominant culture norms, historically underserved families rarely meet specified requirements or desired expectations (Baca & Cervantes, 2003). In frameworks where families like Beatriz's are disproportionately categorized as lacking core resources, knowledge, and skills because of cultural, economic, social, and linguistic differences, resistance is generally reactionary, self-defeating, or conformist (Solórzano & Delgado Bernal, 2001). Each of these types of resistance perpetuates "coercive relations of power" (Cummins, 2009, p. 261) in which the oppressor and the oppressed demonstrate behaviors that obstruct efforts leading to social justice and transformative change.

In the following example a White, monolingual English-speaking social worker visited Beatriz's home to evaluate Megan's progress and to determine a need for additional family resources. Beatriz was excited to engage in a conversation with someone who understood the importance of specific interventions and services. At first, the visit was congenial and the social worker suggested several therapies and treatments from which Megan could benefit. However, when Beatriz mentioned that she did not have a Social Security card, the social worker changed her demeanor (as described by Beatriz), "*No, yo creo que esos tratamientos son muy costosos y ustedes no pueden pagar*" (No, I think that the treatments are too expensive for you to afford). Beatriz concluded that the knowledge she had about Megan's well-being was dismissed by the social worker's inherent biases about Beatriz's documentation status. Relatedly, the social worker stopped listening to Beatriz's recommendations and "never acquired one therapy (for Megan) in the 3 years [they] had her."

Beatriz felt unfairly judged and was upset that Megan would not be able to receive services to improve her communication and social skills. Her resistance to this situation, however, was "self-defeating." Even though she understood the inequity of her situation, she continued to "engage in behavior that [was] not transformational and . . . help[ed] to re-create the oppressive conditions from which it originated" (Solórzano & Delgado Bernal, 2001, p. 317). Beatriz reacted by "complain[ing] to the supervisor and other service coordinators" that the social worker deliberately denied services to Megan. She also informed the supervisor that she would tell other parents about her negative experience if Megan did not receive the assistance she requested. At this point the supervisor intervened where the social worker had not. Under pressure, the supervisor acted quickly and enrolled Megan in two programs that specialized in therapies and interventions for children with autism. However, Beatriz's strategy for getting Megan services perpetuated the type of coercive action generally associated with dominant group oppression. Her resistance was "self-defeating" because it continued to be "destructive to . . . others" (Solórzano & Delgado Bernal, 2001, p. 317) even though the outcomes were favorable for Megan.

***Theorizing resistance in collaborative relationships.*** Collaboration between school personnel and families is a term generally applied to the relationships, interactions, and communication that occur to promote students' academic success. Collaborative relationships have been categorized as parent involvement, parent participation, parent–school partnerships, family-centered partnerships, and school–family–community connections (Epstein & Sheldon, 2002; Turnbull & Turnbull, 2001). The essence of collaboration involves the equal participation of stakeholders who are "voluntarily engaged in shared decision making as they work toward a common goal" (Friend & Cook, 2007, p. 7). Ideal collaboration between school personnel and families is, therefore, equitable, empowering, and transformative as both parties achieve positive outcomes through a mutually beneficial and respectful process. On the other hand, collaboration in which families are invited to be equal partners with school personnel but are not treated with parity engenders misunderstanding and mistrust (Friend & Cook, 2007).

The difficulty with collaboration in school settings is that often families do not enter the relationship on equal footing; instead a type of "turfism" occurs in which school personnel control the interactions and steer conversations in the direction of their choosing (Blue-Banning, Summers, Frankland, Nelson, & Beegle, 2004), attempting to engage families in collaboration that is "family focused" but not "family driven" (Osher & Osher, 2002). Fine (1993) asserts that "The presumption of equality between parents and schools, and the refusal to address power struggles, has systematically undermined real educational transformation" (p. 684). Because many families, especially those who are historically underserved, are not always treated as equals even when invited to collaborate with school professionals, they may resist entering into partnerships while participating in meetings or school events (Santamaría, 2009). Agency plays a critical role in the ways in which families choose to conform to or negate decisions impacting their children. How resistance is manifested depends greatly upon a family's ability to navigate the system by understanding which choices are available to them when confronted with outcomes or decisions that, in their view, are unfavorable.

For Beatriz, there were three distinctive ways in which she and other Mexican-origin parents resisted unequal collaborative relationships in educational settings. Based on a qualitative research study conducted by the author (Santamaría, 2009) in Arizona, five mothers of Mexican origin (two born in the United States, three born and raised in Mexico) including Beatriz explored the specific barriers to participation they faced in schools and their evolving roles as parents over a 16-week period as they critically discussed the origin and manifestation of these barriers. Findings revealed that parents openly sought opportunities for collaboration and support. However, when Beatriz and the other parents did not feel "*confianza*" (trust/confidence) in school professionals who were attempting to communicate or establish relationships with them, they turned to others who could provide them with authentic support (i.e., receptionists who spoke Spanish, parent-support groups outside of the school setting, other parents whom they would speak to in the school hallways or parking lots). School receptionists were strong allies for many of the parents in the study; Beatriz described them as "The only people who support me . . . [and] who translate what the teachers are saying." Beatriz and the other parents would often approach the school receptionists prior to meeting with their children's teachers to get "insider" information or advice about the ways in which they could get the best services for their children.

Beatriz and the other monolingual Spanish-speaking parents would attend the Individualized Education Program (IEP) meetings, write down information during the meeting, and then participate in Spanish-speaking parent-support groups to go over the questions they had written down. Instead of asking questions to the other IEP team members (i.e., school professionals), they felt more comfortable asking members of the support group to clarify specific items on the IEP. As an explanation, one parent offered:

> *Generalmente los hispanos no somos buenos para juntas grandes, porque nos da verguenza levantar la mano, nos da verguenza hacer una pregunta que a lo mejor no es apropiada. Los grupos pequeños y con confianza son más efectivos.*

> (Generally, we Hispanics are not good at big meetings because it embarrasses us to raise our hand, it embarrasses us to ask a question that may not be appropriate. Small groups based in trust are more effective.)

Historically underserved families, of any race or ethnicity, tend to resist systems or people who do not engender trust and instead seek others who will listen and validate them (Harris, 2006; Monzó & Rueda, 2001; Valenzuela, 1999). For the parents in the study, some of the most meaningful and beneficial discussions about their children's IEPs occurred in school hallways or parking lots with other parents. Discussions between parents in these informal spaces influenced parents' decisions whether or not to contest options and outcomes presented by school personnel at IEP meetings.

## Family Resistance as a Tool for Transformative Reform in Urban Contexts

When family resistance is understood as a tool to provide deep insight into the ways in which families provide "feedback or express . . . a differing point of view" (Mauer, 2006, p. 122) subtle and overt behaviors by families that go against expected norms can then be analyzed as valid communication to be considered, discussed, and acted upon. Grounding the concept of "resistance as a tool" within urban reform are at least two assertions. The first is that families' resistance must be viewed as *strength* for authentic change to manifest. Therefore, resistance as an efficient and productive tool in urban school reform should be defined by the creative and unexpected ways in which families "negotiate and struggle with structures and create meanings of their own from these interactions" (Solórzano & Delgado Bernal, 2001, p. 315). Instead of dismissing families' interpretations of the interactions and communications at schools in which they are involved, school leaders and personnel have the opportunity to observe, listen to, and understand these multifaceted and rich landscapes of interpretation as pieces of crucial information necessary to build mutually rewarding relationships.

A second assertion lies in the willingness of the stakeholders involved in the day-to-day interactions that occur within school settings to access *critical consciousness* ("*conscientização*"; Freire, 1970/2000, 1974/2007): an awareness of one's personal agency and an understanding that life's events are not predetermined based on presumably fixed factors (e.g., race, culture, language). Hegemonic belief systems that place individuals or groups of people on immutable and static trajectories based on cultural background and history must be refuted to break oppressive patterns. One of the first steps, according to Freire (1970/2000, 1974/2007), is for the individual to reach critical awareness to take control of his or her life to generate positive changes. This critical consciousness and the realization of the empowerment that is derived from deliberate, positive action is the agency each individual inherently possesses. When accessed, agency is a powerful force through which an individual, through critical reflection and compassionate understanding, can carefully coconstruct with other stakeholders new realities in which every person is respected and valued (Cammarota & Romero, 2006).

***Resistance as a tool and third space.*** In school settings "resistance as a tool" is the interplay between accepting difference as strength and the choice to become critically conscious of the possibilities that exist when individuals from all backgrounds arrive within a space of complete openness to manifest mutual, cocreated realities that benefit everyone—especially the child. This space has been conceptualized as the "third space" (Bhabha, 1994) where the oppressor/colonizer and the oppressed/colonized can negotiate with one another and reposition themselves in ways that disrupt hegemonic structures and practices that lead to disharmony and division. In classrooms, the third space represents the space where students' strengths and experience are relevant and incorporated into the daily curriculum as an important part of student learning (Benson, 2010; Moje, Ciechanowski,

Kramer, Ellis, Carrillo, & Collazo, 2004). For historically underserved families, the implications of third space at IEP meetings, parent-teacher conferences, and school events are vast and deep and serve to inform needed areas of reform. Third space is a shift of perception through which parents and families become leaders within institutional spaces that serve our students. In this space their voices are not only heard but also initiate action, change, and transformation in the schools, at home, and in the spaces "in-between" (Bhabha, 1994, p. 1).

The concept of "third space" is embedded in urban education reform frameworks, such as the Systemic Change Framework (Ferguson, Kozleski, & Smith, 2003), that are transformative and lead to long-lasting, school–community-centered change. Within these frameworks an empowering environment and "a common language" (Kozleski & Smith, 2009, p. 434) among stakeholders who are part of micro- and macrointeractions within school systems are essential to trust building and mutual understanding. Third space can also describe the place in which "the oppressed" awaken to the understanding of their own agency and power (Freire, 1970/2000). In transformational frameworks, however, an additional element must be present for authentic change to occur: "The oppressors" must also "awaken" and become critically conscious of the need for social justice and action in our schools.

Those who are part of the dominant culture or in positions of power must suspend belief systems that create artificial hierarchies in which historically underserved populations are relegated to inferior roles. When parents and families of children with disabilities are stripped of their expertise and knowledge about their own children and are expected to defer to others in positions of authority about what is best for their child, the imbalances and inequities of the system are obvious. The change toward transformation and reform in schools lies in the willingness of the dominant culture to fully accept that the well-being of each child is predicated on the cooperative effort of, informed by and equally distributed among, *all* stakeholders committed to the child's academic and personal achievements. For families, especially for those who are historically underserved, this transformation would manifest through empowering conversations and interactions with school personnel in which families' ideas, insights, and expertise would be considered equally important to information given by a teacher, school leader, or educator. Decisions about a child's academic and behavioral goals would be based on input and feedback provided by all stakeholders to promote mutual trust and to ensure the best possible education for the child. Even new approaches to working with the child that are family or culturally based would be validated by school personnel through their openness to discussing the ways in which this alternative information could be used to strengthen the child's educational plan.

As stated earlier, transformational frameworks provide educators with a multidimensional lens through which resistance among historically underserved families can be analyzed in critically conscious ways that lead to action-oriented school reform. We turn now to present an example of how such a framework may inform practice within urban education reform efforts through the use of participatory action research.

**Resistance as a Tool and Participatory Action Research.** Participatory action research (PAR) is both framework and methodology. "Resistance as a tool" within this framework is a key component to how families' knowledge and expertise is accepted, incorporated, and valued as well as the ways in which families are repositioned as colleagues with school personnel. At its core, PAR is a collaborative approach to research that emphasizes using systematic methods while taking action (Reason & Bradbury, 2001). Conceptually, PAR is a process in which all stakeholders involved have equal status in determining the course of action ultimately taken (Fals Borda, 1991; Maguire, 1987). As an emancipatory approach to taking action against oppressive systems, PAR is centered on providing opportunities for an individual or group to "adapt oneself to reality plus the critical capacity to make choices and to transform that reality" (Freire, 1974/2007, p. 4).

In Freire's (1970/2000) description of PAR, historically underserved groups are integrated into the research process as *"co-investigators"* (p. 106) rather than merely research subjects. The concept of "co-investigation" when applied to relationships between school personnel and families translates as the interactions that occur when stakeholders enter third space as equals to negotiate roles and responsibilities, to investigate the best outcomes for the child, and to take action on decisions reached by consensus. Moreover, co-investigation requires an invested long-term commitment by all stakeholders to take accountability for the decisions agreed upon and the willingness to follow through on actions for which each individual is responsible.

Educators who are interested in authentic collaboration can easily establish communication with diverse families without needing to invite them to participate in a formal research investigation. Although the word *research* is embedded within PAR, working with parents in a systematic and goal-oriented manner is not dependent upon conducting a formal study. PAR is predicated on stakeholders' willingness to work together for the collective good. Educators who are dedicated to the well-being and achievement of all students need only to initiate contact with families who are also willing and able to make the same commitment. There are many ways to contact parents, even those whose first language is not English. Many researchers, however, have emphasized that with Latino families an *official invitation*, whether a phone call, a note home, an email, or one-on-one contact, is

FIGURE 4.1. Plan of Action Worksheet in English and Spanish

POINTS TO BE DISCUSSED/TEMAS DE DISCUSIÓN

- The stated concern/el asunto de interés
- The probable solution/la solución probable
- Timeline for action/la cronología de acción
- Roles and responsibilities/los papeles y responsabilidades
- Location of where the action will take place/ubicación de dónde tomará la acción
- Other ingredients agreed upon/otros ingredientes en que estamos de acuerdo

From *Mexican origin parents with children with disabilities project: Using a critically compassionate intellectualism model to support and foster their participation in U.S. school through a Participatory Action Research Project* [Doctoral dissertation, University of Arizona] by C. C. Santamaría, 2009. Copyright 2009 by *Dissertation Abstracts International, 70*(4), 474. Adapted with permission of the author.

especially effective in eliciting parent participation (Delgado-Gaitan, 1994; Griego-Jones, 2003; Jonson, 1999; Ramirez, 2003).

One important extension of PAR is the creation of an action plan (see Figure 4.1) that is inclusive of all stakeholders' insights and contributions. Incorporating an action plan as part of collaborative relationships with families is highly recommended as a way to structure common goals and to be responsive and accountable to everyone's needs (John W. Gardner Center for Youth and their Communities, 2007). Additionally, action plans are highly effective in documenting change over time as stakeholders are able to demonstrate, in worksheet or spreadsheet form, how goals and objectives are consistently being met. Because an action plan generally is a cowritten agreement among and between stakeholders, all those involved in the process and outcomes of the goals and objectives discussed are consciously aware of their roles and responsibilities. By being critically conscious of the procedural steps taken throughout the process of creating and implementing positive changes that directly impact the child/student, stakeholders take hold of their own agency and witness their actions coming to fruition.

Educators, when located in third space with families, have the opportunity to analyze perceived resistance openly and positively. In PAR, third space is the location where stakeholders become co-investigators or cocreators in the process and outcomes of the decision making. Family resistance as a tool within third space is part of the negotiation process in which differing points of view are discussed critically and constructively allowing stakeholders to equally participate in and contribute to the generation of ideas and their implementation. Disagreements that arise within third space are welcomed rather than feared. Personal or structural barriers are discussed and analyzed as part of the overall process. In third space, stakeholders who are open to the process of reaching consensus understand the importance of dissent if conflicts are resolved through respectful communication and healthy interactions. Successful, long-lasting, urban reform efforts are only possible if resistance among and between stakeholders is accepted as a necessary vehicle through which meaningful discussion can lead to both community building and systemic change.

Another fundamental component of third space within PAR is critical self-reflection about one's role and influence as a stakeholder. Educators or researchers working with historically underserved families of children with disabilities need to be aware of their privileged positions so that thoughts, words, and actions are consciously deliberated and reflected upon. It is not enough to enter into a collaborative partnership with families if underlying good intentions consist of a proclivity toward biases and stereotypes that have never been analyzed genuinely. Educators who commit to urban educational reform take on the responsibility of being conscientious of their motives and should realize that families who volunteer to enter into collaborative relationships for the benefit of their children are likely to have their own expectations. Instead of passing judgment on these expectations, educators can actively listen to the words and meaning behind statements or emotions to uncover possible fears, mistrust, or apprehension on the part of families who may feel vulnerable or uneasy about sharing power with school personnel (Cummins, 2000, 2009). Then educators can demonstrate genuine trust by allowing families to speak their minds, to respond to them in a nonjudgmental manner, and to include families' concerns and ideas as part of the solution to challenging situations (Noddings, 2003).

## BEATRIZ: THE ROAD TO CRITICAL CONSCIOUSNESS AND EMPOWERMENT

For Beatriz, several factors contributed to the shift of perspective she experienced during the 16-week PAR study in which she participated. At the beginning of the investigation, Beatriz demonstrated anger and frustration toward Megan's teacher and other school personnel who provided services to Megan. From her point of view, these educators were quick to discriminate against her because of her cultural and language background as well as her economic, social, and citizenship status. She reacted to their actions and to her perceptions of their motives by resisting communication and interaction that she believed would further disempower her and her family. As a result of her resistance, she had become increasingly isolated from Megan's school which, ironically, contributed to other feelings of disempowerment. Beatriz's fears had reached a heightened state at one of the first IEP meetings she attended in which Megan's teacher, with whom she had not interacted in weeks, told her that Megan needed to be in a self-contained classroom:

*Como siempre he mencionado quiero que [Megan] conviva con niños regulares. . . . La maestra de educación especial me quiso espantar. Me dijo que si [Megan] no se iba a la clase de educación especial, iba a perder todos los servicios. Que ya no iba a tener derecho a nada.*

(As I have always mentioned, I want Megan to be with typical children. . . . The special education teacher wanted to scare me. She told me that if Megan didn't go to the special education classroom, she was going to lose all her services. That I was no longer going to have any rights.)

As a parent who was unfamiliar with the U.S. school system, with special education services and laws, with her rights as a parent of a child with disabilities, and with the language and terminology used at IEP meetings, Beatriz was at a great disadvantage. Feeling intimidated by Megan's teacher led Beatriz to search outside of the school system to find support, security, and validation. She believed the only way to find authentic support was to speak to other parents who were experiencing similar challenges since teachers and other school personnel "only wanted to scare us so that their programs would [appear to be] the only and best ones." Beatriz's perception was that school personnel had already formed biases against certain types of parents. Parents who fell into negative stereotypes were automatically categorized as ignorant, uneducated, and powerless. Because she was unwilling to accept certain outcomes for Megan (i.e., placement in a self-contained classroom), she resisted by reacting against decisions Megan's teacher recommended. She decided to fight for an inclusive setting in which Megan would be integrated for the full day in a general education classroom. To achieve this goal, Beatriz attended support groups for Spanish-speaking parents of children with autism.

*Uno como mamá tiene que buscar un grupo de apoyo. Yo he visto muchos grupos que se reunen en un restaurante, y puede uno compartir sus opiniones, sus experiencias y decir, ¿Puedes ir a este lado? ¿Puedes pedirle esto a tu coordinadora? ¿Hay estos servicios? ¿Hay unas cosas que uno no sabe? Otras mamás nos pueden decir.*

(As a mom, one needs to find a support group. I have seen many groups that gather together in a restaurant, and one can share one's opinions, one's experiences, and say, "Can you go to this side? Can you ask your coordinator this? Are there these services? Is there something that one doesn't know?" Other moms can tell us.)

## Sharing Power in Third Space

The main purpose of the PAR study (Santamaría, 2009) was to analyze the ways in which parent participants of Mexican origin defined parent involvement over time as they critically reflected upon their roles and responsibilities in their children's education through structured discussion sessions that led to specific action-oriented goals. Santamaría Graff entered into third space with these parents and became a co-investigator as she learned, through her *novice* role (Lave & Wenger, 1991), about the structural and personal barriers parents resisted and overcame as they discovered different tools to navigate the educational system.

Santamaría Graff was aware consciously of the importance of sharing power and space as a means to position all participants as equals. By establishing third space at the beginning of the study, co-investigators (including the authors) were able to share intimate accounts of their fears, sorrows, and joys within a safe, trustworthy, and mutually respectful environment. As parent co-investigators created an action plan based on immediate and long-term needs, Santamaría Graff acted as a facilitator to ensure equal representation in discussion and planning sessions and to document the process in various forms so that the information was accessible to all participants.

Another important aspect of third space in the PAR study was the educator's detachment from outcomes derived from traditional expectations of how parents should interact or communicate in the specific venue provided. For example, Santamaría Graff presented an article on parent empowerment so that parent co-investigators could critically discuss the material. During the conversation, parents disagreed with the manner in which "empowerment" was presented. Instead of stepping in to control the outcome of the discussion, Santamaria Graff observed as parents contributed opinions until reaching a place of respectful disagreement. A safe and trustworthy environment was necessary for conversation to flow and for trust among parent co-investigators to unfold as they shared power within the collaborative space created.

## Transformation Through Action-Oriented Change

Beatriz's transformation during the 16-week PAR study was influenced by the opportunity to *convivir* (share meaningful interactions) with other parents who came from similar backgrounds and to feel *confianza* (mutual trust) and *respeto* (respect) as a co-investigator. Through five intense discussion and planning group sessions lasting approximately 1½ hours each, Beatriz was able to share her frustrations, fears, desires, and hopes in a comprehensive and uninhibited manner. Developing strong ties with other co-investigators led her from feeling *aislada* (isolated) to supported and confident.

Beatriz was unable to secure Megan's placement in a general education classroom during the time in which the study took place. However, through discussion and planning sessions she listened attentively to other parents who were going through similar challenges and began to critically reflect upon the ways in which she could take action to forge a better relationship with Megan's teacher. At the end of the PAR study, Beatriz commented on the ways in which she learned from other parents of how to approach Megan's teacher and other school personnel:

> *Lo que he aprendido mucho es cómo dirigirme a las maestras de la escuela de [Megan], cómo pedir las cosas cómo defender los derechos de los niños. Aprendí que hay que comunicarnos más, pedir ayuda, que no estamos solos, por eso hay tantos grupos que nos pueden ayudar y hay que asistir, hay que ir a las reuniones a lo mejor no todos nos sirven pero de algo podemos aprender allí conocer a otras personas para que nos pueda ayudar porque también ellos han pasado por lo mismo que nosotros hemos pasado.*

> (What I have learned the most is how to address the teachers at Megan's school, how to ask for things, how to defend children's rights. I learned that we need to communicate more, ask for help, that we aren't alone, that's why there are so many groups that help and assist us, we need to go to the meetings [and] there is the possibility that not all the meetings can serve us, but we can learn there, get to know other people so that they can help us and also because they have gone through what we've gone through.) (Santamaría, 2009, p. 397)

Beatriz experienced empowerment the moment she understood she was not alone and had the power and knowledge to access others who would support her. According to Delgado-Gaitan (1991), "Empowerment is an ongoing intentional process centered in the local community involving mutual respect, critical reflection, caring and group participation through which people lacking an equal share of valued resources gain greater access to and control over those resources" (p. 23). Delgado-Gaitan's definition of empowerment encapsulated Beatriz's experience during the PAR study as she began to reclaim her inner power as a resourceful and passionate mother who was driven to "give back to the community." Having felt like an "outsider" from the school system because of her cultural and linguistic background, she realized how her experiences as a Mexican immigrant mother of a child with autism could benefit parents who were undergoing similar challenges. At one of the parent-support groups Beatriz attended during the PAR study, a parent approached her about starting her own support group. She shared the following:

*Entonces dije, "Yo tengo que hacer algo." Y fue cuando empecé a
conocer, a investigar, a informarme y tratar de hacer todo lo mejor
que se pudiera, ¿no? Y eso me gustaría más que nada por las familias
que apenas reciben un diagnostico, que no saben que hacer. Que no
sabe adonde ir. Por eso es que decía yo seria bueno, ¿pues alguien no?,
hacer un grupo de las mamás que ya sabemos para la familias que
apenas están empezando o esas familias que reciben un diagnóstico.*

(And then I said, "I have to do something." It was then I began to
learn, to investigate, to inform myself, and to try to do everything
I could better, you know? And what I liked more than anything for
the families that have just received a diagnosis and don't know what
to do. They don't know where to go. For that reason he [a person
from her Spanish-speaking support group] said that I'd be good, well
someone, right?, to start a group with the mothers that we already
know, for families that are just beginning or those families that receive
a diagnosis.)

Toward the end of the PAR study Beatriz confided that she had never
considered herself to be a leader until she heard other parents' validations
of her strengths. She had always known she was a determined and strong-
willed person, but "being Mexican" in the United States made her doubt her
inner voice and expertise. By becoming conscious of systemic inequities and
discrimination within institutions, specifically schools, Beatriz realized her
feelings of disempowerment originated from pejorative messages she was
internalizing from dominant culture media and propaganda. As she gained
awareness of her own power within institutional systems, she also understood that her struggles with powerlessness were not in isolation; rather, she
was connected to historically underserved populations on a global level. In
other words as Beatriz became critically conscious of the "root causes of
social problems" (Ginwright & Cammarota, 2002, p. 83) she, with the support of other parents, developed a sophisticated understanding of how her
challenges on the microlevel were endemic of larger social issues occurring
on the macrolevel. With this realization, Beatriz committed herself to serving other parents whose struggles mirrored her own.

## THE SPIRIT OF PAR IN URBAN EDUCATION REFORM

At its core, PAR presents a blueprint for equity-minded educators who are
committed to establishing and maintaining authentic collaborative relationships with families. The successful implementation of PAR is not predicated
on the involvement of outside researchers. Instead, the goal of PAR in edu-

cation is to liberate all stakeholders, from dominant and minority groups alike, from oppressive hegemonic structures that squelch opportunities for critical collaborative dialogue and inquiry (Hynds, 2010). Emancipation requires that each stakeholder believes that he or she can generate change without the external influence of "experts" (Freire, 1970/2000).

In urban education reform PAR is a strategy that stakeholders can use to engage resistance as a tool in a variety of school settings. Resistance, when conceptualized as a necessary vehicle through which challenges are discussed through acceptance and meaningful dialogue, becomes a powerful tool in reshaping relationships between school personnel and families. Educators who are committed to creating equitable and authentic partnerships with families may instigate the PAR process in a number of ways. Teachers and school leaders begin the process by reflecting upon their privileged positions and the ways in which their roles may be perceived by families from all backgrounds. Then they must be willing to examine school policies and individual practices that impede social justice for historically underserved groups. As the community begins to develop a critical consciousness, discussions with parents and families can genuinely engage shared visions of success for students and begin to deconstruct some of the assumptions that surround what constitutes family involvement. These conversations, within third space, provide equal negotiating power and decision making for all involved and create the opportunity to construct new patterns of local policy development. To ensure that ideas and suggestions lead to transformative changes, a cogenerated action plan can be used as a tool to document goals, responsibilities, and outcomes. If resistance among stakeholders arises and is particularly intense, an objective third-party member who can facilitate or mediate the discussion is critical. This person should be carefully selected and approved by all stakeholders. The PAR process can help create the conditions for families and school personnel to build a common vision for inclusive education that provides the opportunities to learn, participate, and benefit from a robust curriculum and carefully designed learning environments that are differentiated based on the unique characteristics of each child and his or her cultural and linguistic histories.

## CONCLUSION

Historically underserved families who have children with disabilities have been traditionally viewed as existing outside of the system as separate, powerless entities who have had little to contribute. They have proven, time and time again, their strength and worth as they resist oppressive structures and defy negative categorizations of their cultural and linguistic legacies. Their persistence for equality within the educational system has exposed severe institutional gaps. As we realize their marginalization has been socially constructed in both intentional and nondeliberate ways, we awaken to the injustices that impact our schools.

Transformational frameworks, such as the Systemic Change Framework, offer these families an equal and fair opportunity to sit among educators as colleagues and as cogenerators of knowledge. These frameworks call for a paradigm shift in which hierarchies that currently influence school-based institutions are repositioned to reflect an "empowering, horizontal" approach (Figueroa, Kincaid, Rani, & Lewis, 2002, p. ii) rather than the dominant top-down. These collaborative shifts in power will enable historically underserved families to participate and contribute fully to the overall success and empowerment of future students. By establishing a clear and designated space through which genuine trust has been earned and developed over time, families' voices are heard and accepted. Within this positive and collaborative environment, families may no longer need to resist school personnel or the institutions they represent. Instead, as equal contributors to the improvement of school practices, families and school personnel can practice authentic collaboration in the construction of new knowledge inclusive of every stakeholder's input. In this manner, urban school reform is transformative and sustainable.

## REFERENCES

Artiles, A. J., Kozleski, E. B., Trent, S. C., Osher, D., & Ortiz, A. (2010). Justifying and explaining disproportionality, 1968–2008: A critique of underlying views of culture. *Exceptional Children, 76*(3), 279–299.

Baca, L. M., & Cervantes, H. T. (2003). *The bilingual special education interface* (4th ed.). Upper Saddle River, NJ: Prentice Hall.

Benson, S. (2010). "I don't know if that'd be English or not": Third space theory and literacy instruction. *Journal of Adolescent & Adult Literacy, 53*(7), 555–563.

Berkhofer, R. F. (1978). *The White man's Indian.* New York, NY: Random House.

Bernstein, B. (1975). *Class, codes and control: Vol. 3. Towards a theory of educational transmissions.* London, United Kingdom: Routledge & Kegan Paul.

Bhabha, H. K. (1994). *The location of culture.* New York, NY: Routledge.

Blue-Banning, M., Summers, J. A., Frankland, H. C., Nelson, L. L., & Beegle, G. (2004). Dimensions of family and professional partnerships: Constructive guidelines for collaboration. *Exceptional Children, 70*(2), 167–184.

Bourdieu, P., & Passeron, J. C. (1977). *Reproduction in education, society and culture.* London, United Kingdom: Sage.

Cammarota, J., & Romero, A. (2006). A critically compassionate intellectualism for Latina/o students: Raising voices above the silencing in our schools. *Multicultural Education, 14*(2), 16–23.

Cardoso, J. B., & Thompson, S. J. (2010). Common themes of resilience among Latino immigrant families: A systematic review of the literature. *Families in Society: The Journal of Contemporary Social Services, 91*(3), 257–265.

Cummins, J. (1996). *Negotiating identities: Education for empowerment in a diverse society* (2nd ed.). Ontario, CA: California Association for Bilingual Education (CABE).

Cummins, J. (2000). *Language, power, and pedagogy: Bilingual children in the cross-fire.* Clevedon, United Kingdom: Multilingual Matters.

Cummins, J. (2009). Pedagogies of choice: Challenging coercive relations of power in classrooms and communities. *International Journal of Bilingual Education and Bilingualism, 12*(3), 261–271.

Delgado-Gaitan, C. (1991). Involving parents in the schools: A process of empowerment. *American Journal of Education, 100*(1), 20–46.

Delgado-Gaitan, C. (1994). *Consejos:* The power of cultural narratives. *Anthropology & Education Quarterly, 25*(3), 298–316.

Epstein, J. L., & Sheldon, S. B. (2002). Present and accounted for: Improving student attendance through family and community involvement. *Journal of Educational Research, 95* (5), 308–318.

Fals Borda, O. (1991). Some basic ingredients. In O. Fals-Borda & M. A. Rahman (Eds.), *Action and knowledge: Breaking the monopoly with participatory action-research* (pp. 3–12). New York, NY: Apex.

Ferguson, D. L., Kozleski, E. B., & Smith, A. (2003). Transforming general and special education in urban schools. In F. Obiakor, C. Utley, & A. Rotatori (Eds.), *Advances in special education: Vol. 15. Effective education for learners with exceptionalities* (pp. 43–74). London, United Kingdom: JAI Press.

Figueroa, M. E., Kincaid, D. L., Rani, M., & Lewis, G. (2002). *The communication for social change working paper series: Vol. 1. Communication for social change: An integrated model for measuring the process and its outcomes.* New York, NY: The Rockefeller Foundation.

Fine, M. (1993). [Ap]parent involvement: Reflections on parents, power, and urban public schools. *Teachers College Record, 94*(4), 682–729.

Freire, P. (2000). *Pedagogy of the oppressed* (rev. 30th anniv. ed.). New York, NY: Continuum. (Original work published 1970)

Freire, P. (2007). *Education for critical consciousness.* London, United Kingdom: Continuum. (Original work published 1974)

Friend, M., & Cook, L. (2007). *Interactions: Collaboration skills for school professionals* (5th ed.). White Plains, NY: Longman.

Ginwright, S., & Cammarota, J. (2002). New terrain in youth development: The promise of a social justice approach. *Social Justice, 29*(4), 82–95.

Giroux, H. (1983). Theories of reproduction and resistance in the new sociology of education: A critical analysis. *Harvard Educational Review, 53,* 257–283.

Gonzalez, R., & Ayala-Alcantar, C. (2008). Critical caring: Dispelling Latino stereotypes among pre-service teachers. *Journal of Latinos and Education, 7,* 129–143.

Griego-Jones, T. (2003). Contribution of Hispanic parents' perspectives to teacher preparation. *The School Community Journal, 13*(2), 73–97.

Guldberg, K. (2008). Adult learners and professional development: Peer-to-peer learning in a networked community. *International Journal of Lifelong Education, 27*(1), 35–49.

Harris, A. L. (2006). I (don't) hate school: Revisiting oppositional culture theory of Blacks' resistance to schooling. *Social Forces, 85*(2), 797–834.

Harry, B. (2002). Trends and issues in serving culturally diverse families of children with disabilities. *Journal of Special Education, 74*(3), 372–388.

Herrnstein, R. J., & Murray, C. (1994). *The bell curve: Intelligence and class structure in American life.* New York, NY: Free Press Paperbacks.

Hynds, A. (2010). Unpacking resistance to change-within school reform programmes with a social justice orientation. *International Journal of Leadership in Education, 13*(4), 377–392.

Jensen, A. R. (1973). *Educability and group differences.* London, United Kingdom: Methuen.

John W. Gardner Center for Youth and Their Communities. (2007, December). Youth Engaged in Leadership and Learning (YELL): *A handbook for program staff, teachers, and community leaders* (2nd ed.). Palo Alto, CA: Stanford University. Retrieved from jgc.stanford.edu/our_work/yell.html

Jonson, K. F. (1999). Parents as partners: Building positive home–school relationships. *The Educational Forum, 63*(2), 121–126.

Kozleski, E. B., & Smith, A. (2009). The complexities of systems change in creating equity for students with disabilities in urban schools. *Urban Education, 44*(4), 427–451.

Lareau, A. (1989). *Home advantage: Social and parental intervention in elementary education.* London, United Kingdom: Falmer, 1989.

Lave, J., & Wenger, E. (1991). *Situated learning: Legitimate peripheral participation.* Cambridge, United Kingdom: Cambridge University Press.

Maguire, P. (1987). *Doing participatory research: A feminist approach.* Amherst, MA: Center for International Education.

Mauer, R. (2006). Resistance and change in organizations. In B. B. Jones & M. Brazzel (Eds.), *The NTL handbook of organizational development and change: Principles, practices, and perspectives* (pp. 121–138). San Francisco, CA: Wiley.

McKenzie, K., & Scheurich, J. (2008). Teacher resistance to improvement in schools with diverse students. *International Journal of Leadership in Education, 11,* 117–133.

Moje, E. B., Ciachanowski, K. M., Kramer, K., Ellis, L., Carrillo, R., & Collazo, T. (2004). Working toward third space in content area literacy: An examination of everyday funds of knowledge and discourse. *Reading Research Quarterly, 39*(1), 38–70. doi: 10.1598/R R Q.39.1.4

Moll, L. C., Amanti, C., Neff, D., & Gonzalez, N. (1992) Funds of knowledge for teaching: Using a qualitative approach to connect homes and classrooms. *Theory into Practice, 31*(2), 132–141.

Monzó, L. D., & Rueda, R. S. (2001). Professional roles, caring, and scaffolds: Latino teachers' and paraeducators' interactions with Latino students. *American Journal of Education, 109*(4), 438–471.

Noddings, N. (2003). *Caring: A feminine approach to ethics and moral education* (2nd ed.). Berkeley: University of California Press.

Ochoa, G. L., & Pineda, D. (2008). Deconstructing power, privilege, and silence in the classroom. *Radical History Review*, *102*, 45–62.

O'Connor, C. (2001). Making sense of the complexity of social identity in relation to achievement: A sociological challenge in the new millennium. *Sociology of Education*, *74* (extra issue), 159–168.

Olivos, E. M. (2004). Tensions, contradictions, and resistance: An activist's reflection of the struggles of Latino parents in the public school system. *The High School Journal*, *87*(4), 25–35.

Osher, T. W., & Osher, D. M. (2002). The paradigm shift to true collaboration with families. *Journal of Child and Family Studies*, *11*(1), 47–60.

Peña, D. C. (2000). Parent involvement: Influencing factors and implications. *Journal of Educational Researcher*, *94*(1), 42–54.

Ramirez, A.Y.F. (2003). Dismay and disappointment: Parental involvement of Latino immigrant parents. *Urban Review*, *35*(2), 93–110.

Ramirez, A.Y.F., & Soto-Hinman, I. (2009). A place for all families. *Educational Leadership*, *66*(7), 79–82.

Reason, P., & Bradbury, H. (2001). Introduction: Inquiry and participation in search of world worth of human aspiration. In P. Reason & H. Bradbury (Eds.), *Handbook of action research: Participative inquiry and practice* (pp. 1–14). London, United Kingdom: Sage.

Salas, L. (2004). Individualized education plan (IEP) meetings and Mexican American parents: Let's talk about it. *Journal of Latinos and Education*, *3*(3), 181–192.

Salas, L., Lopez, E. J., Chinn, K., & Menchaca-Lopez, E. (2005). Can special education teachers create parent partnership with Mexican American families? *¡Si se pueda! Multicultural Education*, *13*(2), 52–55.

Santamaría, C. C. (2009). Mexican origin parents with special needs children: Using a critically compassionate intellectualism model to support and foster their participation in U.S. schools through a participatory action research project. *Dissertation Abstracts International*, *70*(4), 474.

Smart, J. F., & Smart, D. W. (1995). Acculturative stress of Hispanics: Loss and challenge. *Journal of Counseling and Development*, *75*, 390–396.

Solórzano, D., & Delgado Bernal, D. (2001). Examining transformational resistance through a critical race and LatCrit theory framework: Chicana and Chicano students in an urban context. *Urban Education*, *36*(3), 308–342.

Suárez-Orozco, C. (2000). Identities under siege: Immigration stress and social mirroring among the children of immigrants. In A.C.G.M. Robben & M. M. Suárez-Orozco (Eds.), *Cultures under siege: Collective violence and trauma* (pp. 194–226). Cambridge, United Kingdom: Cambridge University Press.

Suzuki, L. A., & Valencia, R. R. (1997). Race-ethnicity and measured intelligence: Educational implications. *American Psychologist*, *52*(10), 1103–1114.

Tuhiwai Smith, L. (1999). *Decolonizing methodologies: Research and indigenous peoples*. London, United Kingdom: Zed Books.

Turnbull, A., & Turnbull, R. (2001). *Families, professionals, and exceptionality: Collaboration for empowerment* (4th ed.). Upper Saddle River, NJ: Merill/Prentice Hall.

Turney, K., & Kao, G. (2009). Barriers to school involvement: Are immigrant parents dis-advantaged? *Journal of Educational Research*, *102*(4), 257–271.

Valdes, G. (1996). *Con respeto: Bridging the distances between culturally diverse families and schools: An ethnographic portrait.* New York, NY: Teachers College Press.

Valencia, R. R., & Black, M. S. (2002). "Mexican Americans don't value education!" The basis of myth, mythmaking, and debunking. *Journal of Latinos and Education, 1*(2), 81–103.

Valenzuela, A. (1999). *Subtractive schooling: U.S.–Mexican youth and the politics of caring.* Albany: State University of New York Press.

Villegas, A. M., & Lucas, T. (2002). *Educating culturally responsive teachers: A coherent approach.* Albany, NY: State University of New York Press.

Villenas, S., & Deyhle, D. (1999). Critical race theory and ethnographies challenging the stereotypes: Latino families, schooling, resilience and resistance. *Curriculum Inquiry, 29*(4), 413–445.

Yosso, T. J. (2005). Whose culture has capital? A critical race theory discussion of community cultural wealth. *Race, Ethnicity, and Education, 8*(1), 69–91.

Zarate, M. E. (2007). *Understanding Latino parental involvement in education: Perceptions, expectations, and recommendations.* Los Angeles, CA: Tomás Rivera Policy Institute.

# Part III

# TEACHER EFFORTS IN TRANSFORMING URBAN LEARNING ENVIRONMENTS

# CHAPTER 5

# Creating Classrooms for All Learners

*Taucia Gonzalez and Elaine Mulligan*

## MS. NOLAN'S CLASSROOM ON THE FIRST DAY OF SCHOOL

Students walk into the 5th-grade classroom in small groups, talking with their friends. They sit at desks in groups of four as they choose. Ms. Nolan has created a bulletin board of the year's theme, Communities. The bulletin board includes pictures and names of different types of communities (classroom, school, sports team, family, church, town). She takes attendance and then reviews basic classroom rules (respect others, do your best work, ask for help if you need it). Next, Ms. Nolan reviews a list of classroom duties and explains that all students will take turns fulfilling them. Then, she describes the grading and homework procedures and offers times during lunch, before and after school that she will be available for homework help.

## MS. KEATING'S CLASSROOM ON THE FIRST DAY OF SCHOOL

Students walk into the 5th-grade classroom in small groups, talking with their friends. The desks and chairs are stacked against the walls; the walls are bare of decoration. Confused, students ask where they can sit. Ms. Keating replies with a warm smile that they can sit where they choose; the desks and chairs are portable. As the students move desks and get settled, Ms. Keating watches how individual students engage in the process, jotting occasional notes in her notebook. After the students are settled Ms. Keating then begins by introducing herself. As she introduces herself, she writes the categories of information she is giving on a whiteboard: name, people in my home, pets, things I like to do, ways I like to learn, things that bother me. She then asks the students to each introduce themselves, using the categories as guidelines, but to feel free to skip a category if they don't want to address it, or to add other important information about themselves. As she listens to their introductions, she responds to interesting information with nods, smiles, claps, and occasionally jots notes in her notebook. After the introductions, the teacher begins a discussion of "community"; students discuss what is it, who is included, what makes a good community, and so on. Once the students have come to a common agreement about what a community is, the teacher steers the discussion to what is needed to create a good learning community in the classroom. Ms. Keating records student input on poster paper, exactly as it was stated (without editing their grammar). These are posted on the wall. She then poses the question: "What guidelines do we want to have for our community?" She allows the students to debate and decide, noting for herself which students prefer to lead discussions, which like to play "devil's advocate," and other styles and preferences they display. The students create the classroom norms, with very little guidance from the teacher. At times, she prompts them to address an issue such as homework or how and from whom to get help.

Teaching and learning are at the center of the Systemic Change Framework (see Chapter 1). Although what happens in the classroom is connected to many parts of a system, teaching and learning lie at the heart of educating students (Ball & Forzani, 2007). In this chapter, we will explore the roles that teachers play in their classrooms in supporting and designing for student learning. Specifically, we examine how teachers' attention to culture serves as a tool for mediating the instructional dynamic: how they use cultural differences to create instructional and social moves that acknowledge and build on differences as assets to create classrooms where all students are included in meaningful learning. While these two teachers use culture to mediate their classrooms in different ways, these differences provide insight into the range of possibilities for different instructional contexts. Two teachers, Ms. Nolan and Ms. Keating (pseudonyms), open their doors, allowing glimpses into their classrooms, their teaching practices, and their growth as educators striving to create inclusive classrooms where *all* students learn.

The term *inclusive classroom* can be defined and interpreted in a variety of ways. Often it refers to a general education classroom as a space that physically includes students with special needs, or as classrooms where the curriculum is adapted to allow students with special needs to participate in the general education curriculum. Rather than narrowly focusing on place and students with disabilities as parameters, we define *inclusive education* more broadly, drawing on work from Kozleski, Artiles, Fletcher, and Engelbrecht, 2009. Inclusive education ensures that student groups who have been traditionally excluded from and marginalized from schooling are able to access, participate, and engage in the full range of educational opportunities made available within learning environments such as classrooms, schools, and school systems.

Therefore, like the teachers presented in these vignettes, we concern ourselves with creating educational access for the many forms of difference that teachers and students alike will likely encounter in the classroom (Artiles & Kozleski, 2007).

Ms. Nolan and Ms. Keating's stories serve not as goals or exemplars, but rather as anchors for professional reflection. You may, in fact, find similarities and differences between their teaching practices and your own, both of which are wonderful opportunities to pause and reflect on why you engage in those practices. This chapter will borrow Ms. Nolan and Ms. Keating's classrooms as spaces for reflection and conversations about what it means to create a classroom where *all* students learn.

We begin this chapter with a discussion on building a classroom community, but we complicate it by asking you to consider the role culture plays in the everyday practices of teachers and students. We then examine the constraints and affordances that cultural practices can play in creating inclusive classroom communities. We provide you with some guiding principles as tools to help you negotiate the intersection of the school's culture, your own culture, your students' cultures, and the classroom culture you will create. We intend this chapter to be a reciprocal experience between you, the reader; us, the writers; and Ms. Keating and Ms. Nolan, the teachers who have opened up their classrooms to us. We have structured spaces for that reciprocity in the form of questions—moments for you to stop, reflect, and respond with your own thoughts and feelings.

## COMPLICATING COMMUNITY WITH CULTURE

Both Ms. Nolan and Ms. Keating understand how important the first day of school is as a building block for the classroom community that will serve as the learning context for the rest of the school year. Community can just happen or it can be purposefully planned and structured. Everyone who has walked into a school knows that every classroom has a different *feel*, different *interactions*, different *roles* that people play, different *power* dynamics, and different ways of *learning*. Some of those communities feel like places to be and learn, while others may feel chaotic, rigid, or unwelcoming. Visiting Ms. Nolan and Ms. Keating's classrooms provides a glimpse into how two teachers understand the process of building inclusive classroom communities and how their decisions affect students.

Both Ms. Nolan's and Ms. Keating's classroom communities were likely safe and positive for their students, but there were differences in the learning communities. Both teachers made decisions about how to structure their classrooms, what to hang on the walls, and what to do on the first day. Both of them had ample learning occurring on that first day of school. What *differed* was the role *culture* played in guiding how the teachers approached the notion of building classroom learning communities.

What does culture have to do with learning communities? Everything. We are not referring to culture as a "thing" some people have nor as "a craft or historical image that hangs on the wall" (Delgado-Gaitan, 2006, p. vii). We are referring to a more complex, meaningful understanding of culture. The things we do, how we do them, and the things (or tools) that we use to participate in those practices make up our *culture* (Cole, 1996). At-home practices may involve the way language is used, the roles different family members assume, and any other daily practice that a person engages in. It is a common misunderstanding that culture is something *some* people have—often associated with another language, possibly an accent, or a foreign birthplace (Rogoff, 2003). In actuality, every person who walks through the school doors—including you—has his or her own culture. Since the daily practices that people are involved in change according to where they are and whom they are with, people have multiple cultural selves. The classroom is one such cultural context.

Culture is not a passive entity that individuals merely receive. It is both inherited and constructed; "culture is both carried by individuals and created in moment-to-moment interactions with one another as they participate in (and reconstruct) cultural practices" (Nasir & Hand, 2006, p. 450). Your classroom culture may be very different from the one next door because of what occurs in the classroom. Ball and Forzani (2007) call these interactions the "instructional dynamic" (see Figure 5.1). The instructional dynamic is critical in forming the classroom community. Most teachers have understandings of content, students, and their role as teachers—the three corners of the instructional dynamic. The *instructional dynamic* is what happens when those three components intersect. Knowing how to facilitate that intersection is different from just knowing about the three components. In order to create a classroom community where all students learn, we must know how to mediate the instructional dynamic.

Culture is a powerful tool in mediating the instructional dynamic. The relationship between culture and the instructional dynamic is reciprocal in two important ways. First, the instructional dynamic creates the classroom culture. Think about all of the moment-to-moment interactions and decisions teachers make and how students respond and participate. There are teachers who know how to use their understandings of students' lives to mediate the instructional dynamic masterfully. Students are engaged in learn-

FIGURE 5.1. Culture and the Instructional Dynamic Have a Reciprocal Relationship

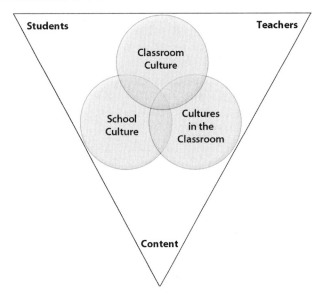

The Instructional Dynamic

ing, they feel valued, and the classroom feels like a safe space. The teacher next door might use all of the same curricular materials and participate in the same professional development, yet she is in a constant struggle to engage her students. These two teachers are negotiating the instructional dynamic in very different ways with very different outcomes. The instructional dynamic creates a classroom culture.

Second, culture can be used to mediate the instructional dynamic. Having a deep understanding of culture can guide not only the moment-to-moment interactions but also how you plan instruction. In order to gain a deeper understanding of how culture can be used to mediate the instructional dynamic, we will turn to Carol Lee's (2007) cultural modeling work in high school classrooms, a powerful example of this mediation. Lee's work demonstrates that all students, even students with histories of low performance, are capable of complex academic engagement in a culturally minded instructional dynamic (see Figure 5.2).

Lee taught high school literature by building understanding and drawing on her students' lives. She describes an example of using cultural modeling to teach satire (Lee, 2007; see Figure 5.3). She begins with a deep understanding of her students' lives to understand how they might already engage in the "habits of mind" required to understand satire. She then uses

FIGURE 5.2. Cultural Modeling

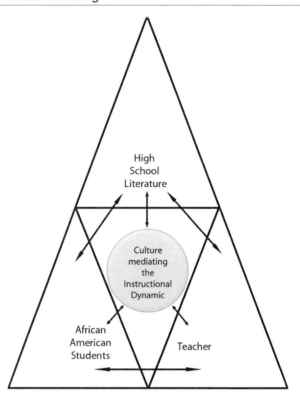

this understanding to form cultural data sets, which are resources from the students' lived experiences that can be used to begin exploring and discussing the target learning concept (e.g., satire). Cultural data sets may be song lyrics, film, television, or another resource that comes from the students' lives. In teaching satire, Lee used rap lyrics, R & B lyrics, a music video, and a made-for-television short film as instructional mediums for beginning discussion of satire. As these discussions took place, Lee continuously scaffolded the discussions with the metalanguage of concept names and highlighting the processes being used. The cultural data sets served as a bridge between the students' lived experiences and the classroom. From their work using the Fugees' song "The Mask," Lee was able to then shift over to the canonical texts that are the required reading in schools

Now that this discussion about creating a classroom community has been complicated with culture, we will narrow our focus to three types of culture that are critical to the day-to-day practices of a classroom: (1) the *cultures in the classroom*, (2) the *school culture*, and (3) the *classroom cul-*

FIGURE 5.3. Connections

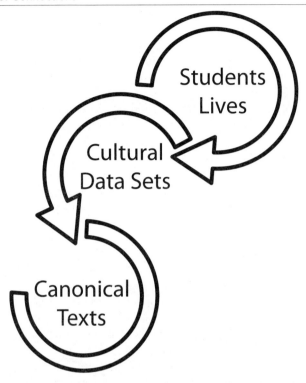

*ture* (Artiles & Kozleski, 2007; see Figure 5.1). These three types of culture can both constrain and afford opportunities to learn. Understanding culture can shape how teachers mediate the instructional dynamic in ways that support all of their students.

We look first at the cultures that each individual (teacher and students) brings into the classroom, or the *cultures in the classroom* (Artiles & Kozleski, 2007). It is very important to remember that using culture to build an inclusive classroom requires us to refrain from thinking of culture as belonging to monolithic groups (i.e., the Latino students, the African American students, the English language learners, and so on). There is actually an incredible amount of within-group diversity (Artiles, Rueda, & Salazar, 2005). Consider Joaquin, a Latino student in Ms. Nolan's classroom. His mother was born in Mexico and his father was born in the United States. Joaquin speaks English as his first language and understands some Spanish, but being Latino does not make his culture the same as his classmate Alejandro's. Latino students may share some cultural similarities, but that does not mean they come from the same culture. Aside from his ethnic culture, Joaquin has other cultural selves. For instance, he has a fascination with wrestling—another cultural self. Youth culture and pop culture are other cultural arenas to consider.

The cultural histories, patterns of transaction, expectations of the way things are "supposed to be," and each person's view of his own identity and role influence the ways in which each person participates in school. Particularly with regard to communication, understandings of the appropriate ways to initiate and respond to others can vary greatly, which can impact both teacher–student and student–student relationships. *Inclusive classrooms connect the curriculum and interaction patterns to the cultures in the classroom, which consist of multiple cultural selves, in authentic and meaningful ways.*

Often, the *school culture* (Artiles & Kozleski, 2007), or the deep-rooted practices of the school, dictates the practices that occur in classrooms. This includes not only visibly recognizable practices such as sitting in rows of desks, walking in single-file lines, and raising hands to speak, but many procedural expectations: sorting students into age-level groups, re-sorting students into ability groups, methods and frequency of assessments, the role of "teacher," the length of time a group stays together (1 year versus looping), roles of teachers, paraprofessionals, volunteers, parents, and students. Every school has its way of doing things. Although some teachers resist the way things are done at a school site, they more often than not conform to the school culture. This can be positive, but it can also be problematic, if an educator decides to veer from the way things are normally done. Administrators likely evaluate classroom teachers based on the school's established norms and expectations.

Reflect for a moment on how Ms. Nolan and Ms. Keating structured their first day of school. Which teacher's practices would be closest to the school culture you know? In many school cultures, the way Ms. Nolan structured her first day of school would be closest to the school's cultural norms and therefore highly valued. If that were the case, imagine how Ms. Keating's first day may be perceived by an administrator? Disconcerting, unorganized, or maybe lackadaisical? A classroom environment that is different from the traditional school culture may at first seem "wrong" to an observer, but it is important to look at the learning happening in the room. *Inclusive classrooms pause to examine how school culture can both afford and constrain learning, with attention to who benefits from the school culture.*

Think about the social work that took place in Ms. Nolan's classroom, which would likely be highly valued by administration. Though she built in support structures and opportunities for students to make decisions and contribute to the classroom community, she was the lone builder and designer of many aspects of the learning space: the desk layout, the wall contents, and the rules they would follow. Ms. Nolan's students were invited into a positive learning community, but as guests.

Now consider the social work that took place in Ms. Keating's classroom. Although she prepared the foundation for what would occur on the first day of school, building did not commence until the students walked in the door. Together they designed and built the beginnings of a learning community: deciding on the physical layout of the desks, sharing their personal identities, deciding on the meaning of community and connecting it to their outside-of-school lives, putting their ideas on the classroom walls, and deciding on the rules they would use to guide their classroom. Ms. Keating's students were invited into a classroom, and together they began designing and building the learning community.

Ms. Nolan and Ms. Keating engaged in somewhat different social work with their students on the first day of school. This social work between teacher and students is the process of building a *classroom culture* (Artiles & Kozleski, 2007), which exists in every classroom (Peterson, 1992). Classrooms that are attuned to the importance of culture can orchestrate social work in a way that creates a classroom that includes *all* students in learning. This social work can vary greatly, as seen in Ms. Nolan and Ms. Keating's classrooms. Not every classroom teacher will feel comfortable allowing as much student control and voice as Ms. Keating, but most teachers will see improved participation and interest in their students if they allow the students to have a stronger voice in creating the classroom community. *Inclusive classrooms are student centered and with all students contributing reciprocally to the community.*

When consciously building a community that is inclusive and supportive for *all* class members, it is important to discover and incorporate the distinct cultures that intersect in a classroom; yours, the students', the school's, and the one you will build together. Throughout the rest of this chapter we will look at how Ms. Nolan and Ms. Keating negotiate these different forms of culture and how you might begin considering the different aspects of culture in learning. These include the *cultures in the classroom,* which are the cultural practices and values that students and teachers bring with them, *the school culture,* or the ingrained practices of the educational system and school building, and *classroom cultures,* the work and activity that students and teachers do together (Artiles & Kozleski 2007).

## THE CULTURES IN THE CLASSROOM: MOVING FROM CATEGORIES OF DIFFERENCE TO A DIFFERENT KIND OF CLASSROOM

Ms. Nolan's class is doing a vocabulary warm-up exercise at the beginning of their literature block. Ms. Nolan has written the word *perspective* on the board in front of the class. Each of the students looks the word up in his or her desktop dictionary, then writes down the word and definition on a 3 x 5 card. After most of the students have finished writing, Ms. Nolan models pronouncing the word and asks for volunteers to explain what *perspective* means. She calls on several students to get a variety of descriptions, then asks for volunteers to give examples of how to use *perspective* in a sentence. If any student has difficulty explaining the definition or using the word, the student can ask for help from a classmate and then explain what he hears the classmate say.

Ms. Keating's class is also beginning their literature block. The class has chosen *The Circuit: Stories from the Life of a Migrant Child* by Francisco Jiménez. Ms. Keating begins the class by reading a chapter aloud. Students follow along in their own copies of the book. A few pairs of students follow along together sharing a copy. When students read or hear a word that they are not familiar with, they mark it with a post-it. At the end of the chapter, Ms. Keating asks students to write or share unfamiliar words that they've found on the board in the front of the class. One student writes *frontera* on the board. Ms. Keating asks if any students are familiar with this word. Several students report that they know this word, and they describe what it means to them and how they have heard it used. A conversation ensues about one student's experience with his family when crossing the *frontera* (border). After the class discussion, Ms. Keating encourages the students to write what they understand about the word and idea of *frontera* in their literature journals and to continue using the word with their classmates in conversation.

Ms. Nolan and Ms. Keating teach in an urban school that, similar to many urban schools throughout the nation, has changed dramatically over the past decade (Aud et al., 2011). The number of Latino students, many of whom are English language learners (ELLs), has steadily increased as the number of White students has declined. Ms. Nolan and Ms. Keating teach students that look, sound, and have likely had many life experiences that differ from their own (Davis, 2006). Teachers encounter difference through race, gender, language, youth culture, sexual orientation, and more. These differences, if not attended to, can negatively affect both teaching and learning, while the reverse side of the same coin is that if teachers attend to culture, they can create rich teaching and learning experiences.

Ms. Nolan and Ms. Keating, both White females, are representative of the majority of elementary and secondary teachers' race and sex (Coopersmith & Gruber, 2009). Like many urban teachers, Ms. Nolan and Ms. Keating have classes that are predominantly Latino and African American, while the number of White students continues to decrease, also representative of urban classroom demographic shifts (Aud et al., 2011). There are many layers of difference widening the gap between these two teachers and their students. There are shades of brown and black skin, hair, and eyes that contrast with their own, the students and parents dress and act differently than the teachers' own families, and the neighborhood surrounding the school differs significantly from the neighborhoods they drive home to each afternoon.

Teachers respond to differences in a variety of ways. For example, Ms. Nolan strives to create a classroom where equality reigns, "Everyone in here is equal. We don't pay attention to color." Sometimes well-intended educators, like Ms. Nolan, can miss opportunities to create more inclusive classrooms. With equality come expectations of equal behavior, equal norms, and equal understanding. "Insistence on a lack of difference means the destruction of the realities of communities other than their own" (Rogoff, 2003, pp. 347–348). While equal may have positive historical connotations (i.e., equal pay, equal rights), in the classroom equal is based on normative cultural beliefs at the expense of other beliefs. Therefore "equal" does not allow students' cultural identities to participate meaningfully in the classroom. Ignoring race as insignificant serves as an example of "equal" used in a way that neglects a social marker of who a person may be culturally. "Equal" can sometimes mean you need to look, act, and talk like the teacher in order to be fully included in a classroom, making inclusion synonymous with assimilation (Artiles, Kozleski, & Gonzalez, 2011). We instead encourage race consciousness (Singleton & Linton, 2006), because inclusive classrooms acknowledge, explore, and celebrate the differences in the classrooms as reflections of the pluralistic society we live in (Richards, Brown, & Forde, 2006). As educators, how do *we* respond to differences? We can pretend differences do not exist or we can acknowledge, celebrate, and build on the similarities and differences that exist in both the classroom and world. *Inclusive classrooms connect the curriculum to the cultures in the classroom, which consist of multiple cultural selves, in authentic and meaningful ways.* In this section we will pay thoughtful attention to how our actions and our discourse are powerful messaging tools we use to respond to the *cultures in the classroom.*

Often classrooms become spaces where students need to leave much of their cultural selves at the door if they want to be included. Sometimes the cultural selves are related to dress, language, or interests. Classrooms and the people in them send continuous messages to students. Who and what is allowed within the space of the classroom? Reflect on the following scenarios:

1.  At recess Alejandro's teacher overhears him describing his weekend to a peer, "*Fuimos a comer* pizza, *y luego* we went to the

   *parque.*" (Standard English translation: "We went to eat pizza,
   and then we went to the park.")
2. During the reading block, three boys huddle together speaking
   excitedly as they look at a magazine. The teacher approaches and
   sees they are reading a *Lowrider* magazine.

What was your initial reaction to these scenarios? Your own belief system, which is guided by your culture, shapes your reaction. Your reaction
or response to these fleeting moments with students is so much larger than
the 5 seconds it takes to respond. Students leave these moments with understandings about their relationship with you, with their classroom, with
school, and with learning. These scenarios can result in an array of responses (see Table 5.1) and therefore indirect or unintended messages directed at
the student (Johnston, 2004).

Language, be it African American English, Spanish, or a combination of
languages, is a part of a person's cultural identity. Scenario 1 is a vivid example of some of the thousands of interactions teachers and students experience daily. Those moments when teachers decide how they will respond are
powerful community building blocks. What do those blocks whisper to the
children throughout the day? The classroom can be a place where academic
English is the only language allowed, and where students are expected to
leave their linguistic selves at the door if they want to be a part of the classroom community. Another option is a classroom where academic English is
learned and engaged with, while other languages or language variations are
also accepted as legitimate ways of being and communicating. Classrooms
can be community spaces where students are able to connect their own cultures and interests to their learning experiences, and where who they are is
not labeled as "deviant" or "in need of fixing." Teachers create inclusive
classrooms not only in their formal instruction but also in their everyday
interactions with students. Students attempt to display not only who they
are as academic learners, but also who they are as people in their daily lives.
Educators seeking to create inclusive classrooms have the opportunity to
communicate *who you are is right and an important part of this classroom.*

Much learning that occurs outside of school is language based. From
a very young age, we are taught using words to create meaning. From a
child's first spoken word to her first professional résumé, learning is con-
veyed through language. The average number of words used by a 3-year
old child of professional parents in the United States is 1,100 words (Hart
& Risley, 1995). The children didn't learn any of these words by looking
them up in a dictionary; they learned them by hearing them used in context
several times, practicing including them in speech, and receiving feedback
from others about how successfully they used them ("No, honey, that's not
a ball, it's an apple."). In essence, literacy emerges through interactions with

TABLE 5.1. Teacher Responses and Student Interpretations of Responses to
Sample Scenarios

| Possible Teacher Responses | Possible Alternate Messages the Student Receives |
| --- | --- |
| *Scenario 1* | |
| "Alejandro, you are mixing English and Spanish. Choose one or the other, but it's incorrect to mix the two at the same time." | You must choose one language. Both languages cause problems. |
| "You say *park*, not *parque*." | The way you (your family and community) speak(s) is incorrect. |
| "Try that again in English, Alejandro." | You were close, but not quite there. Refrain from using your native language and try to use English. |
| "We went to the park too since the weather was so nice. What else did you do with your family?" | You are communicating something that matters to me. |
| *Scenario 2* | |
| "That is not appropriate school reading material." | Your interests are deviant. You do not know right from wrong. |
| "You need to put that away. It's reading time." | The reading you engage in is not really reading. Reading has a narrow definition. Schools have the power to define what is considered reading. |
| "Let's sit down and look through this magazine together so that we can figure out how you can read what you enjoy but also make sure we are following school policies." | As a reader you have an interest that may also have some aspects that break school policy, but we can figure out how to make this work. |
| "Those magazines have half-nude women, and you could get suspended for having them." | There is no place for your reading interest in school, and your deviance warrants disciplinary measures. |

the world. As teachers, we have opportunities to connect literacy instruction to the world our students encounter in their daily practices. Despite the power in broadly conceptualizing literacy as "reading the word and world" (Freire & Macedo, 1987), we often end up narrowing literacy to a set of skills disconnected from the world, or being able to decipher words.

The processes that we typically use in school are often very unnatural ways for children to learn about language. Like Ms. Nolan, when teaching vocabulary we often give students a format for gathering information about a word, something like this:

Word: **Perspective**

Spelling: _____

Part of Speech: _____

Pronunciation: _____

Definition: _____
_____

Use in a Sentence: _____

We assign vocabulary words, give students the format, and instruct them to look them up in a dictionary in order to gather the information. For a student who does well with traditional academic learning formats, the completed work might look like this:

Word: **Perspective**

Spelling: <u>Perspective</u>

Part of Speech: <u>Noun</u>

Pronunciation: <u>p r-spek-tiv</u>

Definition: <u>The capacity to view things in their true relations or</u>
<u>relative importance</u>

Use in a Sentence: <u>I have a different perspective than she does.</u>

What evidence do we have to indicate that she knows how to use this word in her life? She has given the correct definition for the word, and her sentence is grammatically and syntactically correct, but how can we be confident that she will be able to incorporate this word into her own speaking and writing vocabulary?

For a student who is less comfortable or experienced in mainstream academic learning formats, the completed work might look like this:

Word: **Perspective**

Spelling: *<u>Perspective</u>*

Part of Speech: *<u>n</u>*

Pronunciation: *<u>\per-spek-tiv\</u>*

Definition: *<u>neut. Of perspectivus of sight, optical, fr.</u>*

Use in a Sentence: *<u>I have a perspective.</u>*

How did using a dictionary help this student? She appears to have learned where to find the appropriate categories of information, but she does not seem to understand the word enough to explain it in her own words or use it meaningfully in a sentence. If literacy is understood to be a set of technical skills, or "reading the word" (Freire & Macedo, 1987) unrelated to the social world, this may suffice.

If the instructional goal is to have the students add the selected words to their personal vocabularies, creating learning experiences like Ms. Keating's that demonstrate how readers interact with the world to learn new words is not only more effective but more meaningful, both for the nontraditional learner and the traditional learner. Ms. Keating reminds us to use natural learning processes such as modeling with a contextual tool that connects to students' lives (e.g., rich literature, poetry, a scenario), opportunities to engage in social practice (e.g., oral application of vocabulary with peers), moments for students to share their working understanding and receive teacher and peer feedback (e.g., class coming together for students to share out), and more practice to solidify those working understandings.

Vocabulary lessons that are prompted in context, by students identifying unfamiliar words in text or conversation, are naturally occurring learning opportunities that have meaning. Teachers often choose vocabulary words by prereading the material themselves and identifying the words that are most likely to be unfamiliar to the students, but this "helpful" planning removes the opportunity and the expectation that students will work to find out about words in order to make meaning of text, which is how we want readers to interact with the world outside of school.

If literacy is understood to be a social and meaningful practice that links to students' places in the world, or "reading the word and the world" (Freire & Macedo, 1987), we must find ways to make learning experiences connect to the world outside the classroom. Ms. Keating understands that inclusive classrooms connect the curriculum to students' lives in authentic and meaningful ways. In what ways was using Francisco Jiménez's *The Circuit: Stories from the Life of a Migrant Child* to teach the same vocabulary standards as Ms. Nolan's more inclusive for her students? An initial response to this question might be that she has Latino students and the book is about a Latino student. While that is true, using that book as a tool for vocabulary instruction is authentic and meaningfully connected to students in many ways (see Table 5.2).   ·

In Ms. Keating's lesson the example of the Spanish-language vocabulary word, *frontera,* illustrates an opportunity for students to learn from one another that is often overlooked. Words in other languages frequently arise in literature books. If there are students in the class who are familiar with those words, they are natural resources for the rest of the class. This method of learning is much richer, as students not only learn the literal translation

TABLE 5.2. Meaningful Connections of *The Circuit* to Students

| Tool for Vocabulary Instruction | Meaningful and Authentic Connection |
|---|---|
| Author has Latino name: Francisco Jiménez | Students see that diverse names and lives have a place in the literary world. |
| Story has complex characters. | Students are able to experience characters that negotiate the world, including tensions, in different ways. Students have an opportunity to engage in a reciprocal relationship with text, responding with emotions, questions, and so on. |
| Story has code-switching between English and Spanish. | Students receive the message that linguistic differences are a part of both the literary world and their own world, and that their classroom recognizes and validates this difference. Students who speak languages other than English are validated as intelligent and having linguistic strengths. |
| Vocabulary study comes from the text. | Students read with the dual purpose of "reading the world" and monitoring when there is a breakdown in meaning based on a word. Students learn that this is how reading and vocabulary might function outside of school. |

of the word ("border"), but often engage in conversation about other possible meanings or uses of the word (i.e., "frontier") and develop a deeper understanding of both the English and the Spanish words.

We build meaningful relationships with others and with learning itself through our words and actions. Educators will continue to encounter students who are culturally different from them. How will you use your discourse and your curriculum to respond to them as cultural beings? What indirect messages do your words and actions communicate? The cultures in the classroom can be built on as resources to create a different kind of classroom.

## THE SCHOOL CULTURE:
## MOVING FROM HOW IT HAS BEEN TO HOW IT COULD BE

During Ms. Nolan's social studies time, her class sits in rows of desks and copies notes from the whiteboard at the beginning of class; then, participates in a daily lecture and discussion of a section from the district-mandated textbook. Ms. Nolan is a very animated and knowledgeable lecturer, and students are comfortable asking questions during the lecture. Every quarter, the students write a three-page research paper about their state's history. They can work with a partner or alone and Ms. Nolan arranges computer lab time for online research as well as library times to gather print resources. Ms. Nolan is available to help students on research projects during her lunch hour and prep period, which she often spends helping two boys with learning dis/abilities progress on their reports. She has few behavioral issues with her classes, and students like her and tend to earn fairly good grades.

Ms. Keating's social studies class sits in small "discussion groups" and begins class by choosing a topic for brief discussion from several posted on the whiteboard. Topics include: "In what ways have human modifications (e.g., dams, mining, air conditioning, irrigation, agricultural practices) affected Native populations in Arizona?"; "What evidence can you find that Native populations contribute to our daily lives today in Arizona?"; and "How do you think Native Americans felt about human modification to Arizona land?"(Arizona Department of Education, 2012). Students often debate loudly and passionately, and Ms. Keating circulates to prompt students to back up their assertions with facts. Every quarter, the students complete a research project on a topic of their choice from the era being studied that quarter. They may work individually, in pairs, or in small groups. Project format options include a written paper, video presentation, display model, or poem. References are required for each type of project. Ms. Keating is available to help students on research projects during her lunch hour and prep period. She has few behavioral issues with her classes, and her students like her and tend to earn fairly good grades.

Ms. Nolan and Ms. Keating know that they are accountable for student learning and for documenting evidence of that learning. This is a reality in just about every U.S. school, but as is evident in these teachers' classrooms, there are different ways of achieving school expectations.

Conventional U.S. schools are structured around teacher-controlled transmission of knowledge culture, supported by independent practice, assessment, and reteaching. This is not a natural cycle of learning. When we learn skills outside of school (walking, talking, playing baseball, belly dancing), we watch others perform the activity, attempt it with supports, practice with others, and continue improving over time based on feedback from others. There is not a "test" to measure mastery of walking; you know you can walk because you are doing it.

In spite of the fact that assessment may seem incongruent with the everyday learning that takes place outside the school walls, it has become an inescapable part of the *school culture*. Most teachers enter the work force and are enveloped into a school culture, eventually falling into the rhythm of "this is how we do things here." As educators we must remember, *inclusive classrooms pause to examine how school culture can both afford and constrain learning, with attention to who benefits from the school culture.* This "pause" is particularly useful in determining that instructional planning and assessment practices will benefit all students.

The rhythm of the school culture can become natural, like the beating of a drum or a heart. It carries you through the day-to-day things you want to do and the other things you are expected to do. It influences the verbal exchanges that pass between teachers in the hallway, the relationship you have with administration, the tools you use in your instruction. The school culture heavily influences the teachers, staff, and students; the way things are done; and the tools used for getting them done.

It is common to become so in sync with the rhythm of a school culture that we begin to begin to perform most day-to-day practices on autopilot. This can be a survival mechanism for teachers, so that they do not need to put their full attention and energy into every little thing they are doing. If we asked you to throw the brakes on right now and make a list of all of the things you did as a teacher today, what would be on the list? Would some of the things on the list make you smile? Would others make you cringe? What if we then asked you to add to that list explanations of *why* you did each of these things? Which of those things are done because the school expects you to, and which are done for strong pedagogical reasons? Would you struggle thinking of a good reason for some of the things on your list?

Creating an inclusive classroom requires a hand brake. If you can throw on the brakes during your teaching day, or even just slow things down enough to reflect on what you are doing and for what reason, you have the opportunity to make decisions that will benefit all learners.

Consider Ms. Nolan's social studies practices. When she became employed at her school, she quickly learned what was expected of her from her colleagues, students, parents, and administrative staff. Some of these expectations included following the state standards, using the resources at her disposal, and measuring student learning through assessment. Ms. Nolan's practices fell in line with her colleagues, with the school culture, and consequently she received high reviews from administration.

Ms. Keating started working as an educator at the school years before Ms. Nolan. When she joined her grade-level team, she offered different ways of doing things that had worked for her. Although she often heard, "This is how we do things here," she constantly interrogated her practice with, "Who benefits from doing this? Is there a different way that would benefit all kids?" Consequently, her instructional practice veered from how things had been done because of how she thought things *could* be done.

When we pause or slow down to interrogate who is benefiting from how things are done at a school, we must pay particular attention to more marginalized or vulnerable populations. Our competitive, assessment-based educational culture may not be inclusive of students who come from cultures that value cooperation over competition. These students may be from a different country, a Native American culture, a religious group that lives cooperatively, or a family structure that focuses on cooperation. It is important to consider how different aspects of the school culture are benefiting (or constraining) individual students.

Students with learning differences or disabilities might not benefit from the traditional paper-and-pencil assessment practices dictated by many school cultures. Instead, they might benefit from demonstrating their learning through cooperative learning structure demonstrations. Often, these students are very bright and successful at learning outside of the school structure. If a student easily learns games, acquires mechanical skills, or memorizes lines for a play but does poorly on written assignments or tests, that student learns in ways that her teachers are not teaching:

> Exclusion happens when uniformity and standardization are valued and when learning differences are stigmatized. Inclusion, on the other hand, is a teachable process in any classroom. Accepting attitudes that embrace diverse learning styles diffuse the stigma that students with learning disabilities are less than everyone else because they require special accommodations. (Delgado-Gaitan, 2006, p. 45)

This is not to say that students shouldn't be assessed; it is important to measure skill development, both to identify remediation needs and to provide feedback. The point is to reflect on the instruction and assessment practices of the school culture and consciously ask if "how things are done here" benefits all of your students. If not, what can you do?

Like Ms. Keating, you can plan for a variety of points of entry into learning and a variety of assessment measures. Rather than "showing" the skill, assigning independent practice, and assessing, we need to provide opportunities for students to experience the skill in a variety of formats so that they can develop an understanding of the skill and be able to generalize it (Wiggins & McTighe, 2005). If we give the students a chance to figure out how the skill works, they will have a much deeper mastery than if we expect them to replicate their teacher's model of performing the skill.

When planning for the broad range of abilities and talents that we encounter in a classroom, the most effective starting point is to define the learning outcome. State standards or Common Core standards are helpful tools that most teachers and curriculum planners use to define learning goals. From there, many teachers rely on prepackaged curricula to determine learning activities and methods. Generic curricula are designed with the "average" student in mind; they cannot anticipate the many variations in background, prerequisite skills, language and dialect differences, and learning challenges that are present in any one classroom. A more effective way to plan learning activities so that all students are included is to use the principles of Backward Design:

### THREE-STAGE PLANNING SEQUENCE OF THE BACKWARD DESIGN PROCESS

1. Identify the desired results (learning outcome).
2. Determine what is acceptable evidence that students have achieved the outcome (appropriate assessment).
3. Plan learning experiences and instruction (activities that will build the necessary knowledge and skills).

What makes this process effective in improving learning outcomes is the careful planning and thought that the teacher brings to the process *from her specific knowledge of the students in her class.* All students and their differences can and should be considered in planning and assessment.

For example, Ms. Keating's backward design process served as a tool for reflecting on her school's culture of formal pencil-and-paper assessment. She recognized that many of her students were capable of learning the standards but would not benefit from using only a pencil-and-paper assessment. Her backward design process allowed students to demonstrate the learning outcomes (Step 1) in a variety of ways (Step 2). Who benefits from Ms. Keating's "pause" (Step 3)? Ms. Nolan, on the other hand, is providing one entry point into learning and one way of demonstrating learning. Who benefits from planning and instruction when teachers do not pause and interrogate "the way things are done here"?

Students with physical disabilities may find paper-and-pencil tasks difficult. For example, students with some types of cerebral palsy have difficulty with motor control and visual tracking, but have no intellectual delays or learning disabilities. Which classroom would facilitate these students being able to access the curriculum and demonstrate learning? Some students are in the process of learning English and, though capable of learning social studies curriculum, would not be able to successfully demonstrate their learning in a formal essay. Which classroom would facilitate these students being able to access the curriculum and demonstrate their learning?

An inclusive classroom requires us to pause and interrogate who's benefiting from "how it's been" at a school, and use purposeful instructional design and assessment to imagine "how it could be." *Inclusive classrooms pause to examine how the school's culture both affords and constrains learning for all students.* This may require a different type of planning, with broad, flexible objectives and timelines.

## THE CLASSROOM CULTURE:
## MOVING FROM WHAT I WANT TO WHAT WE BUILD

Ms Nolan's class is learning about word choice in writing. She is reviewing sentences on the board, asking students to identify words that can be revised with more precise words. As students offer suggestions, she writes them beneath the underlined word. She leads a discussion of how adjectives can provide a more precise meaning to the readers. When several students have described the function of the revised words, Ms. Nolan asks them to work in pairs to revise their personal narratives with more precise words. The students return to their desks and begin working with their "elbow buddies" to make their words more interesting. A few students who are receiving Title I or special education services are working in a small group with a paraprofessional to identify words they may want to revise.

Across the hall in Ms. Keating's class, students are spread throughout the classroom. One pair sits on the beanbag in the corner of the room working through a pile of books reading excerpts and marking pages with yellow post-its. A group of four students has taken over Ms. Keating's table as they argue their stances on which poet they feel uses words in an interesting way, pointing to and reciting their evidence from their poetry folders. One pair of students is reading three different versions of the introduction from a story they are coauthoring to find out which version has words that help readers "see a picture in their head." Other pairs are entrenched in their own exploration of how writers choose words. One boy leaves a book open on his desk, walks to the supply cabinet, pulls out an index card and marker, writes down a word that he pins to the word wall, and returns to his open book. Ms. Keating and a paraprofessional walk around to help guide students' conversations. Ms. Keating calls the class back together to share out "what word choice means to them as readers and writers."

One of the most fundamental responsibilities of a teacher is to create a *classroom community*, an environment where everyone is engaged in learning. While every teacher does this in his or her own way, inclusive teachers do so with careful thought, planning, and flexibility. When a group of people (i.e., a teacher and their students) spend 180 days together in a room engaged in activities and work, a culture is formed that is unique to that group. That culture may be nurturing or critical, curious or obedient, supportive or dismissive. The *classroom culture*, or "community of practice" (Wenger, 1998), is created through the social work that you do with your students (Artiles & Kozleski, 2007). This social work looks and feels different in every class you walk into. Some classroom cultures, like Ms. Nolan's, are pleasant and safe, an enjoyable community to be in. Then you have classroom communities like Ms. Keating's, which buzz with a certain kind of energy. These are communities where you walk in and students are too busy with learning to look up; where the teacher's presence is intentional yet subtle; and where students own the learning space, moving about it and using it to accomplish their learning. Classroom communities like this, where everyone contributes to create the community, are places where all students can learn.

*Inclusive classrooms are student centered with all students contributing reciprocally to the community.* This is not a "pipe dream" or an artificially imposed goal; it is a reflection of the reciprocity of life in a complex world. People of all backgrounds, abilities, personalities, and dreams live together in homes, neighborhoods, towns, states, and nations. We use our unique individual traits in reciprocity with others to build a balanced whole:

- You cook and I'll clean.
- One neighbor helps the other with taxes, who in return shows the first how to do an oil change on his car.
- The "bread basket" of farming states provides food for the industrial cities of the East, while the East manufactures the equipment essential to food production.
- Swiss banking is world famous, while Japan is known for high-tech manufacturing.

In each of these cases, both entities benefit from their own and others' strengths. Relationships are reciprocal—a constant, although maybe not even, back-and-forth, back-and-forth. It is through this back-and-forth that we build meaningful relationships with others, with learning, and with the world. Relationships with students are the building blocks of your classroom community. The reciprocal nature of the world can be reflected in our interactions with students and in their learning experiences.

Let's examine the principle of reciprocity in the classroom. Ms. Nolan understood this basic premise of reciprocity, but not in the organic sense. Instead, she attempted to ascribe roles in the classroom. She decided Cynthia will care for the plants and Jaime will sharpen the pencils. Is this a reflection of the world? Of course not! You were not *assigned* your role as an educator, but rather your life experiences, interests, and interactions with others shaped that desire. If you were to wake up tomorrow and be assigned the role of politician, you could probably figure out how to do it, but it would very likely be a role with little meaning and certainly not utilizing your passion for working with students.

How then do we create inclusive classrooms that are organic, reciprocal communities? We begin by knowing, really knowing, who our students are and what their strengths and interests are. This is very similar to how strengths develop in the world outside of school. A child might show musical inclination, someone notices it and reinforces it; the child might even begin investing more time and interest into that strength. As teachers we already closely monitor so many aspects of our students; how many words they read per minute, what they scored on their benchmark exams, in which reading group they work. You can take this well-honed skill and expand your lens to include: *Who is this child? What are his interests? Who does he talk to?* Whether you write this down in a notebook like Ms. Keating or keep it mentally, focus on getting to know who your students are beyond their test scores or school lives. Your list might look something like this:

*Dominique:*   Has Chihuahuas, is an only child, loves drawing
*Marcos:*       Loves WWE wrestling, hangs out with Hector on the weekends
*Samantha:*     Lives with her grandmother, gardens

Once you start understanding more about your students as people outside of school, what can you do with this information? Start affirming it, finding space for it in the classroom, and building on it for learning. This does not need to be a public display. Maybe this information can later be connected to a role in the classroom, "Marcos, since you have a good understanding of how tag teams work in wrestling, how do you think we could arrange the classroom furniture so that people can work with different partners or groups more easily?" Or maybe even though Dominique is a resistant writer, during writing time she can have an important coauthoring role where she creates most of the illustrations. This allows Dominique to experience having a writing identity. Everyone in the classroom can use this "lens" or way of being in the classroom community. Consider beginning or ending the day with community circles that provide students with a space and time to share out things they learn about their peers. Samantha might share, "Today at recess I noticed Elizabeth is really good at soccer." Elizabeth then becomes known as someone who is athletic or strong or fast, traits that can eventually be connected to a role in the classroom. Samantha, the classmate who shared this observation, might be someone who can help others analyze literary characters or develop characters in student writing.

Planning instructional activities is also much more effective and meaningful when done with the unique classroom composition in mind. Each classroom culture has its own personality, which can be used to inform instructional decisions. If you have a classroom full of "talkers" who process information by discussing ideas and negotiating understanding out loud, you will want to include group-work, debates, and demonstrations. If you have a classroom that includes a lot of individualistic, artistic students, you will want to plan activities that include diagramming, creating, and displaying. If your class enjoys spending time on computers, by all means, plan activities that allow them to research information online. It is evident that when Ms. Keating plans using backward design, she not only considers different learning needs but also different student personalities and interests. If you use your students' strengths and interests to plan your instruction, you will see much deeper student engagement, fewer classroom management issues, and improved learning outcomes.

Both Ms. Nolan and Ms. Keating receive positive teacher evaluations and are well liked by students, but they have very different approaches to developing a learning community. Ms. Nolan creates a safe space for students and sets very clear expectations and procedures in her classroom, and students tend to do well. Ms. Keating, on the other hand, allows students much more autonomy and encourages them to look at curricular materials from different perspectives. She consciously poses questions that will prompt discussion between students of different racial, linguistic, and cultural backgrounds. She challenges them to look at history (and life) from various points of view.

Student-centered classrooms require structuring activities so that students are involved in deciding what they need to learn about and all students are treated as full members of the learning community. Students with academic difficulties can gain information through classroom discussion or peer interaction, rather than just through written work. Students who are learning English have more opportunities to practice using new words in a natural language-acquisition format. Difference becomes strength through reciprocity.

By working with the students to create a "positive peer culture," teachers benefit from the students' own social interdependence; "the peer group has the strongest influence over the values, attitudes, and behavior of most youth" (Vorath & Brendtro, 1974, p. 8). Students' natural affinity for each other and their intrinsic desire to "do good" for others can be utilized when setting norms. For example, when setting norms about appropriate behavior during work time, teachers may elicit student opinions about acceptable behavior during students' concentration on difficult tasks. Then teachers may ask what behaviors students consider appropriate when they are finished with their work, but their best friend is still struggling to understand the work. In this way, the teacher not only gives students opportunities to express their own needs, but also prompts consideration for others and engages the students' compassion and peer allegiance.

Building a classroom community takes time, and it may seem inefficient to invest precious days and weeks developing relationships and norms rather than diving right into the dense amount of curriculum to be covered. Time spent as a class discussing, negotiating, revisiting, and even arguing about how you (all of you) want to do things in your classroom community will reap exponential benefits creating a learning community where all students learn.

By structuring learning activities to be student oriented and reciprocal, we can engage students in developing intellectual curiosity and sharing their own knowledge. Ms. Nolan understands how to build a safe, organized classroom where students learn. Ms. Keating understands that an inclusive classroom is less concerned with what she wants and more concerned with what she and her students will build together through an ongoing reciprocal process.

## THE CLASSROOM COMMUNITY:
## A CULTURAL CONSTRUCTION ZONE

The classroom is an amazing construction zone where cultures intersect and begin the daunting yet exciting work of building a classroom community. Ms. Nolan and Ms. Keating flagged us through their construction zones, allowing us an understanding of how two teachers go about negotiating individual and school cultures within the instructional dynamic to create inclusive classroom cultures based on their own understanding. While Ms. Nolan made categories of difference invisible, Ms. Keating built on difference to create a different kind of classroom. They waved us through the stop and go signs that the cultures in the classroom might encounter. Ms. Nolan fell into the rhythm of "how it has been," while Ms. Keating used "how it could be" to change her practices to benefit all students. They demonstrated that slowing down the pace of your work can create the reflective space needed for negotiating the school culture. Finally, we saw Ms. Nolan build community based on what she felt comfortable with, while Ms. Keating and her students used the social space of the classroom to build "what we want"—making evident the difference between construction zones with one builder versus many builders.

As you reflect on your own negotiation with culture to create a classroom community where all students learn, we encourage you to reflect on how you are negotiating the instructional dynamic. What tools are you using to negotiate the intersection? Are your tools culture-free or do you use culture as a mediating tool? How does an understanding of different forms of culture afford and constrain how you negotiate the instructional dynamic?

Both culture and instruction are dynamic, constantly changing. Understanding how the *cultures in the classroom*, the *school culture*, and the *classroom culture* are both inherited and created is a powerful tool in creating inclusive instructional dynamics that do the following:

- Connect the curriculum to the cultures in the classroom, which consist of multiple cultural selves, in authentic and meaningful ways
- Pause to examine how school culture can both afford and constrain learning, with attention to who benefits from the school culture
- Demonstrate that they are student centered, with all students contributing reciprocally to the community

We end this chapter with our thanks for engaging in this reciprocal relationship between reader and writer—writing and reading, questioning and reflecting, posing ideas and responding to them. We hope that the scenarios we have examined provide you with opportunities for critical thought, both about your own practice and about the possibilities for better engaging students in learning.

## REFERENCES

Arizona Department of Education. (2012). Arizona's common core standards English language arts and literacy in history/social studies, science, and technical subjects: Kindergarten–12th grade. Phoenix, AZ: Arizona State Department of Education. Retrieved from http://www.azed.gov/azcommoncore/elastandards/

Artiles, A. J., & Kozleski, E. B. (2007). Beyond convictions: Interrogating culture, history, and power in inclusive education. *Language Arts, 84,* 351–358.

Artiles, A. J., Kozleski, E. B., & Gonzalez, T. (2011). Para além da sedução da educação inclusiva nos Estados Unidos: Confrontando o poder, construindo uma agenda histórico-cultural [Beyond the allure of inclusive education in the United States: Confronting the power, building a historical-cultural agenda]. *Revista Teias, 12*(24), 285–308.

Artiles, A. J., Rueda, R., & Salazar, J. J. (2005). Within-group diversity in minority disproportionate representation: English language learners in urban school districts. *Exceptional Children, 71*(3), 283–300.

Aud, S., Hussar, W., Kena, G., Bianco, K., Frohlich, L., Kemp, J., & Tahan, K. (2011). *The condition of education 2011* (NCES 2011-033). Washington, DC: U.S. Department of Education, Institute of Education Sciences, National Center for Education Statistics.

Ball, D. L., & Forzani, F. M. (2007). What makes education research "educational"? *Educational Researcher, 36*(9), 529–540.

Cole, M. (1996). *Cultural psychology: A once and future discipline.* Cambridge, MA: Harvard University Press.

Coopersmith, J., & Gruber, K. (2009). *Characteristics of public, private, and Bureau of Indian education elementary and secondary school teachers in the United States: Results from the 2007–08 schools and staffing survey* (NCES No. 2009321). Washington, DC: U.S. Department of Education, Institute of Education Sciences, National Center for Education Statistics.

Davis, B. (2006). *How to teach students who don't look like you: Culturally relevant teaching strategies.* Thousand Oaks, CA: Corwin Press.

Delgado-Gaitan, C. (2006). *Building culturally responsive classrooms: A guide for K–6 teachers.* Thousand Oaks, CA: Corwin Press.

Freire, P., & Macedo, D. (1987). *Literacy: Reading the word and the world.* South Hadley, MA: Bergin & Garvey.

Hart, B., & Risley, T. (1995). *Meaningful differences.* Baltimore, MD: Brookes.

Johnston, P. (2004). *Choice words: How our language affects children's learning.* York, ME: Stenhouse.

Kozleski, E. B., Artiles, A. J., Fletcher, T., & Engelbrecht, P. (2009). Understanding the dialectics of the local and the global in Education for All: A comparative case study. *International Critical Childhood Policy Studies Journal, 2*(1),15–29.

Lee, C. D. (2007). *Culture, literacy, and learning: Taking bloom in the midst of the whirlwind.* New York, NY: Teachers College Press.

Nasir, N. S., & Hand, V. M. (2006). Exploring sociocultural perspectives on race, culture, and learning. *Review of Educational Research, 76*(4), 449–475.

Peterson, R. (1992). *Life in a crowded place: making a learning community.* Portsmouth, NH: Heinemann.

Richards, H. V., Brown, A. F., & Forde, T. B. (2006). *Addressing diversity in schools: Culturally responsive pedagogy.* Tempe, AZ: National Center for Culturally Responsive Educational Systems.

Rogoff, B. (2003). *The cultural nature of human development.* New York, NY: Oxford University Press.

Singleton, G. E., & Linton, C. (2006). *Courageous conversations about race.* Thousand Oaks, CA: Corwin Press.

Vorath, H. H., & Brendtro, L. K. (1974). *Peer Culture.* Chicago, IL: Aldine.

Wenger, E. (1998). *Communities of practice: Learning, meaning, and identity.* New York, NY: Cambridge University Press.

Wiggins, G., & McTighe, J. (2005). *Understanding by design.* Alexandria, VA: ACSD.

# CHAPTER 6

# Teacher Learning in Urban Schools

*Kathleen King Thorius and Samantha Paredes Scribner*

Middleton High School (a pseudonym, as are teacher names) is a comprehensive high school in a U.S. midwestern city school district. With a student body of 1,800, the district is directing resources toward stemming attrition rates and increasing graduation rates. The student population is relatively diverse: 62% African American, 16% Latino, 21% White, and 1% other ethnic/racial designation. Eighty-three percent of the student population qualify for free or reduced price lunch. Sixteen percent of the students receive special education services, and 7% are designated English language learners. Graduation rates and student achievement on state accountability exams fall well below state and national norms. Among the faculty, 79% of the teachers are White, 17% are African American, 3% are Latino, and 1% is Asian. As in many schools in the district (and across the country) the demographic composition of the student population is not reflected in the teaching ranks. Additionally, 25% of the teachers have less than 5 years of experience, 24% have more than 20 years of experience, with the remainder ranging between 6 and 20 years of experience.

Over the past several years the school district dedicated professional development resources toward curriculum articulation across the K–12 continuum in an effort to close gaps in instruction across grade levels and align curriculum objectives with state accountability exams. While these efforts yielded some improvement at the elementary and middle school levels, student attendance, dropout rates, and overall performance remained problematic at Middleton. Ms. Lyons, the principal at Middleton, and the Middleton leadership team agreed that departmental and team-level discussions needed to continue the curriculum articulation work, but not at the expense of focused and collaborative discussion and learning centered on students. As Ms. Watson, the 9th-grade biology teacher said, "We can align all we want, but Joey still isn't getting it the way we are teaching it. And Shana is still frustrated." In other words, knowing what students need to know and be able to do at each grade level and within each course is important; however, it is measurably less complex an endeavor than translating that into meaningful teaching and learning in a classroom full of diverse learners.

To this end, 9th-grade teachers began to restructure their team meetings to center conversation, inquiry, and collaborative practice on topics and actions that explicitly connected their students' lives, community contexts, and learning objectives. They figured there was much they did not know about their students beyond how they performed in their classes. And several of the teachers were aware that, growing up, they had vastly different experiences than their students were living.

## THE PRACTITIONER LEVEL OF SYSTEMIC REFORM IN URBAN SCHOOLS

All too often, educational reforms have underinvested in teacher learning (Lieberman & Mace, 2010). Ensuring that all students have access to highly qualified teachers requires attention to more than technical capacity and content mastery (Sleeter, 2008). Narrowly defined technocratic conceptions of teaching ignore important cognitive, emotional, and dispositional dimensions inherent to the complex practice of teaching, which are necessary for systemic improvement. A broadened definition of teaching well in urban settings includes not only "a conviction in the intellectual abilities of students from historically underserved communities" (Cochran-Smith, Davis, & Fries, 2004, p. 217), but also multitheoretical fluency; creative problem solving; data-driven, reflective, and inquiry-based teaching; self-management; and ongoing professional growth. Educational systems that are situated in urban centers require particular ways of attending to how and what teachers learn, driven by explorations of identity and sociocultural, political, and economic histories of urban systems and schools, as well as individual and cultural views about difference. Based on our collective experiences as researchers and educators, the vignette woven throughout this chapter illustrates how a group of educators engages in what we assert are necessary features of reform-oriented urban teacher learning.

Because the ways in which policy and practice reforms are implemented rests heavily on the skills and creativity of teachers (Coburn & Stein, 2006), spaces within which teacher learning occurs are critical variables in the interpretation and translation of education reform for equity, and in turn, improved and equitable student access, participation, and outcomes (Hindin, Morocco, Mott, & Aguilar, 2007; Ross, Bruce, & Hogaboam-Gray, 2006). Yet a solid understanding of urban educational systems and the policy arenas that must be engaged across all levels is necessary to solving problems related to intractable, culturally bounded issues like educational equity. Such issues exist in all schools; however, they are magnified in urban school contexts due to high concentrations of students of color, students from families living in poverty, sociolinguistically diverse students, and a disproportionate amount of students identified as having some sort of disability. Urban schools are more likely to be underresourced and staffed by professionals who do not share the demographic characteristics of their students. Thus urban schools represent a convergence of differences and histories that cross racial, socioeconomic, and linguistic lines, introducing a unique political, cultural, and organizational context.

The Systemic Change Framework (Ferguson, Kozleski, & Smith, 2003) is a useful theoretical tool for understanding the complexities of urban educational systems, and is comprised of five nested levels of systemic effort and six policy and practice arenas that cut across these levels. This chapter on teacher learning in urban schools is grounded in the practitioner level of the Systemic Change Framework, which consists of professional elements that affect student learning; the framework emphasizes six arenas of practice at this level: (1) teaching design and practice; (2) leadership for learning; (3) group practice and professional learning; (4) family connections and partnerships; (5) design and use of time and space; and (6) inquiry on equity in schooling.

Across the systemic levels and arenas of focus, transformative change in people, policy, and practice combine to impact student achievement and learning. Over time this framework has been expanded and applied to equity-focused work and resources developed in systems across the United States with success in improving results for underserved and supported students (e.g., King, Capulo, Kozleski, & Gonzales, 2009).

## A TEACHER LEARNING FRAMEWORK
## FOR URBAN EDUCATIONAL SYSTEMS

There is no shortage of research on teacher learning. An exploration of the current literature on teacher learning situated in urban schools reveals at least three key areas to be addressed in order to effect transformative changes in practice, thus improving outcomes for all students while redressing entrenched equity issues. First, while ongoing teacher learning is more and more localized in classrooms rather than in traditional professional development workshops, the continued development of the teachers' role as learner requires teacher learning frameworks that move learning from isolated professional development activities disconnected from experience toward the sphere of daily practice (Webster-Wright, 2009). Next, given a history of inequity across multiple spheres of urban life (i.e., access to housing, schooling, health and human services, and so on), teacher learning that is *situated* in urban schools also requires attention to the intersections of geographic, social, and political realities within which teachers work. Finally, although the importance of teacher inquiry into student outcomes has been demonstrated in much of the research discussion about teacher learning, it is with little regard for critical concerns related to educational equity. As a result, the outcomes of teacher learning result in improvements to systems operations (i.e., what already exists) rather than improvements in how the system is organized to achieve equity in its outcomes (Kozleski & Artiles, 2012). This focus "deflects attention from equity as a core value of a public education system within a democracy," contributing to teachers' view of their work "in terms of operational tasks while outcomes that benefit the most oppressed groups of students can become tangential to technical improvements to the system" (Kozleski & Artiles, 2012, p. 409). This inquiry into equity is deepened when teachers engage in critical identity work to understand the roles that their cultural memberships and experiences play in shaping their views of teaching and learning, as well as students, families, and communities.

Below, we discuss each of these areas and provide the rationale for their inclusion in a teacher learning framework for urban school reform. In doing so, we draw from and expand upon the opening vignette to demonstrate how teacher learning has the potential to address unequal access to resources and power that are internal and external to urban schools.

## Situating Teacher Learning in Practice Arenas

Teacher learning is often viewed by educators as fragmented, decontextualized, and irrelevant to real issues and problems teachers encounter daily in their work (Lieberman & Mace, 2008). Individual teachers pursue content-oriented training and/or learn the latest strategies out of context. At the same time, scholars and policymakers increasingly acknowledge that teacher learning is a critical element in the policy implementation efforts aimed at changing teacher practice (Coburn, 2001; Coburn & Stein, 2006). This assumption demands that teacher learning is both coordinated and embedded in the policy implementation context. Too often, however, attempts to influence teacher practice through policy have produced organizational mechanisms designed to ensure compliance and "one-size-fits-all" methods (Lieberman & Mace, 2008) rather than learning that enables teachers to negotiate complex and diverse problems of practice.

Adult learners in particular need to connect their learning to the communities in which they practice or work (Donovan, Bransford, & Pellegrino, 1999); isolated professional development activities are less likely to transfer to practice than activities engaged alongside a community of teacher learners, and then implemented in concert with other learners engaged in developing the same sets of practices. Accordingly, the conceptualization of teacher learning as situated practice is essential for systemic reform efforts in urban schools because it recognizes teachers as those who enact the policies of schooling in their everyday interactions with students, and as such, those whose daily practice has the potential for greatest impact on student learning as a result of systemic reform.

Organizational learning theory informs a framework for teacher learning (Johnson, 2009), including the construct of "learning-in-working," (Brown & Duguid, 1991, p. 41), which aligns with sociocultural theoretical views of development via participation in communities of practice (Cuddapah & Clayton, 2011; Lave & Wenger, 1990). We suggest such a theoretical orientation is crucial to an understanding of teacher learning in urban schools, and necessary for improving teacher learning frameworks for at least three reasons. First, a sociocultural theory of teacher learning recognizes that improving practice is a social process. Learning is facilitated as teachers collectively make sense of new policies, instructional resources, and demands, and learn with and from each other how to translate interpretations into their practice. Second, it acknowledges that increasingly the impetus for teacher learning originates outside the teacher communities. Teachers' work is embedded in varying organizational contexts and informal teacher communities are one of these contexts (Jurasaite-Harbison & Rex, 2010). A sociocultural view of teacher learning accounts for the introduction of new or shifting demands, problems, or instructional resources from outside local settings (e.g., the policy and/or research community, districts, textbook companies, other organizations, and so on). The extent to which teachers can collectively make sense of real problems of practice and link these shared understandings with larger structural issues will shape the degree to which teacher learning in urban schools accounts for the complexities inherent to such settings.

Finally, the social and embedded aspects of teacher learning point to a third rationale for a sociocultural theory of teacher learning: Teacher communities of practice increase capacity for the learning to accommodate complexity and diversity and allow for participants to exercise judgment and some authority in negotiating local interpretations that align with wider goals (Coburn & Stein, 2006). As teachers engage in patterned social interactions, within and across communities, they enhance the learning that can occur at the organizational level. As teachers socially construct both the meaning of reforms or new and persistent problems, they also are always constructing their identities as colleagues and professionals. Amid many pressures to retreat into compliance, a collaborative and collective stance toward learning positions teachers to negotiate authority, exercise judgment, and span boundaries in large and complex urban school systems.

Equity concerns infuse policy and practical contexts in urban schools. Collective teacher learning that explicitly encompasses questions of equity includes attention to the details of teacher conversations and the artifacts with which teachers focus their learning. For example, Horn and Little (2010) document that conversational routines shaped the ability of urban high school teachers to learn ways to increase access and success in core academic subjects. Investigating the conversations between two different groups, the researchers found that their talk positioned teachers differently in relation to their stated goals, and thus influenced the quality of their learning and practice. El-Haj's (2003) work with an urban teacher network found that teachers' collective learning that centered equity concerns squarely engages the messy ethical dilemmas of focusing on children within a system that "assumes failure." She described teachers employing a phenomenological approach "through processes of observation and description of the particular" amid accountability pressures, and in doing so, developing a "dual consciousness" that acknowledges and engages the constrictions at the intersection of equity and standardization. This approach allowed teachers to "develop ways of practicing, [and] pushing against educational inequality" (p. 842).

***Organizing schools for situated teacher learning.*** Given the appropriate organizational conditions pertaining to structural arrangements (e.g., time, frequency, space, autonomy) and human resources (e.g., intellect and experiences), such learning communities are a productive force for school improvement (Bryk, Sebring, Allensworth, Luppescu & Easton, 2010; Louis & Kruse, 1995), as is evidenced in reflective dialogue, interdependence, and shared practices focused on student learning. When a school is organized to support practice-embedded teacher learning, several conditions are in place so that educators are able to experience incentives and access resources through the way teaching assignments are defined and organized, the intellectual and material supports made available to them, and the structures for how professional time is organized (Little, 1999; Stoll, Bolam, McMahon, Wallace & Thomas, 2006). For example, with regard for the first condition, that teachers teach and learn best when they are assigned to a content area they feel competent in and a group of students they feel competent to teach, yet inexperienced teachers are often assigned to the most challenging classes, which contributes to inequities in student learning (Murnane & Steele, 2007). To exacerbate matters, Achinstein and Ogawa (2012) found that new teachers of color who participated in a 5-year study faced a "double bind," as they negotiated policy/practice tensions in their attempts to practice culturally relevant teaching, tensions that took a measurable toll on each teacher. Teacher assignments should provide opportunities not only for teachers to expand their repertoires of practice, but also to configure educators in ways that allow for maximum professional dialogue, support, and other forms of shared practice (Little, 1999). Otherwise, the contradictions of prescriptive policies and culturally relevant practices (both of which are commonly encountered and/or advocated for in urban schools) will continue to take a toll on teachers (Achinstein & Ogawa, 2012).

Beyond strategic teacher assignment, the creation of routinized shared professional learning time further enhances teacher learning. One approach that has gained traction over the last decade is the development of professional learning communities that are centered around formalizing communities of educators who work collaboratively and that place learning at the center of teachers' work (Hord, Roussin, & Sommers, 2010; McLaughlin & Talbert, 2001.

> In response to dialogue between Middleton educators and administration, the superintendent convinced the school board to codify "professional learning community" time by requiring that schools regularly organize for collaborative discourse that is driven by teacher learning around high-quality curriculum and instruction. Once a week, students are released an hour earlier, so that teachers can engage in professional learning, and on this particular day, the 9th-grade teams convened to discuss their agenda for learning about their students, thinking about curriculum, and connecting this knowledge to their understanding of district policies and the community context. At each grade level, there are four grade-level teams, each composed of a mathematics teacher, a biology teacher, a language arts teacher, and a social studies teacher. A guidance counselor is assigned to each team, and most teams also include a special education and/or English as a second language (ESL) teacher in their weekly team meetings. Teachers are also affiliated with content area departments, and meet regularly with these colleagues to discuss content standards and accountability.
>
> Today at Middleton, teachers file in and sit with their teams. The teaching experience ranges from teachers beginning their 2nd year of teaching, to teachers with 10 years of experience. For the first 4 weeks, teams of teachers collected student work, tracked attendance and discipline referrals in their classes, and kept a log of contacts with parents. The counselors assigned to each team have information about each student's academic progress in middle school as well as students' interests and circumstances and information to promote college-going culture to share with the teachers. With the first grading period approaching, teachers begin by discussing the range of student performance they are encountering in their classrooms.

As the discussion ensues, teachers share stories about students who have recently become homeless, suspicions that a group of male 9th-graders are taking steps toward being "jumped into" local gangs, and bubbling conflict between a group of parents and a team of teachers, alleging structural racism in the scheduling of students. The discussion becomes lively, and the teachers alternately try to explain, defend, or critique the various situations and their relationship to student performance. While they did not all agree, it is not long before the group of teachers does reach consensus that teaching at Middleton presents unique and messy problems of practice.

## Situating Teacher Learning Within Macro- and Local Contexts

Especially relevant to teacher learning frameworks in urban education settings, however, are understandings that teachers' work is situated not only in the educational system, but also within the contexts of urban centers. As the vignette above illustrates, the convergence of social, political, and economic factors in urban schools creates particular contexts where access, participation, and outcome disparities exist across racial and ethnic groups of students, and where increasingly, accountability structures impact the ways in which students are sorted and educated in different settings on the basis of measures of ability and language proficiency. For these reasons, a crucial aspect of urban school reform is educators' access to learning opportunities that facilitate the interpretation of reform efforts situated in the macrocontexts within which policy is designed, and the microcontexts within which it is implemented, and how both compete to hinder and afford the design of learning environments in which students experience equitable educational opportunities (King, Artiles, & Kozleski, 2009).

Understanding teacher communities of practice as occupying a space within the nested communities (Fink & Resnick, 2001) that constitute urban school systems illumines the processes and conditions necessary for changes in practice induced by broader social, political, and historical concerns. These settings are characterized by high concentrations of racially, ethnolinguistically and culturally diverse students, high rates of poverty, high rates of teacher turnover, dense bureaucracies and lack of adequate funding (Kozol, 1992; Milner, 2006; Weiner, 2003). Given the density and intersections of multiple policy streams in urban schools and school districts, teachers encounter multiple and sometimes contradictory demands, not the least of which pertains to eliminating achievement disparities among students of color. Add to the policy context the structural features related to tracking and sorting of students by dis/ability or language proficiency; disciplinary procedures; assessment procedures and associated decision-making practices; graduation requirements; attendance procedures; promotion criteria, and so on. Compounding these intersecting policies and practices are structural effects of poverty (i.e., students' and families' access to basic needs and resources allowing them to participate in school fully (Kozol, 1992; Lareau, 2011) and institutionalized racism and sexism that often pervade hiring, governance, and matriculation practices.

In such complex contexts, teacher learning must integrate educational policy demands with an understanding of social and community dynamics manifested in practices intended to engage students, families, and community stakeholders in efforts to reform urban schools. This includes critical reflection and examination of practices and factors that reproduce inequitable access and/or disproportionate limitations of educational opportunities. This also allows educators to view their practice beyond a purely technical perspective, toward a contextual and critical perspective that seeks to understand the nature of the learner from her or his potential, cultural/historical background, cognitive and socioemotional development, and the nature of the context and curriculum in which students are expected to perform (Freire, 1970; McLaren, 2000).

## THE INQUIRY-BASED NATURE OF URBAN TEACHER LEARNING

Organizing teacher learning around inquiry into student work is one particular way to situate learning in practice (Lin, 2002). Much has been written about such practices, which include alternative versions of Japanese Lesson study (Fernandez, Cannon, & Chokshi, 2003) and their importance in impacting changes in teaching. Because of the extensive literature on this area of inquiry in teacher learning, we turn toward an area of inquiry all but neglected in studies of teacher learning, but crucial in urban school reform.

### Equity-Oriented Inquiry

Related to understandings of the role of macro- and local context in shaping teacher practice are the design of teacher learning opportunities that facilitate the exploration of such contexts, their relationship to student outcomes, and the outcomes that are troubling and that require critical attention. Central to these learning opportunities is the role of inquiry, and more specifically, equity-oriented inquiry, as teachers examine legacies of troubling student outcomes in urban education systems: namely, disparities in achievement between racial, ethnic, economic, and ability groups of students, as well as disproportionate identification and placement of students from historically underserved groups in special education (Teese, Lamb, & Duru-Bellat, 2007). As we illustrate below, while part of this inquiry is focused on better understanding social forces outside school walls, more important is exploring the relationship between these forces and the social and institutional patterns of policies, practices, and belief systems within urban schools that create conditions for inequities in student outcomes to persist. In our experiences, data displays such as the one described below are useful in spurring such inquiry.

Before teachers get started looking at the student data they have collected over the first 4 weeks of school, the lead counselor calls the group to order and explains that before the teams begin working independently, she wants to share a new tool that may inform some of their discussion. She directs their attention to a projection of a map of Middleton High. This map, produced in partnership with the school district and the National Institute for Urban School Improvement's LeadScape project, depicts a blueprint of Middleton with each classroom shaded in one of several colors.

"As you know," the counselor explains, "as one of our efforts to better understand and eliminate academic achievement disparities, and intervene early with struggling students to eliminate our disproportionate rates of students of color in special education, we've been working to figure out ways to more carefully analyze student achievement data. One of these strategies is the use of mapping software to analyze different data patterns. This map is intended to get our conversation started. The colors on this map represent the total percentage of students, by classroom, who passed the benchmark assessment administered last week. In those classrooms that are shaded green, over 90% of students passed, while in the dark blue, between 50 and 60% passed, and in red classrooms, under 30% passed.

"We'd like you to discuss with your teams the types of data that you believe would give us a nuanced picture of the things we need to be addressing when it comes to equitable access, participation, and outcomes in education for our students."

As the teams convene, there is a buzz. The map raises new questions that make their way into the discussions of student performance. How might disciplinary patterns relate to the variety (or lack thereof) of learning activities required in a given classroom? Might the maps depict variables of concern across gender, as well as racial and ability groups, illuminating where disparities in achievement, discipline, and special education identification and placement patterns exist? How can we explore the ways teachers interact with families? How might various data displays facilitate changes in our practice?

As teachers are generating their questions they begin discussing the various sources of data available were they to pursue these lines of inquiry. An English teacher, Mr. Myers, wonders aloud whether they can track an academic advising "pipeline"— where are the decisions made and by whom? This makes Ms. Browning, a fellow 9th-grade teacher, respond, "What do we really know about our students' strengths or interests? Where do they come from? How do they get to school?" This generates a lively discussion about the history of the neighborhood around the school. The departure of a major manufacturing firm and the boom of tract homes 40 miles east of the city induced a major emigration out to the suburbs over the last decade. Only recently have community colleges and state universities become more visible throughout the city and in its high schools, through early college programs and partnerships. A couple of teachers on the faculty grew up near this neighborhood, but the majority of the faculty members commute into the city from surrounding suburban communities, so these patterns are not foreign to them, but somehow become less abstract as they converse about the conditions their students and their families navigate daily.

The group of 9th-grade teachers decides to pursue a few related lines of inquiry. First, a few of them agree to investigate demographic and employment patterns in the neighborhood. They wondered, what kinds of employment opportunities are available to adults in the community? Where do families access support for finding employment or getting job training? Second, a small group decides to construct a student survey about student interest, familiarity with postsecondary options, and student networks that include adults in and around the school. One teacher shared that even though students interacted with their teachers daily, several of his students claimed to know of no one who attended college. He suspected that the relationships between teachers and students and how students imagined themselves as potential college students may not be so unrelated. A third group agreed to work with a local community historian to collect oral histories of community members, family members, and graduates of the school. In addition, they all committed to identifying several sources of data related to student performance, including student work, test scores, progress toward mastering standards, and so on. The three groups agreed to reconvene after they had gathered some of this information so that they could begin to situate their students' progress within a deeper and more complex understanding of the educational context.

## Reflective Identity Work

Beyond a focus on student work, and on concerns for equity in patterns of data on student access, participation, and outcomes in urban schooling, evidence from a variety of studies on practitioner inquiry have demonstrated the role of teachers' critical reflective learning in relating inclusive and culturally responsive beliefs about teaching to conscious action in the classroom (Darling-Hammond & Bransford, 2005; Souto-Manning & Dice, 2007). Accordingly, another area key to teacher inquiry in urban schools is in the form of reflective identity work. As the majority of teachers in urban schools continue to come from different, and dominant, sociodemographic groups as compared to their students (Strizek, Pittsonberger, Riordan, Lyter, & Orlofsky, 2006), it is crucial that teachers examine ways in which their own identity, including their beliefs about the nature of teaching and learning and assumptions about students, families, and the communities within which they work, are connected with troublesome student outcomes. Yet, while most P–12 teachers have been prepared to reflect upon their practice in order to improve their practice (e.g., see Zeichner & Liston, 1996), reflection on issues of equity and diversity are seldom taught or practiced (Milner, 2003).

> The 9th-grade teachers adjourn for the day, with a clear mission to continue their inquiry into data patterns that may serve to identify problematic practices and policies related to student outcomes. A few days later Mr. Myers and Ms. Browning return from a walk in the one-block radius that surrounds the school, the goal of which was to map the social and material resources they noticed along the way. As they returned to Middleton, they began to draw their own map, noting the one church and one mosque many of their students attended, the variety of languages they heard spoken on different sections of the street, and the ways in which people were socializing on front porches, sidewalks, and corners. But although she'd begun reading a book describing a process by which teachers might engage in such an activity, Ms. Browning felt unsettled. "I have to confess," she told Mr. Myers, "even though we are talking about these things we saw as strengths, I can't quite put my finger on why, but I felt uncomfortable when we were walking through the neighborhood."

As the example above depicts, a necessary feature of teacher inquiry in urban schools includes the exploration of racial identity. This is especially crucial for White teachers, many of whom do not consider themselves as racial beings, which allows them to dismiss notions of race in their work, as does adopting, color-blind ideologies in which they do not "see race"

(Lewis, 2001). Further, reflection on racial identity in connection with teacher practice is also relevant for teachers of color who are subject to discrimination, oppression, and misunderstandings in relation to their race and, as a result, often benefit from purposeful unlearning of internalized stereotypes about themselves (Tatum, 2001). Suggested practices for critical self-inquiry include teacher dialogue about race in professional learning communities and race reflective journaling (Milner & Smithey, 2003), facilitated through questions that may guide reflection, such as "How might my students' racial experiences influence their work with me as the teacher?" (Milner, 2003, p. 178).

Another example of critical identity work as a teacher learning strategy is an analysis of discourse patterns between oneself as the teacher and one's students, by examining the role of evaluation versus feedback that one provides in response to students' classroom comments. Feedback, as opposed to evaluation, not only signals to students that learning is about analyzing and expanding upon ideas, but also allows teachers to examine their beliefs about the roles of teachers as partners in students' learning and work to dismantle power structures based on authoritative views of teaching (Tabak & Baumgartner, 2004). This examination may take place as part of supportive collegial relationships formed around data collection and analysis activities like the neighborhood walk-through and the related debriefing detailed below.

> Ms. Browning and Mr. Myers talked about this unsettled feeling, wondering what impact it had on their interactions with students and the way they might be perceived by students' families. Ms. Browning shared that she could not stop thinking about a recent special education referral she had initiated for a Black male student whom she had persistent difficulty reaching in her class. She and Mr. Myers commiserated around the notion that sometimes they make referrals because they just don't know what else to do, and the students' struggles in class can often bubble up into a conflict. Ms. Browning, perhaps spurred by an emerging critical awareness of her own discomfort in the neighborhood, was troubled by how quickly it seems she and her colleagues jump to referrals for special education, especially in the case of struggling male students of color. Sometimes these referrals do not result in eligibility for special education services, but often they do. In the cases when a student is not found eligible for special education, Ms. Browning recalls teachers (including herself) being frustrated. In this moment, she wonders with Mr. Myers, if there is more to learn about the students and the identification process that may address the root of the problems they encounter in the classroom.

At the next convening of the 9th-grade teachers' learning community, Mr. Myers and Ms. Browning shared some of their reflections and conversation. Ms. Browning explained that she wanted to know more about why and how often students were referred for special education services between 8th and 10th grade. She explained that she worried that the identification process was being used in ways that avoided other difficult issues related to how students and teacher perceive each other, interact, and build authentic relationships in the context of this community. The teachers struggled with the implications of Ms. Browning's concerns, but eventually agreed that with the help of counselors, special education teachers, and administrators it would be worthwhile to investigate trends related to special education referrals and practices, beginning in the 9th grade.

## PUTTING IT ALL TOGETHER

As we have discussed throughout this chapter, a framework for teacher learning in urban schools is complex and moves beyond goals of technical improvements in teacher practice driven by policy shifts and research developments. The use of a vignette that captures many of the teacher learning efforts we have engaged ourselves as urban education practitioners and researchers, along with involvement in structured partnerships between the NIUSI and large urban school districts, was meant to illustrate the complex nature of urban schools, which requires that teacher learning structures facilitate: (1) learning opportunities and activities embedded in teachers' daily practice; (2) explicit attention to equity in student access to, participation in, and outcomes as a result of schooling; (3) exploration of structural institutional legacies of oppression and discrimination in urban contexts; and (4) critical identity work within which teachers not only explore their cultural experiences, but also the relation of these experiences to practice and beliefs about students. Explicit and integrated attention to these areas increases the power of teacher learning to play a meaningful role in urban education reform, and to impact and respond positively to the students and families they engage and the urban communities within which they work.

## REFERENCES

Achinstein, B., & Ogawa, R. (2012). New teachers of color and culturally responsive teaching in an era of educational accountability: Caught in a double bind. *Journal of Educational Change, 13,* 1–39.

Bransford, J. D., Brown, A. L., & Cocking, R. R. (Eds.). (1999). *How people learn: Brain, mind, experience and school.* Washington, DC: National Research Council.

Brown, J. S., & Duguid, P. (1991). Organizational learning and communities-of-practice: Toward a unified theory of working, learning, and innovation. *Organization Science, 2,* 40–57.

Bryk, A. S., Sebring, P. B., Allensworth, E., Luppescu, S., & Easton, J. Q. (2010). *Organizing schools for improvement: Lessons from Chicago.* Chicago, IL: University of Chicago Press.

Coburn, C. E. (2001). Collective sensemaking about reading: How teachers mediate reading policy in their professional communities. *Educational Evaluation & Policy Analysis, 23,* 145–170.

Coburn, C. E., & Stein, M. K. (2006). Communities of practice theory and the role of teacher professional community in policy implementation. In M. I. Honig (Ed.), *New directions in education policy implementation: Confronting complexity.* (pp. 25–46). Albany: State University of New York Press.

Cochran-Smith, M., Davis, D., & Fries, K. (2004). Multicultural teacher education: Research, practice, and policy. In J. Banks (Ed.), *Handbook of research on multicultural education* (3rd ed., pp. 931–975). San Francisco, CA: Jossey-Bass.

Cuddapah, J. L., & Clayton, C. D. (2011). Using Wenger's communities of practice to explore a new teacher cohort. *Journal of Teacher Education, 62*(1), 62–75.

Darling-Hammond, L., & Bransford, J. (2005). *Preparing teachers for a changing world: What teachers should learn and be able to do.* San Francisco, CA: Jossey-Bass.

Donovan, M. S., Bransford, J. D., & Pellegrino, J. W. (Eds.). (1999). *How people learn: Bridging research and practice.* Washington, DC: National Research Council.

El-Haj, T.R.A. (2003). Practicing for equity from the standpoint of the particular: Exploring the work of one urban teacher network. *Teachers College Record, 105,* 817–845.

Ferguson, D. L., Kozleski, E. B., & Smith, A. (2001). *On . . . transformed, inclusive schools: A framework to guide fundamental change in urban schools.* Newton, MA: Education Development Center, National Institute for Urban School Improvement; Washington, DC: U.S. Dept. of Education, Office of Educational Research and Improvement, Educational Resources Information Center.

Ferguson, D. L., Kozleski, E. B., & Smith, A. (2003). Transforming general and special education in urban schools. In F. Obiakor, C. Utley, & A. Rotatori (Eds.), *Advances in Special Education: Vol. 15. Effective education for learners with exceptionalities* (pp. 43–74). London, United Kingdom: JAI Press.

Fernandez, C., Cannon, J., & Chokshi, S. (2003). A U.S.-Japan lesson study collaborative reveals critical lenses for examining practice. *Teaching and Teacher Education, 19,* 171–185.

Fink, E. & Resnick, L. (2001). Developing principals as instructional leaders. *Phi Delta Kappan, 82,* 598–606.

Freire, P . (1970). *Pedagogy of the oppressed.* New York, NY: Continuum.

Hindin, A., Morocco, C. C., Mott, E. A., & Aguilar, C. M. (2007). More than just a group: teacher collaboration and learning in the workplace. *Teachers and Teaching: Theory and Practice, 13*(4), 349–376.

Hord, S. M., Roussin, J. L., & Sommers, W. A. (2010). *Guiding professional learning communities: Inspiration, challenge, surprise, and meaning.* Thousand Oaks, CA: Corwin Press.

Horn, S. H., & Little, J. W. (2010). Attending to problems of practice: Routines and resources for professional learning in teachers. *American Educational Research Journal, 47,* 37–64.

Johnson, B. L., Jr. (2009). Understanding schools as organizations: Implications for realizing professional learning communities. In C. A. Mullen (Ed.), *The handbook of leadership and professional learning communities* (pp. 17–28). New York, NY: Palgrave Macmillan.

Jurasaite-Harbison, E., & Rex, L. A. (2010). School cultures as contexts for informal teacher learning. *Teaching and Teacher Education, 26,* 267–277.

King, K. A., Artiles, A. J., & Kozleski, E. B. (2009). *Exemplar brief series: Professional learning for culturally responsive teaching and learning.* Tempe, AZ: National Center for Culturally Responsive Educational Systems (NCCRESt).

King, K. A., Capulo, K. Kozleski, E. B., & Gonzales, J. (2009). Inclusive education for equity. *Professional Learning for Equity Module Series.* Tempe, AZ: Equity Alliance at ASU.

Kozleski, E. B., & Artiles, A. J. (2012) Technical assistance as inquiry: Using activity theory methods to engage equity in educational practice communities. In S. Steinberg & G. Canella (Ed.), *Handbook on critical qualitative research* (pp. 431–445). New York, NY: Peter Lang.

Kozol, J. (1992). *Savage inequalities.* New York, NY: HarperCollins.

Lareau, A. (2011). *Unequal childhoods: Class, race, and family life* (2nd ed.). Berkeley: University of California Press.

Lave, J., & Wenger, E. C. (1990). *Situated learning: Legitimate peripheral participation.* Palo Alto, CA: Institute for Research on Learning.

Lewis, A. E. (2001). There is no "race" in the school-yard: Colorblind ideology in an (almost) all White school. *American Educational Research Journal, 38,* 781–811.

Lieberman, A., & Mace, D. P. (2008). Teacher learning: The key to education reform. *Journal of Teacher Education, 59*(3), 226–234.

Lieberman, A. & Mace, D. P. (2010). Making practice public: Teacher learning in the 21st century. *Journal of Teacher Education, 61,* 77–88.

Lin, P. (2002). On enhancing teachers' knowledge by constructing cases in classrooms. *Journal of Mathematics Teacher Education, 5,* 317–349.

Little, J. W. (1999). Organizing schools for teacher learning. In L. Darling-Hammond & G. Sykes (Eds.), *Teaching as the learning profession: Handbook of policy and practice* (pp. 233–262). San Francisco, CA: Jossey-Bass.

Louis, K. S., & Kruse, S. (1995). *Professionalism and community: Perspectives on reforming urban schools.* Thousand Oaks, CA: Corwin Press.

McLaren, P. (2000). *Che Guevara, Paulo Freire, and the pedagogy of revolution.* Lanham, MD: Rowan & Littlefield.

McLaughlin, M. W., & Talbert, J. E. (2001). *Professional communities and the work of high school teaching.* Chicago, IL: University of Chicago Press.

McLaughlin, M. W., & Talbert, J. E. (2006). *Building school-based teacher learning communities.* New York, NY: Teachers College Press.

Milner, H. R. (2003). Teacher reflection and race in cultural contexts: History, meanings, and methods in teaching. *Theory into Practice, 173–180.*

Milner, H. R. (2006). Preservice teachers' learning about cultural and racial diversity: Implications for urban education. *Urban Education, 41*(4), 343–375.

Milner, H. R., & Smithey, M. (2003). The process and results of a course curriculum to challenge and to enhance preservice teachers' thinking and experience with diversity. *Teaching Education, 14,* 293–305.

Murnane, R., & Steele, J. (2007). What is the problem? The challenge of providing effective teachers for all children. *The Future of Children, 17*(1), 15–43.

Ross, J. A., Bruce, C. D., & Hogaboam-Gray, A. (2006). The impact of a professional development program on student achievement in grade 6 mathematics. *Journal of Mathematics Teacher Education, 9,* 551–577.

Sleeter, C. E. (2008). Equity, democracy, and neoliberal assaults on teacher education. *Teaching and Teacher Education, 54,* 1947–1957.

Souto-Manning, M., & Dice, J. L. (2007). Reflective teaching in the early years: A case for mentoring diverse educators. *Early Childhood Education Journal, 34*(6), 425–430.

Stoll, L., Bolam, R., McMahon, A., Wallace, M., & Thomas, S. (2006). Professional learning communities: A review of the literature. *Journal of Educational Change, 7, 221–258.*

Strizek, G. A., Pittsonberger, J. L., Riordan, K. E., Lyter, D. M., & Orlofsky, G. F. (2006). *Characteristics of schools, districts, teachers, principals, and school libraries in the United States: 2003–04 schools and staffing survey* (NCES 2006-313 Revised). Washington, DC: U.S. Department of Education, Institute of Education Sciences, National Center for Education Statistics..

Tabak, I., & Baumgartner, E. (2004). The teacher as partner: Exploring participant structures, symmetry, and identity work in scaffolding. *Cognition and Instruction, 22,* 393–429.

Tatum, B. D. (2001). Professional development: An important partner in antiracist teacher education. In S. H. King & L. A. Castenell (Eds.), *Racism and racial inequality: Implications for teacher education* (pp. 51–58). Washington, DC: American Association of Colleges for Teacher Education (AACTE).

Teese, R., Lamb, S., & Duru-Bellat, M. (Eds.). (2007). *International studies in educational inequality, theory, and policy* (Vols. 1–3). New York, NY: Springer.

Webster-Wright, A. (2009). Reframing professional development through understanding authentic professional learning. *Review of Educational Research, 79,* 702–739.

Weiner, L. (2003). Why is classroom management so vexing for urban teachers? *Theory into Practice, 42*(4), 305–312.

Zeichner, K., & Liston, D. (1996). *Reflective teaching: An introduction.* Mahwah, NJ: Lawrence Erlbaum.

# PART IV

# BUILDING AND DISTRICT LEADERS' ROLES IN URBAN REFORM

# CHAPTER 7

# The Role of the Urban Principal in Leading School Change

## The Efforts and Tensions of Principals in Disturbing the Status Quo

*Dorothy Garrison-Wade, JoEtta Gonzales,*
*and Cynthia Alexander*

### TALES FROM TWO URBAN SCHOOL PRINCIPALS

School principals play a significant role in the development of inclusive and culturally responsive schools. Without a concerted effort by the principal and leadership team, schools cannot change or improve to address the needs of all students by ensuring they are meaningfully participating in essential academic and nonacademic lessons and are attaining equitable outcomes. This chapter focuses on the efforts of the school principal in promoting and sustaining equitable change, and explores the tensions involved in leading this change through disturbing the status quo. Through the stories of two urban principals (the names of the schools and principals in these stories are pseudonyms), we spend some time exploring ideas related to the importance of the school principal in leading change, key patterns of change essential for creating inclusive schools, and the use of a systemic change framework (Ferguson & Kozleski, 2003; Kozleski & Smith, 2009) as a tool to promote the sustainability of change efforts.

La Paz Elementary School
Dr. Elsa Barraza, Principal

When I first came to be the principal of La Paz School, I immediately familiarized myself with demographic information. La Paz School was

153

located in an urban part of one of the largest cities in the United States. Single-family homes surrounded this community school, and many of these homes housed several generations of family members. Domestic violence plagued the overcrowded homes and poverty prevailed in this neighborhood tattooed with graffiti and debris. More than 85% of the students were eligible for free or reduced price lunch. Reflecting the population of the neighborhood around the school, the student population was just over 75% Latino. Many of the families were recent immigrants, and over 35% of the students were English language learners. The population of Black students was just under 17%, which dropped considerably over the past 5 years as the Latino population burgeoned. Students of Asian, Pacific Island, and Native American descent made up about 4% of the population, and White students made up the remaining 4%.

When Dr. Barraza became principal of La Paz School, her first priority was to get to know more about the school. She met with each staff member individually, conducted observations in classrooms and throughout the school, and asked parents and other professionals for their input. She used these interactions to perform a cultural assessment that would inform the moves she would make initially to embark on the journey of change. Through this assessment she noticed teachers making decisions for the sake of convenience, and identified teacher behaviors that were restrictive and controlling in nature. There were few opportunities for student leadership or meaningful participation. She also took note of an achievement gap. Students at La Paz School performed poorly on state and district assessments, with an average of only 35% of the students meeting state and district standards. There was also a glaring discrepancy in the number of discipline referrals, with Black males being overrepresented by about 50%, and the school environment appeared rigid and controlled by adults not wanting to lose power to the students. The foundation of the school was grounded in oppression, and heavy-handed practices were deeply embedded in the attitudes and values of the staff. She knew changes needed to occur throughout the school, and understood that every decision made needed to be carefully thought out. Her determination would be imperative.

## Hope Middle School
### Dr. Genevieve Collins, Principal

When I first accepted the challenge of taking on Hope Middle School, I knew it was considered a "high priority and failing" school according to the standards set by No Child Left Behind. Only 57% of all students were proficient in math and 67% proficient in reading;

both academic areas were below the state expectations for student achievement. The school community was largely African American (just over 80%), and over 15% of the students were English language learners. Students of Asian, Pacific Island, and Native American descent made up about 5% of the population.

Dr. Collins was faced with numerous challenges at Hope Middle School: The school's inspection did not meet district standards; teacher absenteeism was extreme; and the special education program was out of compliance. She expressed a no-excuses mentality to teachers and staff, and began her work with a sobering assessment to acquire the information necessary to turn the school around. Data were gathered from all stakeholders to get a true picture of the school community. Dr. Collins listened to the concerns of parents, teachers, staff, and students, and concluded that the expectations for the school were much loftier than what was evidenced through observation. In other words, her new community was talking the talk, but their walk was not up to par. It would be her job to position the stakeholders to recognize the school's shortcomings in order to build a plan to make excellence in teaching and learning a reality.

The story of the urban school principal is one of accepting challenges—challenges that often are accompanied by systemic disarray such as run-down facilities, low levels of family engagement, disproportionate discipline patterns, dispirited staff morale, and inferior academic performance. Although La Paz and Hope schools are geographically separated by about 1,500 miles, the experiences of the two principals are similar. In this chapter we explore the role that principals play in leading transformation in their schools. We take a look at two principals from different geographic regions of the United States who eagerly accepted the challenge of leading urban schools in need of improvement and change. The two principals, Dr. Barraza and Dr. Collins, open the doors of their school and allow us insight into their thinking and planning. As their challenges unfold and stories of courage emerge we ask the reader to engage the necessity of disturbing the status quo in order to lead school change that is equitable and inclusive of all students.

Our chapter develops by exploring the urban school context and uncovering some of the key barriers and bridges associated with attaining equitable outcomes. Understanding more about notions of educational equity, evidence of culturally responsive practice, and the foundation of inclusive schools may help parents, educators, community members, and policymakers support the work of the school principals in more meaningful and comprehensive ways. In this chapter, we discuss the role of principals in building a school's capacity to meet the personalized needs of all learners, and emphasize the strategies and resources that successful principals use to develop a reflective and supportive learning community. Because inclusive practices represent a considerable shift in practice for some schools, we begin by helping you understand more about the complex process of school change, and introduce a systemic change framework that can serve as a guide for principals working toward equitable outcomes. We spend considerable focus on several strategic arenas that promote sustainable change for culturally responsive and inclusive practice, and discuss the role of the school principal in championing change that is student centered. In discussions of change related to educational equity, attention must be given to notions of equity and how this thinking becomes rooted in the daily work of principals. Finally, we offer considerations about the complex process of school change that, if intentionally engaged by the principal, have the potential to disturb the status quo and bring about the change necessary for all students to be served well.

## URBAN SCHOOL CONTEXT

We use the term *urban* as a descriptor for schools that share several features, including high concentrations of young people from low-income families; a diverse racial, ethnic, and linguistic mix of students in the school population; and many people living in close proximity. In many cases, urban schools are also characterized by students and families in which abundant signs of stress are experienced (e.g., family dysfunction, crime, poor nutrition). Students attending urban schools are the most culturally and ethnically diverse in the country. Yet our school systems struggle to meet their needs for a variety of reasons. In some cases, many of the teachers and principals in these schools lack the professional training and experience to effectively teach students who are culturally and ethnically diverse (Ferguson & Kozleski, 2003). In other instances, approaches to family engagement have not been adapted to meet the needs of an ever-changing student population. Still, in many schools and districts, policies and practices at federal, state, and local levels exacerbate inequities in school funding and student access to rigorous educational programming. Consequently, children in urban schools as a whole often continue to perform poorly on standardized assessments at the state and national levels.

The term *school principal* refers to individuals who assume formal positions of influence within a school setting, and who direct, lead, and support the work of themselves and others in pursuit of continuous change and improvement. We pay special attention to the role of principal, noting that inhabiting this role is not necessarily the same as exercising inclusive leadership. We define *inclusive leadership* as the shared work and commitments that shape the direction of a school community and engage effort and energy in pursuit of a school where all students are meaningfully engaged and served well. In this chapter we pay particular attention to the deliberate actions of principals Barraza and Collins, who have recognized a calling to promote equitable student outcomes.

We approach our examination of urban school leadership from a particular vantage point we refer to as *leadership for inclusive and equitable schools*. This set of ideas places emphasis on leaders that focus time and attention on *all* learners, including those in the "margins, students who traditionally are separated out into 'special' programs; uncategorized, unlabeled, yet unsuccessful students in the regular classroom; students who come from families that do not speak English; as well as high performing students who push the margins in the other direction" (Salisbury & McGregor, 2005, p. 6). It also contends that leaders who concern themselves with educational equity, that is, accommodating and meeting the specific needs of specific students, understand that addressing and responding to the individual needs of all learners is a complex challenge that involves several key arenas for change involving decision making, the allocation of resources, professional learning, and improved classroom practice. Principals for inclusive and equitable schools are centrally concerned with the learning of students, the instructional staff, support staff, and themselves as a professional learning organization.

Student learning is at the center of leadership for inclusive and equitable schools and it also encompasses the center of the Systemic Change Framework (Ferguson & Kozleski, 2003; Kozleski & Smith, 2009). We use the framework to structure the principals' stories about change and articulate a pathway for other principals to consider. In order for systemic change to occur, schools must ensure that student learning is a top priority. The principals at La Paz and Hope schools were emphatic about articulating the importance of placing focus on the students in the schools in which they served. To promote student learning, the principals realized that they had to assist their staff members in creating a learning environment that was supportive of and responsive to the various backgrounds and cultures of all students. It involved carefully examining the culture of their schools, the instructional practices of teachers, and the expectations of staff, while also aligning inclusivity and cultural proficiency with everyday practice.

> I knew I had a lot of teaching to do and a lot of ground to cover in order to create an inclusive learning environment for all students. My vision of an inclusive, student-centered school grew out of my own experiences of exclusion; I knew the damaging effects of it as I had been excluded numerous times as a learner. Conveying a vision that was different from the status quo created tensions among the staff. Still, I sought to make sure teachers were emotionally invested in the need to do things differently, and I knew the change had to become a seamless blending and weaving of practices that would best suit

the needs of the student learning community. I was hoping to create a lasting change—one that permeated the culture and stood the test of time. —Dr. Barraza, La Paz School

Dr. Barraza started this process by asking staff members to think back to their own experiences in elementary school. Who were they as learners? What were their hopes and fears? What types of experiences helped them successfully navigate the system? What were some of the barriers or obstacles they had to overcome? Was their participation always meaningful, or were there times when they felt disenfranchised or perhaps even excluded? The idea was to get teachers and staff members talking about their own identities and how their identities shape the ways in which they view and respond to student differences.

Consider what principals might do to help teachers develop new ways of knowing and understanding students who come from backgrounds that are unfamiliar to them. Because culture is constantly changing, staff members also need opportunities to examine their attitudes, beliefs, and dispositions over time to address disparities in new and innovative ways. Anticipate the ways in which the principals and their leadership teams reframed deficit-grounded assumptions about students and their families. At La Paz and Hope Schools, the principals understood that ongoing, job-embedded professional learning was necessary to shift their school communities away from deficit thinking. An important part of the work was listening to and understanding practitioners, family members, and students.

I knew that to turn around Hope Middle School, I would need to focus on improving the academic perception of the school. Hope had many good teachers, yet many teachers had grown discouraged after years of failing performance. I noticed teachers placing blame on students for their academic struggles. Planting seeds for inclusive leadership, I told my teachers, "Don't get distracted by the negative, but be responsible for positive solutions because the success or failure lies within your vision as instructional leaders."

Interviews with teachers, students, and parents revealed some disturbing trends about the ways in which particular students were viewed and treated: (1) There were no safety nets for English language learners; they either caught on to instruction or sat in silence as others learned; (2) students considered to be gifted were not seen as a priority for teachers, and there were no personalized plans designed to challenge their thinking or push rigorous knowledge acquisition; and (3) African American male students made up the vast majority of discipline and special education referrals, and teachers expressed relief and enthusiasm when they were successful in plac-

ing students in restrictive programs. The fact that these trends were not off-putting to many in the community told me that there were some deeply held mindsets and beliefs that needed to be examined.
—Dr. Collins, Hope School

Inclusive education encapsulates schools that value every student contribution in the learning community. Every child, regardless of race, ethnicity, national origin, gender, ability, socioeconomic status, or religion, is offered opportunities for success in inclusive schools (Sands, Kozleski, & French, 2000). Both principals at La Paz and Hope schools sought to change the ways teachers and staff approached student learning so that all student contributions were appreciated and respected, and in doing so they both began with teachers and staff members exploring their own thoughts and attitudes about education through the exploration of their individual identities. The principals' goals involved building capacity by starting at ground zero—the individual staff member and all of the cultural affiliations and legacies that combine to make him or her the person that exists today.

Mindsets and beliefs about confirming the membership and belonging of every student in the school community are essential for the journey toward the development of inclusive schools. These dispositions are bolstered by federal laws that require schools to provide an appropriate education for students who have traditionally been marginal members of many schools: students with disabilities, students who are culturally and linguistically diverse, and students who bring alternate ways of knowing and being into the school and classroom settings. These laws outline requirements for monitoring the progress of all students and providing additional services and supports to students who may need them. Yet the laws and mandates cannot and do not articulate the attitudes, beliefs, and dispositions necessary for principals and practitioners to fully understand and respond to the needs of diverse learners. Notions of equity, fairness, objectivity, and justice require discourse at the school level with the intent to better understand ourselves and students in order to address unique social and academic needs.

The high expectations that come with both the values and mandates to achieve equitable outcomes for students require highly accomplished principals who are familiar with the research and theory related to inclusive schools. They must also be able to confront systemic practices that exacerbate inequities and are in conflict with best practice. In addition to beginning with teacher identity, the principals at La Paz and Hope schools understood the importance of breaking cycles of disparity in a systemic approach.

While engaging staff members in reflection and collaboration with others, principals Barraza and Collins also addressed six unique arenas for change, reflected in the Systemic Change Framework that anchors this book (Ferguson & Kozleski, 2003; Kozleski & Smith, 2009). These include: (1) governance and leadership for equity, (2) building a culture of change and improvement, (3) creating new school and community connections and partnerships, (4) examining the design and use of time and space, (5) the equitable distribution of resources, and (6) facilitating a process of inquiry around equity and inclusiveness. Each of these arenas is present in the Systemic Change Framework, and by connecting their stories to this framework, we offer examples to help the reader better understand the importance of addressing efforts in each arena. In using the framework to plan for and implement change, the notion of inclusive learning communities receives a laser focus in which change initiatives are more likely to take hold.

## GOVERNANCE AND LEADERSHIP FOR EQUITY

Schools across the United States are experiencing an increase in students of diverse cultural, linguistic, and economic backgrounds. The percentage of students who identify as racial/ethnic minorities increased from 22% in 1979 to 46.5% in 2010 (U.S. Department of Education, NCES, 2011). Nearly 10% of students enrolled in our nation's public K–12 system are receiving services as English language learners, and in our urban schools the percentage grows to over 14% (Aud, Fox, & KewalRamani, 2010). As the number of students from diverse backgrounds increases in U.S. schools, leadership for equity is essential. Leadership for equity entails deliberate attention to shared governance and decision making. It is the first arena within the Systemic Change Framework that we will explore.

> The ways that decisions are made in a school have a strong impact on the school's culture, and I was interested in modeling collaboration and value for the La Paz School community. By including teachers, staff members, and family members on our school leadership team, I was hoping there would be greater ownership of student outcomes. I was also hoping to change the oppressive culture that was working to keep students and family members from positions of leadership. It was difficult getting family members to engage, though. They were used to being passive participants in the leadership of the school. They appeared intimidated to voice opinions within the group. It took a lot of finessing, and occasionally I had to meet individually with some members of the team, but it was important to involve and listen to members of the community that were often reluctant to get involved. I wanted to offer voice to individuals who otherwise might not have been involved. —Dr. Barraza, La Paz School

The style of governance and leadership that school principals use has a tremendous impact on the school culture and learning environment, and as Dr. Barraza modeled an inclusive approach for decision making, she was also hoping to model inclusive approaches for working with students and their families. She was intentional about promoting a positive school climate that could lead to inclusive and culturally responsive daily practice. Furthermore, she acknowledged the relevance of herself as a cultural being whose positionality (e.g., race, gender, class, sexual orientation, ability, and position as principal within the school) shaped her priorities and leadership for school reform (Taylor, Tisdell, & Hanley, 2000).

Throughout her own education, Dr. Barazza experienced patterns of inattention which she contributed largely to her background as a Mexican American female student. She also experienced this in the workplace during meetings in which two or three staff members with very assertive personalities—and privileged positionalities—talked almost the entire time with no sign from anyone that anything was wrong. So she understood her that her positionality could lead to a sense of credibility (she had been there and done that), or it could lead to a perception that the only way she might get attention is to make an issue of how disparate situations were for students with similar backgrounds.

Dr. Barraza had a grasp of the ways in which power and privilege surface in school settings. Privilege exists when one group has something of value that is denied to others simply because of the groups they belong to, rather than because of anything they've done or failed to do (McIntosh, 2003). Privilege shows up everywhere and touches every life in various ways. It exists within families, communities, churches, governments, businesses, civic organizations, and workplaces. Because it is part of the social fabric that we live in, it is also deeply entrenched in schools where students have their first experiences with people who are unlike themselves. Difference is negotiated socially since difference exists in the eye of the beholder. Who gets to decide what is different and what it is different from is part of the process of norming or determining what will be called "normal." The encounters that students have with difference involve privilege and power since some groups have the privilege of determining what is normal and what is different. That also means that some groups have more power than others and this power accrues across generations.

Addressing the ways in which certain students and families in schools are privileged over others is a complicated task. The political ramifications of these conversations create fear that can hold school systems back and keep educators from looking deeply into what's going on. For example, students who struggle in school are often blamed for choosing not to apply themselves, electing not to care, and ultimately deciding whether or not they are going to be successful. However, students understand that their differences from the school's dominant norm are a reality and not something they've chosen. Yet students must learn from teachers who may not understand or attend to the social fabric of power and privilege and their roles in perpetuating it. Without a school community commitment to revealing the pernicious effects of power, privilege, and beliefs that success is determined entirely on the basis of one's hard work, and thus merit, teachers may continue to misunderstand their students, their histories and experiences, and how that influences how and what they learn (Kozleski, 2011).

Leadership for inclusive and equitable schools also involves a continuous cycle of planning, implementation, and evaluation of the school change process. It also means pushing for innovative solutions to issues that exclude learners who differ in myriad ways.

> I wasn't afraid to involve district-level administrators and support in helping turn around Hope Middle School. In fact, I believed it was imperative to open up our school to honest critique from outside experts. I also believed it was important for our existing staff members to engage in careful examination of our own practices. We started by auditing our own programs on an inclusivity scale, then asked our curriculum and instruction department to analyze classroom practice in terms of inclusive practice. We took this data and spent time in reflection—at the individual level, department level, and school level. We went through a process of selecting programs that enhanced our vision of an inclusive school and eliminating the programs that did not. Getting everyone on board with the elimination of programs that were exclusionary in nature was probably the most challenging, as often educators hold on to practices because "it's always been done this way" or because they couldn't be convinced that it wasn't right. It took great skill to lead the staff through this process. It also took a great deal of time and courage.
> —Dr. Collins, Hope School

Dr. Collins took deliberate actions to work with her staff, parents, and other school district professionals. While many principals shy away from eliciting the support of divergent groups for fear of the vulnerability it might cause, Dr. Collins welcomed the opportunity for group problem solving and collaboration. In the past decades, leadership literature pointed to school leadership in ways that were largely principal-centric, sometimes narrowly focusing on what amounts to "instructional coaching" or "clinical supervision" of individual teachers. Sometimes, this literature also referred to a wider range of functions that promoted instructional improvement across the school (Gordon, 2002; Leithwood & Duke, 1999; Sergiovanni, 1987). As Dr. Collins modeled in her example, we expand this notion to treat instructional leadership as *inherently distributed* among different staff in the building and throughout the district (Spillane, 2006), who bring attention to the shared approach to the development of inclusive and equitable schools. Dr. Collins modeled the distribution of leadership as a fact of school life, not an administrative action (like the delegation or distribution of responsibilities), though she was certainly able to shape the way participants engaged. She spent the time up front building trust by getting to know all the stakeholders and then listening carefully to them in order to find workable ways to tap into their strengths and use their ideas to evoke a sense of commitment toward change. She shared information candidly with members of her school community, and was willing to work on projects at the ground level with students, teachers, and families to address the barriers to inclusive practice.

## INQUIRY ON EQUITY

Like many principals across the United States, the principals of LaPaz and Hope schools faced a complicated challenge in confronting the systemic pattern of underachievement in their schools. Patterns of varying levels of academic success for students, in many cases, is determined by race, ethnicity, socioeconomic status, and/or language background, and the patterns persist despite years of effort to reform practice. The principals in LaPaz and Hope schools deliberately initiated different approaches than many schools in similar circumstances. In many schools, the approaches are void of the consideration of the role of culture in teaching and learning, highly technical, and lack critical awareness of students' lived experiences (e.g., implementation of highly scripted curriculum, increased use of "test-prep" materials and strategies).

> Teachers and staff members at La Paz were eager to turn the school around, and in many instances they expressed their enthusiasm with the words, "Just tell me what to do, and I'll do it." But for me, that expression was part of the problem. My staff members and teachers were used to being told what to do. But I wanted them to be *thinkers*, and I knew that in order to make a difference in student achievement, our staff members would have to take responsibility for their planning, instruction, assessment, feedback, and outcomes. Collaboration among and between students, paraprofessionals, families, and teachers was paramount to helping our staff members think about

their practice differently and become more reflective. I wanted my teachers to engage in inquiry in order to make the changes necessary to respond to student needs. —Dr. Barraza, La Paz School

At LaPaz the staff spent time engaged in inquiry on equity in teaching all students effectively, grounded in teachers' views of themselves as learners, including what, where, and how they learned. For example, a strong commitment to group practice helped teachers seek out the new knowledge and skills they needed to better meet the needs of students. Teachers at the school were used to working solo in the classroom, so the ideas of collaboration and group practice took time and transition. Many teachers felt uncomfortable discussing their data or other teachers' data. They also had difficulty opening their classroom doors for peer observations. Yet as they practiced together, and communicated openly about their vulnerabilities, their daily practices began to change, and there was a stronger focus on student learning—more of a team commitment to achieve the best results for students. Rather than working harder, teachers were able to work smarter by planning together, problem-solving with one another, and serving as supports when lessons didn't go as planned.

It was important to make teaching and learning more public. Our school leadership team read up and discussed best practices, and in doing so incorporated opportunities for students to track their own progress. We also looked for ways in which teachers could display student progress in their classrooms and in the hallways of the school. This included students establishing quarterly goals for themselves and then having their photos attached to the goal as it was attained. For example, as kindergarten students learned their letter sounds, their photos were on display in the hallway for all members of our school community to acknowledge their accomplishment. It was accountability and celebration all wrapped up in one. —Dr. Barraza, La Paz School

Decisions regarding performance and/or goals were linked explicitly to the data collected. Teachers and staff learned how to interrogate data; that is, they learned to ask deep questions about the data to uncover patterns and trends that could lead to inequities. Then they used these data to drive dialogue around student learning and classroom practice. Every grade level or vertical team meeting involved data, and we found it enhanced collaboration by offering teachers a springboard for learning about their own and others' practice, while also offering opportunities for reflection and research about common practices within our school.

## CULTURE OF CHANGE AND IMPROVEMENT

Another arena on the Systemic Change Framework involves creating a culture of change and improvement. The notion of creating a culture of change and improvement involves a school's commitment to evaluate progress, examine school culture and climate, and constantly strive for improvement. At La Paz and Hope schools, it involved sharing ideas and learning from one another. It was a vital component of the principals' plans to create an inclusive school because the principals acknowledged the fact that change is constant, and educators need to be able to embrace change and use it as a springboard to improving practice.

> I was looking for examples of the ways in which teachers brought students' cultural histories into the classroom and into La Paz School in general. I recognized that if the culture wasn't overtly supportive of diverse learners, our students would likely flounder. The process of assessing the culture felt somewhat slow and arduous; but I understood the importance of watching and listening as an integral component of building trust. I also knew better details provided for a stronger foundation for which change and improvement could occur. Collecting adequate baseline data was essential. —Dr. Barraza, La Paz School

Both La Paz and Hope schools initially had school cultures that relied on excuses related to why student performance wasn't better, or why the school struggled with making gains in achievement. In both schools, the excuses about students were abundant, and in many cases the students themselves began to accept low expectations.

> I started by creating a questionnaire to use with the faculty, staff, and parents of Hope Middle School regarding the cultural practices of the school—the activities that folks enjoyed, the practices that needed time and focus, and the traditions that would be disastrous to eliminate. These interviews were scheduled throughout the summer and were approximately 30 minutes in length. They served two purposes: (1) They allowed me the opportunity to meet individually with key stakeholders and learn about the cultural histories of individuals, teams, and the school in general; and (2) they offered me the opportunity to demonstrate my care and concern for the routines, systems, and customs that stakeholders perceived important. Because perceptions about school culture impact the morale of students, teachers, and family members, the time spent assessing the culture in this way was invaluable. —Dr. Collins, Hope School

Consider the practice of carving out time to meet individually with as many individuals as possible prior to the first day of school. Knowing that you cannot possibly meet with every individual connected to the school, how would you go about prioritizing whom you meet with? In asking questions about what is working well in the school, what needs refinement, what traditions are important, and what the prevailing attitudes and beliefs are about the school, you will have a clearer picture of the work ahead. The information gathered could also be fantastic data to share with your leadership team and staff during the first meetings.

At both La Paz and Hope schools a cultural change was necessary in order to improve the mindsets of teachers and students relating to high expectations and increased student achievement. Staff members spent many faculty meetings talking about the beliefs they had regarding students. They began to build a common language as they spoke about creating a culture of possibility throughout the school. The notion of focusing on academics had to permeate the building—and the focus had to change from compliance and behavior to ideas for teaching and learning. Every decision made in the school had to pass a litmus test for academic impact, and every staff meeting contained a professional development component intentionally designed to introduce ideas of cultural responsiveness, collaborative lesson design, and continuous improvement.

> After listening to the stories of the students, family members, and staff members, I knew a cultural change needed to occur at La Paz, but I also understood that I ran the risk of creating a divisive culture if I was not inclusive of all stakeholders in the process. Besides meeting individually with stakeholders prior to the start of school, I needed to continue to take time to sit with folks individually in order to continue getting to know their strengths and passions. It was essential for me to listen to individuals in order to find ways to include their ideas in our plans for change. I made a point to be visible throughout the building —in classrooms, on the playground, and in areas where teachers, students, and families congregate, and I built relationships by being available before, during, and after school. —Dr. Barraza, La Paz School

Both principals spent a great deal of time talking to parents and students to let them know that their voices and opinions mattered. As inclusive principals, they understood their responsibility to respond to students' diverse needs (Leithwood & Riehl, 2003), and went out of their way to listen to those who were perceived as disenfranchised. Changing parents' attitudes and perceptions may involve a cultural shift; a school interested in a culture of change finds various ways to personally invite parents in and encourage their involvement.

I recognized early that the same students and parents were voicing their opinions about what was occurring at Hope Middle School, while other parents and students appeared reluctant to share. It was important to me to find out the cultural patterns of communication in the school in order to invite and include all members to participate. By asking lots of questions about family engagement, I discovered many parents felt a sense of hostility toward the school. They had wanted to be involved, but felt that the doors had been closed to their involvement. They were not comfortable sharing in front of others because they had been treated poorly when expressing opinions in the past. In addition, they had no trust that I would be any different from the previous principals. Working to include disenfranchised members of our school would take considerable effort on my part. —Dr. Collins, Hope School

## SCHOOL AND COMMUNITY PARTNERSHIPS AND CONNECTIONS

Families, churches, and community centers all contribute to students' daily lives and are stakeholders in their education. Principals Barraza and Collins both prioritized effective communication with these stakeholders in order to gain insights into students' interests, talents, and challenges. Further, they understood that developing ongoing partnerships with families and community groups would strengthen schools' relationships with students and improve students' performance.

I really wanted to involve all family members at La Paz School, and I knew that in order to do so we had to break down some communication barriers and offer parents something of value. I started by engaging in conversations with parents and other family members before and after school as they dropped off or picked up their children. I found that some initiatives—(1) inviting families in for breakfasts, coffee, workshops, and/or celebrations; (2) giving up office space in the front of the school to develop a parent welcome center; (3) reserving computer and other office equipment for parent volunteers; and (4) providing workshops for parents, such as gang awareness, drug prevention, using the Internet, and lessons on how to navigate the education system—proved valuable to many parents, and engagement started to turn around. We offered our family engagement activities in multiple languages to be inclusive of parents with diverse language backgrounds. —Dr. Barraza, La Paz School

Inclusive principals recognize that student voice is also key in mobilizing the learning community. Dr. Collins listened to students and incorporated their ideas in school improvement initiatives, which ultimately promoted student pride and ownership at Hope School.

> We were interested in getting our community organizations involved in our school, so to do so we listened to our students' ideas about enhancing the school community in a variety of ways. They asserted that if they organized community service projects aimed at helping the organizations in the area, then these community organizations would in turn want to get involved in school projects. They brought in loose change monthly for the privilege of wearing jeans (Hope was a uniform school), and each time their loose change helped various community organizations such as the local food bank, women's shelter, and assisted living center. They also participated in food drives, sock drives, and penny wars. Students volunteered at the senior center by reading to seniors, watering plants through the building, and running small errands for community members. Additionally, they collected blankets for patients in nursing homes and children's hospitals and wrote cards and letters to military staff serving overseas. Students participated in community beautification activities and conducted acts of kindness for "buddies" in and out of the school. The students at the school took on special feelings of belonging and connectedness as they participated meaningfully in efforts to improve and enhance their school. —Dr. Collins, Hope School

## EQUITABLE RESOURCE DISTRIBUTION

Yet another arena on the Systemic Change Framework includes the ways in which resources are distributed so every student has access to the sets of resources needed for learning. The distribution of resources, including the ways teachers get assigned to grade levels or content areas as well as the amount and quality of materials, is a critical component for student access to authentic learning opportunities.

> I was really concerned with the amount and type of support that new teachers would be receiving at La Paz, because when I took over as principal, about 40% of the teachers were new to the school. I understood the fact that new teachers needed time to assimilate into the culture, but also recognized that many of our new teachers had not yet built up a repertoire of skills to address unique student needs, nor had they built up a stockpile of books and materials designed to help

students learn. When I walked through empty classrooms during the summer, I noted a distinct difference between the amount and types of materials our veteran teachers had compared to those of our new teachers, and I knew this disparity wouldn't serve our students well. In setting up the equitable distribution of resources, it was important for me to make sure all classrooms were equipped with the basic set of furniture, equipment, and materials—and that the new teachers received a budget to enhance the basic set of materials and make up for the lack of accrued materials teachers collect over time. It was a goal in our school for every classroom library to have at least 300 books available for students to read throughout the day or to take home as appropriate. We elicited funds from Title I and sought donations through our parent organization to bring interesting and vivid titles into our classrooms. It was important to us that all students, regardless of the amount of time their teacher had been teaching, had access to quality learning materials. —Dr. Barraza, La Paz School

## DESIGN AND USE OF TIME AND SPACE

Another element of the Systemic Change Framework is related to the ways in which schools are organized environmentally so that people can comfortably and regularly interact. In attending to the design and use of time and space in your school building, you should ensure that every area in the school can become a place for student learning and engagement.

I noticed that students and family members were spending a lot of time in the front office to register students, to wait for advising, complete paperwork, or to kill time when waiting to be picked up after school. I noticed that there were no reading materials for students or their parents. This was an easy fix and something our parent organization could get behind. We located books appropriate for all levels and attractively arranged them in a reading corner we designed for students, got in touch with local community organizations to promote activities that were going on locally with flyers and pamphlets for parents, and created a resource center for parents looking to enhance their role as supporters of learners with books, newsletters, and tip sheets for ways in which they might help.

We also took a look at other places where we saw students congregating and not a lot of learning happening. We placed booklets and magazines in the nurse's office so students who were feeling ill had an opportunity to read and reflect while visiting, created a reading nook near the counselors' office so students in crisis could have something to take their minds off their troubles, and strategically placed photos and captions throughout the hallways so students had things to consider as they walked between classes. Staff members really got creative when thinking about all the ways and places throughout the school in which learning could occur. —Dr. Collins, Hope School

Other considerations related to the design and use of time and space include the structure of school calendars, the use of planning time and space for teacher collaboration, the flexible use of facilities and student grouping, the amount of time and quality of interactions between the principal, teachers, and students in classrooms. The way that learning spaces are organized sets the tone for the learning. Paint color, desk arrangement, temperature, and noise can all affect student performance. In addition, the placement of classrooms often indicates the value of the staff and students in those classrooms. For example, music and art classes are usually located in areas away from general education classrooms because of noise and traffic volume. Many times, if the focus at the school includes building 21st-century skills, the computers are not located in labs, but instead classroom sets of laptops or tablets are located on carts and can be brought into the learning space where students are more apt to use technology to enhance their learning rather than separating the acquisition of technology skills and curricular content. Other things to consider include articulation across grade level or subject area.

La Paz was a large, spread out school, so it was important to me that teachers had an opportunity to interact across grade levels. Multiage groupings of classrooms promoted community and articulation across grade levels. Another priority, since we had so many new teachers, was to place mentor teachers in close proximity to their mentees in order to encourage collaboration and increase support. But the most important priority for me when I took over as principal involved moving the special education resource classrooms out of the portables and into the center of the school. I believed that by having these students located on the fringe of the school, we were communicating a message to students, staff, and families about their importance. I wanted them to feel a sense of belonging and connectedness, and if they were having to walk out to the portables in substandard classrooms, then I wasn't doing my job in creating an inclusive school. Another important consideration I had was the amount of time it would take for students needing special support to walk to and from these special classrooms. I understood that if the classrooms were centrally located, time away from instruction would be minimized and communication between general education and special area teachers could be enhanced. —Dr. Barraza, La Paz School

A student-friendly feel is necessary in schools aiming to be inclusive and culturally responsive. Students need to see their work and images of people that look like them displayed in positive ways throughout the school. Sometimes this entails a fresh set of eyes examining the school in order to point out things that can often be overlooked by teachers and staff that are used to their surroundings. Every decision regarding the design and use of time and space should send intentional messages of student importance and high expectations for learning.

## CONCLUSION

Student learning is at the heart of all efforts in schools looking to become more inclusive and culturally responsive. The use of a model such as the Systemic Change Framework can provide evidence-based areas of focus for the school principal and school leadership team. However, in order to embark on change that is inclusive and sustainable, the leadership team and principal must confront the tensions associated with disturbing the status quo. Principals Barraza and Collins were intentional about the relationships they forged, the messages they sent out, and the strategies they took to help teachers, staff, students, and parents understand the urgency of change. Creating a shared school vision that promoted high expectations and academic excellence were merely first steps. These leaders understood the importance of change at multiple levels of the system, and worked simultaneously across several arenas to create the type of cultural change that they wanted to see—change that could be sustainable and stand the test of time. It is this type of knowledge and understanding that is essential for the school leader looking to create a school where all students, families, teachers, and staff feel a sense of belonging, connection, and empowerment, and where all stakeholders share the belief that all students can attain high levels of achievement.

As offered up in story by the principals of La Paz and Hope schools, the idea of building an inclusive and culturally responsive school is complex and multifaceted. There were concerted and intentional efforts that took time, deep listening, and immense commitment. At times, efforts may have been as simple as locating reading materials for the front office. Other times efforts may have been more challenging, such as getting teachers on board with opening up their practice for regular peer observations and discourse. In order to effectively meet the needs of diverse learners, both principals recognized and acknowledged the importance of having critical conversations with staff related to understanding the needs of students who were culturally, racially, linguistically, and ethnically diverse. It took courage for them to open up this discourse, but both had conviction in their rationale for making school a better place for those students in the margins.

In closing, we draw attention to the complexities of our educational system (e.g., geography, cultural historical practices, and interpretations of policy that maintain local customs and practices), and take note of all the ways in which educators spend time examining their systems and grappling with the equity dilemmas associated with the implementation of inclusive and culturally responsive teaching and learning practices. The notion of equity at La Paz and Hope was paramount in the decisions made, and a continuous examination of beliefs, attitudes, and practices took place throughout the tenure of the principal in the school building. Each was deliberate in creating opportunities for ongoing, job-embedded professional learning designed to transform the learning community. Begin with examining the priorities in your school, and ask how they uncover deeply held values and beliefs about equity and inclusiveness.

The principals at La Paz and Hope schools demonstrated the significance of working collaboratively with all stakeholders—students, parents, teachers, and community members—and encapsulated that value for every student contribution in the learning community by offering every child, regardless of his or her difference, ample opportunities for success. They modeled a respect for cultural differences, empowered students to be partners in their own achievement, and promoted buy-in and ownership for accomplishing the school's vision and mission. In these schools, students were eager to learn and were encouraged to learn without having ceilings for their accomplishments. La Paz and Hope schools were welcoming and caring environments where the backgrounds and lived experiences of diverse individuals mattered.

Through the stories of the two principals, this chapter aimed to provide school leaders with authentic strategies aligned within the Systemic Change Framework as a tool in promoting an inclusive and culturally responsive school environment. Aligning your own initiatives to an evidence-based tool such as the Systemic Change Framework should be the first step in promoting sustained and inclusive school transformation.

## REFERENCES

Aud, S., Fox, M., & KewalRamani, A. (2010). *Status and trends in the education of racial and ethnic groups* (NCES 2010-015). U.S. Department of Education, National Center for Education Statistics. Washington, DC: U.S. Government Printing Office.

Ferguson, D. L., & Kozleski, E. B. (2003). Inclusive urban schools: The National Institute for Urban School Improvement. In V. Gaylord., T. Vandercook, and J. York-Barr (Eds.), *Impact: Feature issue on revisiting inclusive K–12 education*, 16(1). Minneapolis: University of Minnesota, Institute on Community Integration. Retrieved from ici.umn.edu/products/impact/161

Gordon, R. D. (2002). Conceptualizing leadership with respect to its historical-contextual antecedents to power. *The Leadership Quarterly, 13,* 151–167.

Kozleski, E. B. (2011). Dialectical practices in education: Creating third spaces in the education of teachers. *Teacher Education and Special Education, 34,* 250–259.

Kozleski, E. B., & Smith, A. (2009). The complexities of system change in creating equity for students with disabilities in urban schools. *Urban Education, 44*(4), 427–451.

Leithwood, K., & Duke, D. L. (1999). A century's quest to understand school leadership. In K. S. Louis & J. Murphy (Eds.), *Handbook of research on educational administration* (2nd ed., pp. 45–72). San Francisco, CA: Jossey-Bass.

Leithwood, K. A. & Riehl, C. (2003). *What we know about successful school leadership.* Philadelphia, PA: Laboratory for Student Success, Temple University.

McIntosh, P. (2003). White privilege and male privilege: A personal account of coming to see correspondences through work in women's studies. In M. S. Kimmel & A. L. Ferber (Eds.), *Privilege: A reader* (pp. 147–160). Boulder, CO: Westview.

Salisbury, C., & McGregor, G. (2005). *Principals of inclusive schools.* Tempe, AZ: National Institute for Urban School Improvement. Retrieved from www.urban-schools.org/pdf/principals.inclusive.LETTER.pdf

Sands, D. J., Kozleski, E. B., & French, N. (2000). *Inclusive education for the 21st century: A new introduction to special education.* Belmont: CA: Wadsworth.

Sergiovanni, T. J. (1987). Will we ever have a TRUE profession? Supervision in Context. *Educational Leadership, 44*(8), 44–49.

Spillane, J. P. (2006). *Distributed leadership.* San Francisco, CA: Jossey-Bass.

Taylor, E., Tisdell, E., & Hanley, M. S. (2000). *The role of positionality in teaching for critical consciousness: Implications for adult education.* Paper presented at the Adult Education Research Conference in Vancouver, Canada. Retrieved from http://www.adulterc.org/Proceedings/2000/tayloreetal1-final.PDF

United States Department of Education (NCES). (2011). *The condition of education 2011 (NCES 2011-033).* Indicator 6. Washington, DC: National Center for Education Statistics.

# CHAPTER 8

# Leadership for Transforming Districts into Inclusive Systems

*Amanda L. Sullivan, Susan L. Abplanalp,*
*and Jack Jorgensen*

I joined Lowell Elementary School as principal in the Madison Met-ropolitan School District (MMSD) after serving 6 years as a princi-pal of a private parochial school. So many aspects of the private and public settings were startlingly different to me in those early months. What stood out most was special education. In my former Catholic school, we didn't provide special education services, so special needs were generally not formally identified. Instead, all staff taught all children regardless of their differences. Moreover, many parents did not want their children identified for special education because of the stigmatization and segregation that accompanied it. They wanted to keep their children in our general classrooms instead of having them moved to specialized settings where they did not expect them to have the same experiences or opportuni-ties. Accordingly, I worked with these parents and teachers to sup-port the learning needs of students with disabilities in our general classrooms. We looked to the literature to understand how to best support these children within our standard curriculum without con-ventional special education. Happily, we saw many of these children flourish. Thus, from the beginning of my time at Lowell, I questioned the school's special education service delivery model because it did not align with my own beliefs about how children with special needs should be educated or with what I knew of the current research on inclusive practices. At Lowell, our students were primarily placed by disability label in multigrade special classrooms—sometimes away from their home schools and almost always away from their age-appropriate, nondisabled peers—and provided different curricu-lum. I could not help but wonder why it happened this way. Why weren't these children in their home school? When I looked to our data, I saw that many of these students were not making academic

gains, and this again made me wonder why they were kept in these settings if it did not appear to help. Wasn't supporting their learning and success our overarching goal? Perhaps I was naïve, but I had to understand why things were done this way. Within a few months, I began to meet regularly with staff to discuss current practices for special education identification and placement and to ask why we were sending these children out of our classrooms and out of our school. What was best for them? Why could we not meet their needs here? How could we improve what we were doing and serve them better? Not surprisingly, I was not the only one with concerns. Together, we explored our beliefs and principles and constructed a vision for a more inclusive system.
—Susan "Sue" Abplanalp

This was the beginning, the spark that would set off years of school change alongside district reform. For Lowell Elementary School, it began with a newcomer asking a relatively simple question about one school's model of special education—*Why?*—and was fueled by the staff's willingness to explore this question and re-envision their service delivery model. Driven by a shared belief that schools should support the learning needs of *all* children— no matter their differences in ability, skills, experiences, or background— this school embarked on a journey of reform. Their efforts paralleled district efforts to produce systemwide change. This is that story. It is a story of leadership for systems change as leaders and educators came together to create a context transforming into an inclusive system.

Situated within the larger context of how school change efforts inform and shape district efforts, and how district efforts drive change, we describe the activities initiated within MMSD over 12 years. In this time, the district successfully restructured a categorical, label-driven special education program model into one that today is nationally recognized as highly inclusive and collaborative. Concurrently, a major change effort also occurred at one of the district's elementary schools as an inclusive model of education was implemented. By illustrating the relationships across and between the district and school levels of an educational system, we describe not only the efforts engaged in at two levels of systems change, but also the strategies for ensuring that reform efforts are embedded across levels of the system. We offer a description of inclusive education followed by brief descriptions of the state, district, and local school contexts to ground the analysis that follows. We explore a framework for complex school change followed by a discussion of processes that foster systemic change at the practitioner, school, and district levels. A final section reminds readers of the role that leadership plays in setting a vision, providing access to resources, gauging progress, and tuning efforts.

## INCLUSIVE EDUCATION FOR STUDENTS WITH DISABILITIES

Federal special education policy requires that students with disabilities receive free, appropriate public education in the least restrictive environment. Prior to the passage of the Education for All Handicapped Children Act of 1975 (P. L. 94-142), an estimated 1 million students identified with disabilities were excluded from schools—thus forced to stay home or be institutionalized—and nearly 4 million more received inappropriate services (Connor & Ferri, 2007). The persistent segregation of students with disabilities compelled Congress to include the requirement that children in special education should be educated in the least restrictive environment to the maximum extent possible along with the requirement that states monitor the placements of students with disabilities (20 U.S.C. 1400-87). In the years that followed, these students were increasingly served in educational settings, but there continued to be wide variability in the nature and level of inclusiveness with nondisabled students and access to general education curriculum.

Empirical analyses have shown that children with disabilities experience better social, communication, and academic outcomes when they are educated in general education settings (e.g., Bennett, DeLuca, & Bruns, 1997; Blackorby et al., 2005; Fryxell & Kennedy, 1995; Peltier, 1997; Wagner, Blackorby, Cameto, Hebbler, & Newman, 1993). Not only did students with disabilities thrive in inclusive settings, their involvement in general education settings did not inhibit the academic achievement of students without disabilities and showed social benefits for all children (Peltier, 1997; Staub & Peck, 1995). Data from a large-scale nationally representative longitudinal study of nearly 10,000 students with disabilities showed that children who spent more time in general education were absent less, had higher achievement scores, and performed closer to grade level than their peers in more restrictive placements (Blackorby et al., 2005). Despite these findings, however, by 2010 only 53% of students with disabilities spent the majority of their time in these settings (U.S. Department of Education, 2011), although in some states, this number is as high as 93% (Gibson & Kozleski, 2011).

The term *inclusion* refers to the integration of students with disabilities in general education settings, but this term is used to represent a range of practices and perspectives related to the degree of involvement children have in general education settings and the level of support provided by educational specialists such as special educators, occupational therapists, or behavior specialists (Sailor & Roger, 2005). There is no one model or definition of inclusive education; implementation varies substantially across sociocultural contexts and levels of educational systems (Kozleski & Smith, 2009). A simple way to think of inclusive education—and one that is consistent with the practices described herein—is that it is concerned with ensuring access, participation, and achievement for students "whose identities have been constructed under oppressive conditions" (Artiles & Kozleski, 2007, p. 355).

Despite the fragmentation of the inclusion discourse, the inclusive education movement has generally focused on issues of social justice, encouraging the service, within general education settings, of students who have a variety of markers of difference such as language, ability, sexuality, religion, and cultural differences (Artiles, 2003). While detractors have argued that the special needs of children with disabilities and English language learners necessitates their treatment in specialized settings outside of the typical classroom, supporters have argued that through appropriate teacher preparation and utilization of teaching technologies such as universal designs for learning and differentiated instruction, all children can excel in general education settings.

Unfortunately, the complexity of such reform can hamper efforts to implement and institutionalize inclusive education. Scholars have shown that many school systems rely on individual expertise rather than policy change or systemic change (Kozleski & Smith, 2009), which can undermine sustainability and scalability of reform efforts. The intent of this chapter is to describe systemic efforts that lend themselves to substantive sustainable change that improves opportunities to learn and outcomes for all students.

## LOCAL CONTEXT

MMSD is located in Wisconsin, a state that is home to more than 5.6 million residents (Wisconsin Department of Administration, 2010). The state's population is predominantly White and most residents (65%) live in urban areas. Statewide, more than 870,000 students are educated in public schools (Wisconsin Department of Public Instruction, 2011). Racial inequities in special education have been a focus of concern for many years (for discussion, see Sullivan, Kozleski, & Waitoller, 2008), but issues of inclusive education received less attention. That said, since 1999, there has been a statewide increase of more than 10% in the percentage of children with disabilities who spend the majority of their time in general education (Sullivan et al., 2008).

### District

MMSD is an urban district in south-central Wisconsin educating approximately 27,000 students. Anyon (1997) described urban schools as those serving students in densely populated urban corridor communities where disparities in resources are widespread. Serving more than 426,000 mostly urban residents in the state's second largest county, MMSD had 32 elementary schools, 11 middle schools, and 4 comprehensive high schools in 2012. Half the student population self-identified as racial/ethnic minorities and 51% came from low-income households (Madison Metropolitan School District, 2011). Student diversity doubled from 2000 to 2010. In addition, more than 16.3% of students were identified for special education, which outpaced the national rate of about 11% (U.S. Department of Education, 2011).

Beginning in 1997, the district's special education delivery model became the focus of a major reform effort. A new superintendent and director of special education were promoted from within the district and built on existing relationships to initiate dialogues regarding the questionable state of special education in the district. Prompted by systemwide concern from families, teachers, and principals, the focus was on identifying challenges and envisioning improvement. Simply put, special education was no longer viewed as responsive to the needs of students with disabilities, and increasingly parents desired an inclusive education in the child's school of residence with age-appropriate, nondisabled peers.

### School

Just as the district was beginning a long-term process of reform, Lowell Elementary was also beginning a process of system change. Spurred by a needs assessment that highlighted lackluster reading skills among students with special needs, the school began to explore how to ensure all students achieved reading proficiency by 3rd grade through an inclusive approach. The previous delivery model had become entrenched in label-driven placements that were disconnected from students' developmental levels or teachers' knowledge and expertise. Achievement data showed that students were not benefiting from such placements. Grounded in the assumption that all students should be educated in the least restrictive environment using research-based curriculum and instruction, the school began to shift policies and practices to move students with special needs back into the general education environment and improve the education of all children. Lowell, as well as other schools, developed and implemented an instructional design model ensuring that all children were educated appropriately in the least restrictive environment. This model was eventually adopted districtwide to support inclusive practice.

Both school and district contexts shape reform efforts at both levels. This chapter explores the interactive efforts to foster inclusive education at the district and school levels in MMSD. The practitioner, school, and organizational changes described throughout were grounded in the framework described below.

## A FRAMEWORK FOR COMPLEX SCHOOL CHANGE

Although inclusive education efforts can be hampered by the complexity of change, this complexity can be managed successfully by using a coherent conceptual framework. Lowell grounded its reform efforts in Knoster, Villa, and Thousand's (2000) framework for managing complex change. This framework conceptualized five elements as essential for true change: (1) vision, (2) skills, (3) incentives, (4) resources, and (5) action planning and identifying the obstacles to be expected if particular elements were missing. Vision provided the foundation for complex change; without it, stakeholders became confused in the reform process. Adequate skills enabled stakeholders to make their vision a reality; without them, stakeholders often became anxious and frustrated. Incentives helped stakeholders become invested in the change process; without them, some stakeholders resisted reform. Appropriate resources, like adequate skills, enabled stakeholders to act on their vision. Such resources included sufficient material, time, and funding to produce the desired change; without them, practitioners experienced ongoing frustration. Finally, the action plan provided the roadmap for reform; without it, stakeholders often had false starts in their reform efforts. Consequently, these five elements were considered necessary for productive, sustainable change efforts.

### Crafting a Collective Vision for Change

Following this framework, Lowell's principal and teachers worked together to identify a vision for the future. This collective effort progressed slowly as members first explored their beliefs, values, and goals for the education of all students. They then worked together to review and critique the conceptual, theoretical, and empirical literature on inclusive education and effective collaborative instruction in order to identify what was needed for an inclusive model. Lowell partnered with experts from the University of Wisconsin, including Alice Udvari-Solner, in crafting their vision. University partners brought to the table their expertise in research and theory while the Lowell staff brought their practical expertise and understanding of their local context.

Over time the staff collectively crafted a vision of inclusive education at Lowell Elementary based on their beliefs and values, and the theoretical bases of inclusive practices. This was an iterative, dynamic process grounded in the local cultural context, shaped by shifting school policies, and influenced by the experiences and expertise of the educators and families within the school community. Through this process, the staff identified their core values that included beliefs about (1) access to the general education curriculum; (2) respecting and honoring cultures, needs, and interests; (3) the critical role of neighborhood schools in serving all children; and (4) the importance of collaborative teaching. In each case, the importance of these beliefs for all children was specific, which staff members incorporated into a set of statements:

- We believe all students must have access to the general education curriculum.
- We respect and honor all children's cultures, needs, and interests.
- We value placement in the neighborhood schools and will design our special education delivery model to reflect a preference for educating students in their neighborhood school.
- We value collaborative teaching to support the diverse needs of all learners in general education settings.

The team realized that the existing system of categorical placements was in direct conflict with their articulation of values. It was no longer acceptable for students with disabilities to be served in self-contained classrooms by an "emotional disabilities teacher" or "learning disabilities teacher." They also rejected the practice of basing educational decisions on students' special education labels. Instead, they developed a collaborative teaching model in which teams of educators worked together to meet the individual and collective needs of all students in a classroom. Thus the school made the collective decision to abandon the pullout model for a model based on collaborative planning and coteaching, always attending to the individualized needs of students.

### Identifying Requisite Skills and Resources

Lowell's staff recognized that enacting their shared vision would necessitate major shifts in practice, and thus new skills and resources would be required. Coplanning and coteaching were central to this vision, so developing collaboration skills would be key to fostering the skills and strategies central to supporting collaborative teaching and other inclusive practices. In addition, an inclusive model necessitated changes in instructional practices to support differentiation and behavior management.

The inclusive model also necessitated the reallocation of resources. Beyond the time needed to develop their collaborative planning and teaching skills, the Lowell staff needed release time for revising the scheduling process and engaging in collaborative instructional design. Shifting from pullout placements with separate curriculum to inclusive placements also meant that additional materials were needed to support students with disabilities in general education settings. Groups of teachers, who later became instructional teams, worked with staff at the district office to delineate clearly needed resources and sources of support.

## Incentivizing Change

Lowell staff recognized that incentives were needed to promote morale throughout the multiyear process of planning and implementation. Returning to the beliefs and values identified in the first phase of this planning process, staff again met in groups to discuss their goals and the outcomes that would reflect those goals in order to make reform personally rewarding for each teacher and support staff. The staff mapped out benchmarks for change that would be needed to track the progress of their change efforts. Benchmarks included level of inclusion of students with disabilities in general education classrooms and achievement gains because these were the problems that spurred the reform efforts. As they moved forward, revisiting these benchmarks and celebrating progress became central to keeping all team members focused on the shared vision for inclusive education. Ongoing examination of student progress showed that all groups of students were improving their literacy and math outcomes as indicated through ongoing progress measures that teachers used in their classrooms. Informal measures of accomplishment, used by the teachers to group and regroup students, change their teaching designs, and connect students with different kinds of literature, translated into improved accountability performance for the school. Statewide assessments validated the efforts on the part of the students, the teachers, and the school to accelerate learning under the new benchmarks. These data confirmed the beliefs of supporters and galvanized skeptics to embrace a more inclusive approach.

As a building principal, I reflect on a day when a special education teacher who was skeptical of our reform initiatives came to me to share news of a student's success in his new inclusive placement. "Look at this piece of writing that I just received from one of my students!" she stated proudly, presenting me with an essay composed in language arts. "I can't believe he came this far in such a short time." She had been teaching this child outside of the classroom with a different reading program for several years prior to our reform. When she taught this child the balanced literacy curriculum of general education among his peers, she realized that this student—and many others—had the capabilities to perform and excel within the general education classroom—capabilities of which she was never aware during years of pullout instruction. This incident, among many others, gave testimony to the fact that we, collectively, as a staff, needed to continue with our efforts to implement inclusive practices. Although there would be bumps in the road, the time had come to be steadfast in our beliefs that all children could indeed learn together without compromising the high standards set forth for every child. —Sue Abplanalp

### Devising and Implement an Action Plan

Over the course of the first year of reform, Lowell staff worked with an outside consultant, Alice Udvari-Solner, to develop an action plan for making their vision a reality. In it, the necessary changes for inclusion were articulated and individual roles were identified so that each member of the staff understood what would be expected as they moved through this change process. This action plan was refined over several meetings of the staff and university partners with the understanding that it was a dynamic document to be revisited periodically as progress was made or obstacles were encountered. This was a dynamic, nonlinear process in which individual and group conceptualizations were constantly in flux as old ideas and reforms were challenged, data were explored, and the needs of students, families, staff, and schools were considered.

Embedded within the action plan were the other three critical elements for change: (1) professional development to foster the skills needed by staff and leadership to enact the vision, (2) guidelines for the reallocation of resources needed to support skills development and change, and (3) timelines for monitoring progress in the student outcomes that served as the incentives for staff to persist in their reform efforts. As the teachers acquired the necessary knowledge and skills for inclusion, the action plan resulted in children being placed increasingly in general education settings in their neighborhood schools rather than in self-contained, category-based, magnet-like programs across the district.

By the end of the yearlong planning process, the Lowell staff had arrived at a collective understanding of their vision for inclusive instructional design, carried out the necessary professional development, and reallocated resources to support the new service delivery model. As they entered year 2, the school began to implement a new model based in the belief that all children should be educated in general education settings. As staff delved more deeply into their data and received feedback from stakeholders, they also saw that the process had resulted in increased levels of parent involvement, decreased special education referral and identification rates, and forged new school and community partnerships, which further fueled their reform efforts. By year 2 of the reform initiative, staff at Lowell began to serve all children in their neighborhood school regardless of labels rather than assigning them to self-contained programs in other schools. As the district moved toward systemic implementation of an inclusive model underpinned by a comprehensive literacy program, Lowell would serve as a model for change across school buildings.

> By this time, we frequently had visitors from the central office and other schools who came to observe our model in action. It was not uncommon for them to remark that they could not discern the child with special needs from those without, nor could they determine which teacher was the special education teacher and which was the general education teacher. The lines of delivery were clearly merged.
> —Sue Abplanalp

## FOSTERING SYSTEMIC CHANGE

While Knoster and colleagues' (2000) framework provides a map of the processes necessary to initiate school change effectively, it did not represent the full scope of challenges inherent in systemic change at multiple levels of school systems. The Systemic Change Framework developed by the National Institute of Urban School Improvement, grounded in Bronfenbrenner's ecological theory (Ferguson, Kozleski, & Smith, 2003; Shanklin et al., 2003), described the multiple layers and dimensions of activity necessary to produce improved outcomes for students (see Chapter 1). In the description that follows, the focus was on the district, school, and practitioner levels, and the elements necessary to support coherent, sustained systemic change for inclusive education.

### Practitioner Effort

Teachers' dialogues regarding the needs of learners, effective practices, and core values drove the change process in MMSD, as exemplified by the process enacted at Lowell. In envisioning their goal of developing an inclusive school, Lowell practitioners realized the value of collaboration. Thus the design and delivery of their teaching was reconceptualized in a collaborative teaching model featuring shared/group planning time, shared expertise, and coteaching. General and special education staff met regularly to revisit students' individualized education plans (IEPs), plan for instruction, and monitor the progress of all students.

### School Effort

School organization can support teachers' efforts by creating contexts where sustained, critical, reflective practice can occur through shared decision making, collective practice, and appreciation for continuous improvement (Ferguson et al., 2003). At Lowell, for instance, the tool presented in Figure 8.1 facilitated teacher reflection by prompting ongoing examination of their perspectives on and values regarding inclusive practices. In order to establish an active collective dialogue about practice and outcomes, in the initial stages of the reform process at Lowell, school staff met regularly to discuss outcomes, practices, and procedures in order to understand why the current system was not effective for their students with disabilities. Lowell's efforts to implement inclusive education emphasized teacher leadership through the teaming process. Professional development centered on improving capacity for collaboration and instructional design. In response to the collaborative efforts of teachers, school leadership made coplanning and coteaching a priority in the master schedule. Teaming strategies and successes were highlighted in all staff meetings. Professional development became the topic of all staff meetings with leader teachers asked to lead learning activities and to initiate conversations around the school's changing philosophy of special education. In particular, these conversations emphasized the need for clear expectations and accountability for all students' learning.

For some, this shift in roles and expectations created discomfort that resulted in highly conflicted meetings. The literature on organizational change emphasizes that reform is met with an individual reaction process that may include denial, resistance, explorations, and eventually acceptance and commitment (Bovey & Hede, 2001). *Resistance* should be seen as a natural aspect of the change process as professionals within the system are faced with abandoning known processes and roles for those largely unfamiliar to many. Whereas maintenance of the status quo is a relatively effortless state, change requires an infusion of cognitive, emotional, temporal, and material resources (Strebel, 2006), which is objectionable to many. Thus the initial pushback against the school's inclusive model was to be expected as it necessitated major changes to the school's policies, procedures, and practices.

Within any organizational change process, it is important for school and district leaders to be mindful that individuals vary in their cognitive and emotional responses to change and that effective leadership requires navigating both the organizational and interpersonal obstacles. Without attention to the dynamics of resistance, school reforms are often slow and temporary; indeed, failure is the norm in a milieu of conflicting ideologies and interests and constant policy change (Starr, 2011). Principals in particular must embrace their roles as catalysts and mediators in this complex process of transforming systems through sensitivity to both organizational and individual reactions to paradigm shifts (Starr, 2011).

There are a number of behavioral manifestations of emotional resistance to change (e.g., arguments or refusal to participate) that were enacted in the staff meetings as both individuals resistant to and supportive of the

FIGURE 8.1. Self-Assessment of Inclusive Perspectives: A Tool for Informing Professional Learning

| Inclusive Education: Coplanning and Coteaching for All Students | |
| --- | --- |
| *Directions:* Think about each of statements presented. Select the numerical value below (1 = lowest, 5 = highest) corresponding with the extent to which you value this feature as an educator. In the right-hand column, check the three statements you believe to be most critical in the subsequent work/professional development in the school. | |
| Value | Top 3 |
| All students in my classroom spend the majority of the day in general education environments with appropriate learning expectations, material, and support. <br><br> Low Value  1      2      3      4      5  High Value | |
| I regularly coplan curriculum and instruction with my teammate (e.g., general education along with specialist–special education, ESL, Title I) in advance of teaching. <br><br> Low Value  1      2      3      4      5  High Value | |
| Team meetings focus on upfront planning and differentiation of curriculum and instruction that meets the unique learning needs of all students in the general education classroom. <br><br> Low Value  1      2      3      4      5  High Value | |
| Before considering the need to pull students out for specialized instruction, teaching teams exhaust all options in the general education classroom. <br><br> Low Value  1      2      3      4      5  High Value | |
| Students and adults together share a strong sense of community, respect, and belonging with one another. <br><br> Low Value  1      2      3      4      5  High Value | |
| When there is more than one adult in the classroom, we plan for varied ways to coteach, sharing roles and responsibilities with one another. <br><br> Low Value  1      2      3      4      5  High Value | |
| I have shared ownership and responsibility for all students' progress as well as their challenges in the classroom(s) in which I work. <br><br> Low Value  1      2      3      4      5  High Value | |

*Note:* Based on 2004 planning tool from the MMSD Collaborative School Reform Project.

new model were engaged in dialogues about student needs and professional responsibilities. Individuals' responses ranged from overt aggression to silence. For some at Lowell, this pushback was voiced through explicit rejection of certain proposed changes; others lashed out at the individuals supporting the change. While the conversations were guided by leader teachers, the overall process was mediated by support staff to alleviate interpersonal conflicts. Conversations were redirected to the process when interpersonal skirmishes emerged because it was the process that had triggered the negative responses. Administrators emphasized the need for cohesion and continuity in order for the inclusive model to be successful. In the face of this resistance, commitment to improving student outcomes motivated persistence on the parts of administrators. Such a *hopeful* forward-looking orientation was essential to dispelling resistance and motivating sustained change (Calabrese, 2003).

> I knew that for every spoken complaint, there were likely more unspoken from the silent dissenters, and that made me sad. I had to constantly remind myself of all of the underserved children of the past and our responsibility to do better. It was this thought that kept me motivated despite the complicated, messy process of change. I knew it was going to take persistent, consistent support and nurturance on my part to establish clear expectations and commitment to inclusion throughout our journey together. —Sue Abplanalp

## District Effort

*Inquiry on equity in schooling.* MMSD's district reform was driven by questions about what works, under what circumstances, and for whom, which revealed the strengths and weaknesses of the old model. The driving concern was how to best educate all students, underpinned by the collective belief that all children should be educated effectively in general education. Efforts centered around collecting input from key stakeholders, convening committees of stakeholders to identify needs, values, and evidence-based practices, and communicating with district administration. Teachers, principals, and administrators were continually engaged in the processes of critically examining their values, beliefs, and practices about placement and instruction. Through this process, the district identified the following hallmarks of an inclusive school community:

- Share a common vision and goals for high levels of student engagement, learning, and relationships
- Have a common understanding of student outcomes: what we want students to know and be able to do for each lesson

- Have a common understanding of inclusive practices that wrap services around each child
- Agree with each other about how to assess students so we know they are, in fact, learning
- Assess each child and have in-depth conversations about what the next teaching points and learning levels are for each child
- Implement timely, systematic interventions based on what is learned from assessing the child and what we have agreed upon that students should know and be able to do in the lesson
- Agree to and act upon the commitment that we must address the needs of every student who is not reaching the outcomes. Engage in collaboration to surround each child with the power of shared responsibility and the expertise of a team of teachers and other key adults

These hallmarks emerged and were refined through an iterative process of group reflection, and were revisited throughout the process of re-envisioning the district's special education programming and used to guide the school's development of new instructional designs. These elements were underpinned by a vision of equity in which all individuals within the school community were respected and valued.

***District–community partnerships and participation.*** District leadership developed community and districtwide partnerships to facilitate communication as part of the process of implementing system change for inclusive education. Led by Executive Director of Special Education Jack Jorgensen, they convened focus groups of key stakeholders—general educators, special educators, district administrators, principals, and paraprofessionals—to ascertain the perspectives, concerns, and needs of particular groups. The focus groups were led by district administrators from general and special education in order to communicate a unified front. Specifically, the Special Education Parent Advisory Council met directly with the executive director. These efforts, led by Jorgensen, signaled the district commitment to respecting the voices of multiple stakeholders throughout the reform process. Jorgensen and others met with the parent council to discuss candidly the shortcomings and needs of the district's special education program. What occurred were frank conversations about the experiences and priorities of children with disabilities and their families, highlighting the need to reflect critically on the structure and quality of the opportunities to learn that were provided to students with disabilities. As a result of these discussions, six overarching priorities for change were identified to guide organizational efforts to reconceptualize the participation and learning among students with disabilities:

- Establish a district vision for special education that is supported by clear values and beliefs.
- Regularly provide general education staff with individualized planning information related to the needs of the students with disabilities in their classrooms.
- Establish a districtwide positive behavior interventions and supports (PBIS) system that responds to the needs of students with serious behavioral challenges.
- Establish a cross-categorical special education service delivery system at all schools.
- Develop and implement a comprehensive plan for recruiting, training, and retaining paraprofessionals (i.e., special education assistants—SEAs) to more effectively support students in inclusive settings.
- Establish a reliable and equitable staff allocation formula (i.e., special education teacher, paraprofessionals, related services staff, and so on) to support special education at all schools that is responsive to the needs of students and is not driven by labels and a separate pullout program model.

In addition, schools already engaged in the shift toward inclusive practices, like Lowell, were consulted to identify successful practices for addressing identified concerns. The district used these data and the priorities above to guide their development of an operational plan for instituting systemic change. Then a committee of stakeholders examined student outcome data, research, and best practice guidelines to develop specific recommendations for change. For each of the six priorities, a detailed improvement plan was created that included: (1) desired outcomes, (2) improvement activities, (3) resources, (4) persons responsible, and (5) a timeline for completion.

Additionally, the district fostered community partnerships to support the complex needs of children. For instance, a multiyear partnership with the Dane County Mental Health Center provided social workers to assist district-based behavioral supports, which in turn strengthened the coordination of services between home, school, and community. The goal was to provide seamless, comprehensive, and coordinated services to the child and family.

MMSD also partnered with the National Institute for Urban School Improvement (NIUSI) to strengthen efforts to foster culturally responsive inclusive schools and reduce the disproportionate representation of students of color in special education. Thus the district's vision of inclusion was broadened to encompass other aspects of student diversity, thereby strengthening the commitment to improving outcomes for all learners. Attendance at NIUSI-sponsored national conferences was supplemented by site visits and professional development activities provided by NIUSI staff. These were instrumental in promoting positive perceptions, attitudes, and practices among teachers and administrators related to enhancing culturally responsive practices in classrooms and schools.

## Equitable Resource Development and Distribution

Support from district administration was vital to supporting the re-distribution of resources and execution of professional learning plans. For instance, a more equitable staff allocation formula was developed to ensure that each school had the staffing necessary to support students in the more inclusive placements because the old formulas based on the pullout program model often resulted in understaffing, and thus underservice. Additionally, a state grant supported districtwide development and dissemination of coteaching strategies. Furthermore, schools received additional resources from the district to build capacity for collaborative teaching. Within individual schools such as Lowell, coteaching teams identified the resources and skills necessary to implement their coteaching plans. In addition, the district implemented a comprehensive plan for recruiting, training, and retaining paraprofessionals to support students with disabilities in inclusive settings. This was a crucial element of the inclusive model alongside teacher planning and coteaching.

## Inclusive Leadership for Equity and Accountability

The district engaged in strategic planning to establish a blueprint for change. Building on feedback from focus groups and the advisory committee, the district leadership team developed a plan for scaling up inclusive education. Central to this plan was a comprehensive, multiyear research-based professional development program utilizing action research and peer coaching. Specifically, the staff engaged in study groups, planning teams, classroom observations, and curriculum development. This program was grounded in the goal of improving student outcomes and was bolstered by continuous data monitoring. The focus of this multiyear plan was to build capacity to serve students in age-appropriate regular classrooms through a collaborative, coteaching model. To deliver the support necessary for this plan, the central office provided facilitators of professional development activities for school and district staff. Also, for the first time, special education teachers were included in districtwide professional development activities, previously targeted only for general education staff, to build knowledge and skills in the curriculum content areas. Such change emphasized that these were no longer separate units that trained and functioned independently.

## Culture of Change and Improvement

It was also important for district leadership to foster an orientation toward incremental and ongoing change. Efforts in this domain focus on inquiry, goal setting, and accountability. District administration set forth a district vision of inclusive education that was research based and data driven. Individual school leaders were encouraged to strive for improvement on their own site-based goals related to the district vision. The notion of ongoing change and improvement was underscored in the unveiling of the plan introduced with a retrospective video montage of the major milestones in the district's special education program in the preceding 25 years. This presentation emphasized inclusive reform as the next phase of a program long oriented toward improving services for students with disabilities. The goal of the unified professional development plan for general and special education teachers was to promote student achievement through best practice and compliance with state and federal special education statutes. Ongoing professional learning was emphasized, in which critical inquiry, evaluation, and collaboration were central to the district's results-oriented framework of professional development. Student achievement data were continually examined to gauge the effectiveness of these efforts and guide potential revisions to school action plans.

## System Infrastructure and Organizational Support

Organizational support was communicated in a variety of ways. Central office administrators were involved in all aspects of planning and communicated their commitment to collective dialogues and continuous improvement. For example, in having administrators conduct the focus groups mentioned above and meet regularly with the Parent Advisory Council, leaders communicated their commitment to listening to the multiple voices of their stakeholders and their desire to put this input to constructive use. Organizational support was also provided for school-level innovation. When Sue Abplanalp approached central office administrators with her concerns about Lowell, she was not only encouraged to undertake the reform described above, but was provided district personnel and grant support to assist in the process.

As the special education program was transformed, new challenges would emerge. It quickly became apparent, for instance, that school teams needed more assistance in supporting challenging behaviors in general education settings. In response, the district established a positive behavior interventions and support (PBIS) system to provide systemwide services and staff development. Such systemwide support efforts were critical to preventing reversion to past practices.

As more students with disabilities were moved into general education classrooms, building principals requested guidance in instructional planning. Central office staff developed an instructional design tool (see Figure 8.2) to guide the decision-making process for assigning staff and students to specific classrooms. This tool provided a structure for the redistribution of human and material resources in annual scheduling and class assignments. Through the application of this tool, each building was able to ensure that all students with special education needs were assigned to age-appropriate general education classrooms with appropriate supports regardless of their eligibility category or function level.

## LEADERSHIP FOR CHANGE

Systemic change for scalable, sustainable inclusive practice requires flexibility, innovative leadership, and an orientation toward reflection and continuous improvement at all levels of the system (Kozleski & Smith, 2009). In MMSD, inclusive education was and is perceived as a work in progress. Consequently, continuous feedback was critical. Educators and families within the district and school communities were engaged in an ongoing partnership in which accomplishments and concerns were shared. This is essential as leaders cannot force change but must instead provide models and guidance through the process of organizational and individual paradigm shifts required for systemic change (Calabrese, 2003).

Even within a single school system, individual buildings vary substantially from one another by virtue of the diverse participants in each school community and histories of leadership policy and practice. As such, district leadership must be responsive to the unique characteristics and needs of individual school buildings during the reform process, providing different levels of scaffolding as policies and resources are re-examined and shifted. Collaboration and collective expertise are central to inclusive reform as staff must come together to coplan, develop, and evaluate instruction. This occurs through major shifts in assumptions, practice, policy, and use of time and space, the complexity of which is mediated by leadership so that all actors in the school community are heard (Ferguson, Kozleski, & Smith, 2003).

Thus systemic change is a complex process in which top-down policies need to coincide with changes in the knowledge, skills, and commitment among staff and the surrounding school communities in order for changes to be substantive and sustainable. Leaders must be responsive to the cognitive and emotional reactions to change among personnel (Bovey & Hede, 2001). Resistance is to be expected; it is the leadership response to this resistance that will determine whether organizational transformation eventually

FIGURE 8.2. Guiding Principles and Considerations for Instructional Design in Inclusive Settings

GUIDING PRINCIPLES

- Every student has membership in age-appropriate general education classrooms. Students are to be first scheduled in general education classes. Any alternate instructional arrangements (e.g., community-based instruction or small groups for preteaching, reteaching and/or reinforcing) will be developed and scheduled as necessary.
- All students are assigned to classroom sections in heterogeneous groupings based on the available data about each student.
- Each general education classroom should be composed of no more than:
  » 30% of students who receive cross-categorical special education services
  » 60% of students who are English language learners
  » A combined ceiling density of 50% of students who receive cross-categorical special education services and students who are English language learners
- Teachers (general classroom teachers, special education teachers, ESL/bilingual teachers, and Title I teachers) are assigned to Instructional Teams on the basis of shared students, grade levels, or departments in ways that promote team membership, collaboration, communication, and coplanning of curriculum and instruction. Special attention must be given to:
  » Matching teacher skills and interests with students needs and characteristics
  » Grouping compatible adult team members for Instructional Teams
  » Building capacity in all staff members to work with diverse students
  » Instructional Teams are dynamic and may change throughout the year and from year to year in response to (1) students' needs, (2) changes in student population, and (3) changes in staffing.

SPECIAL CONSIDERATIONS FOR STUDENTS WITH DISABILITIES

- Supporting students in the least restrictive environment is a legal entitlement and cannot be based on staff preference or comfort level.
- Special education case management assignments and the corresponding instructional support for students are defined by students' needs as outlined in their IEPs, not disability labels.
- The assignment of students with disabilities to classroom sections results in a balance between the range of students in terms of the intensity of their needs and equitable case management assignments for special education teachers.
- Special education teachers are assigned to students in no more than three classroom sections and move with the students across their instructional settings. Alternate instructional arrangements are counted as one of the settings.

SPECIAL CONSIDERATIONS FOR STUDENTS WITH DISABILITIES WHO ARE ENGLISH LEARNERS

- Each ESL teacher is assigned to no more than 6 classrooms that have clusters of ESL/bilingual students.
- Bilingual Resource Specialists, who provide translation to ESL students and teachers, are assigned to specific grade levels to foster familiarity with the curriculum and strong relationships with their Instructional Teams.

occurs. Both levels of change must be bolstered by appropriate resource allocation and a collaborative sense of agency in order to move forward and foster substantive sustained change. The reform discussed here was driven by systemwide commitment to thoughtful consideration of the needs of all learners, and the balancing of the resultant tensions. Further, district leaders leveraged the expertise and experience of building leaders in successfully fostering inclusive practice to augment district reform efforts, thus ensuring a bidirectional flow of knowledge throughout the school and system change process. Throughout the process through which MMSD instituted inclusive education, there was recognition of this dynamic, bidirectional nature through the actions of school and district leaders. In fostering systemic change, school leaders made strategic choices about levels of change, how to foster collaboration and buy-in, and how to ensure that changes were maintained.

A commitment to equity and improving outcomes for all learners was essential to creating an inclusive system in MMSD. The focus was not just on *change*, but *transformation* of the system. Ensuring access and participation for students with disabilities served as an ethical imperative underpinning transformative leadership at practitioner, school, and district levels and fostered reflective, collaborative professional effort. As Calabrese (2003) noted, this sense of purpose is an important distinction:

> The transactional school administrator has no direction other than to move from point to point; the transforming school administrator has a moral compass and seeks to lift the followers, raise them to higher levels of purpose and achievement. . . . They know when change is necessary to bring benefit to all members of the school community. They are willing to act on their belief that the considered change is the right thing to do. (pp. 8–10)

It is this sense of purpose, this compass, that is essential to navigating the complexity of change and the resistance and other obstacles encountered throughout the process so that inclusive education does not become another failed reform effort.

## REFERENCES

Anyon, J. (1997). *Ghetto schooling: A political economy of urban educational reform*. New York, NY: Teachers College Press.

Artiles, A. J. (2003). Special education's changing identity: Paradoxes and dilemmas in views of culture and space. *Harvard Educational Review, 73*, 164–202.

Artiles, A. J., & Kozleski, E. B. (2007). Beyond convictions: Interrogating culture, history, and power in inclusive education. *Language Arts, 84*, 351–358.

Bennett, T., Deluca, D., & Bruns, D. (1997). Putting inclusion into practice: Perspectives of teachers and parents. *Exceptional Children, 64,* 115–131.

Blackorby, J., Wagner, M., Cameto, R., Davies, E., Levine, P., Newman, L., . . . Sumi, C. (2005) *Engagement, academics, social adjustment, and independence: The achievements of elementary and middle school students with disabilities* (SRI Project P10656). Menlo Park, CA: SRI International. Retrieved from www. seels.net/designdocs/engagement/All_SEELS_outcomes_10-04-05.pdf

Bovey, W. H., & Hede, A. (2001). Resistance to organizational change: The role of cognitive and affective processes. *Leadership & Organization Development Journal, 22,* 372–382.

Calabrese, R. L. (2003). The ethical imperative to lead change: Overcoming the resistance to change. *International Journal of Educational Management, 17,* 7–13.

Connor, D. J., & Ferri, B. A. (2007). The conflict within: Resistance to inclusion and other paradoxes in special education. *Disability & Society, 22,* 63–77.

Ferguson, D. L., Kozleski, E. B., & Smith, A. (2003). Transforming general and special education in urban schools. In F. Obiakor, C. Utley, & A. Rotatori (Eds.), *Advances in Special Education: Vol. 15. Effective education for learners with exceptionalities* (pp. 43–74). London, United Kingdom: JAI Press.

Fryxell, D., & Kennedy, C. (1995). Placement along the continuum of services and its impact on students' social relationships. *Journal of the Association for Persons with Severe Handicaps, 20,* 259–269.

Gibson, D., & Kozleski, E. B. (2011). *2011 Part B annual performance report (APR) analysis: Indicator 5, Part B.* Tempe, AZ: Equity Alliance at ASU.

Individuals With Disabilities Education Act, 20 U.S.C. § 1400 (2004).

Knoster, T., Villa, R., & Thousand, J. (2000). A framework for thinking about systems change. In R. Villa & J. Thousand (Eds.), *Restructuring for caring and effective education: Piecing the puzzle together* (pp. 93–128). Baltimore, MD: Brookes.

Kozleski, E. B., & Smith, A. (2009). The complexities of systems change in creating equity for students with disabilities in urban schools. *Urban Education, 44,* 427–451.

Madison Metropolitan School District. (2011). *Enrollment information* [Enrollment tables]. Retrieved from infosvcweb.madison.k12.wi.us/enroll

Peltier, G. L. (1997). The effect of inclusion on non-disabled children: A review of the research. *Contemporary Education, 68,* 234–239.

Sailor, W., & Roger, B. (2005, March). Rethinking inclusion: Schoolwide applications. *Phi Delta Kappan, 86*(7), 503–509.

Shanklin, N., Kozleski, E. B., Meagher, C., Sands, D., Joseph, O., & Wyman, W. (2003). Examining renewal in an urban high school through the lens of systemic change. *International Journal of School Leadership and Management, 231,* 357–378.

Starr, K. (2011). The principles and politics of resistance to change. *Educational Administration & Leadership, 39,* 646–660.

Staub, D., & Peck, C. A. (1995).What are the outcomes for non-disabled students? *Educational Leadership, 52,* 36–40.

Strebel, P. (2006). *Why do employees resist change?* Boston, MA: Harvard Business School Press.

Sullivan, A. L., Kozleski, E. B., & Waitoller, F. (2008). *State profile of efforts to create culturally responsive educational systems: Wisconsin.* Tempe, AZ: National Center for Culturally Responsive Educational Systems. Retrieved from http://ea.niusileadscape.org/docs/FINAL_PRODUCTS/LearningCarousel/WisconsinProfile.pdf

United States Department of Education. (2011). *30th annual report to Congress on the implementation of the Individuals with Disabilities Education Act, 2008.* Washington, DC: Office of Special Education and Rehabilitative Services, Office of Special Education Programs.

Wagner, M., Blackorby, J., Cameto, R., Hebbler, K., & Newman, L. (1993). *The transition experiences of young people with disabilities: A summary of findings from the national longitudinal transition study of special education students.* Menlo Park, CA: SRI International.

Wisconsin Department of Administration. (2010). *Demographic Services Center's 2010 final estimates summary.* Madison, WI: Division of Intergovernmental Relations. Retrieved from www.doa.state.wi.us/docview.asp?locid=9&docid=7269

Wisconsin Department of Public Instruction. (2011). *WINSS data analysis.* Retrieved from data.dpi.state.wi.us/Data/GroupEnroll.aspx?OrgLevel=di&GraphFile=GROUPS&S4orALL=1&SRegion=1&SCounty=47&SAthleticConf=45&Qquad=demographics.aspx&Show=COMM&RevExp=4&Group=AllStudentsFAY&FULLKEY=05368903%60%60%60%60&DN=Montello&SN=None+Chosen

# PART V

# INTERSECTIONS OF MACRO, MESO, AND LOCAL POLICIES FOR URBAN REFORM

# CHAPTER 9

# Educational Systems Change at the State Level

*Donna Hart-Tervalon and David R. Garcia*

## PROLOGUE

I was working in my office at the Wisconsin Department of Public Instruction in the summer of 2006 when I received a call from a special education director of a Wisconsin school district. He called to share with me the major changes occurring in the district due in part to the assistance they had received from our Disproportionality Workgroup. He said that district staff were beginning to initiate candid conversations about the relationship between race and the disproportionate representation of students of color in special education. To me, this simple phone call was an affirmation of our extensive efforts to support and encourage frank conversations about the relationship between race and the disproportionate representation of students of color in special education.

—Donna Hart-Tervalon

This chapter chronicles how a State Education Agency (SEA) facilitated systemic change to address disproportionality issues statewide. We examine the collaboration among Wisconsin's 462 school districts, including a number of urban school districts that presented a particular constellation of issues, and the Wisconsin Disproportionality Workgroup, an ad-hoc collection of state-level consultants and administrators from the Wisconsin Department of Public Instruction (WDPI) with common expertise in special education. The Wisconsin example is a case where an SEA spearheaded a statewide initiative to address racial disproportionality in special education in multiple ways. This work offers important lessons for practitioners, policymakers, families, advocates, and researchers that illustrate how to navigate the complex relationships between the interconnected levels of the educational system.

The Wisconsin workgroup created a nurturing environment where local officials could openly address the relationship between disproportionality and racial inequalities and explore the ways in which institutionalized practices contributed to troubling outcomes for some students. This work highlighted the integral role in facilitating systemic change that is the particular responsibility and purview of SEAs. Within the Systemic Change Framework (see Chapter 1 of this book; Kozleski & Smith, 2009), the SEA addresses several key arenas of policy and practice within the SEA itself (i.e., horizontally), as well as facilitating changes in district policy and practice (i.e., vertical reform) through the distribution of resources, technical assistance, and professional learning intended to inform and influence district reform. Also, the SEA interprets and appropriates federal level reform efforts, acting as a filter between macrolevel policy shifts and localized interpretations of such shifts.

The chapter contributes to the discussion of education reform by considering the ways in which SEAs can serve as transformative change agents. This is an important contribution to deep change work in which all levels of the educational system fuel the transformational process. It provides a counterexample to cases within the urban reform literature in which the SEAs' role is either not considered or, as agents of the state, they are regarded as an obstacle to local reforms (Maxcy, 2009). The role of SEAs, referred to as state departments of education in some states, is of interest in the study of urban education reform because SEAs present a paradox; they are both powerful and peripheral in their role and influence in local reform efforts. As powerful organizations, SEAs "control substantial resources, regulate schools' adherence to laws, and are dominant within the hierarchy of K–12 education" (Hamann & Lane, 2004, p. 429). Furthermore, the No Child Left Behind Act (NCLB) expanded SEAs' responsibilities by placing them in a pivotal position to implement federal education reforms (Sunderman & Orfield, 2006). SEAs face an authoritative paradox, however, because they do not have direct control at the local level. They must traverse a contradictory organizational balance among enforcement, leniency, flexibility, and scope of influence to encourage and support local reform efforts.

## CONCEPTUAL FRAMEWORK: THE ROLE AND POSITIONING OF SEAS IN EDUCATIONAL REFORM

From a systemic standpoint, SEAs are positioned between the state legislative bodies and local school districts in the public education system. While state policymakers, legislators, and/or state boards of education charge SEAs with interpreting and administering legislative mandates, SEAs have little direct authority over school districts and only mediated authority over individual schools where reform efforts must ultimately produce results. SEAs do not control schools directly and never influence schools without the intervening filter of district administrators. Successful education reform, however, requires behavioral changes at the school level. Yet teachers and school staff are employees of the district, meaning that those ultimately responsible for improving student academic achievement respond to SEA initiatives according to the manner in which those initiatives have been interpreted by their respective district. For SEAs, "The problem presented by complex school reform, then, is the problem of how the SEA can bring about specified changes in the practice of a large number of practitioners over whom it has little, if any, direct control and to whom it has no proximity" (Lusi, 1997, p. 10).

To negotiate the complicated organizational structure of public education systems, effective SEAs share five common characteristics. First, the agency takes on substantive work that is characterized as knowledge centered and uncertain. Second, the agency builds capacity to focus on outcomes rather than processes. Third, the agency creates organizational flexibility by developing structures "that are more team oriented and less hierarchical" (Lusi, 1997, p. 17). Fourth, the agency moves away from compliance to focus on building capacity at the local level. Fifth, the agency relies upon external collaborations for support. These characteristics help SEAs tailor their approach to encourage early adopters (those districts that engage with the state early), push the status quo cases (those that comply but do not lead), and support the troubled cases (districts that either are resistant or lack the capacity to implement new initiatives) (Lusi, 1997).

The Systemic Change Framework's (SCF's) broad and interactive view of education reform is a useful tool for understanding how changes at one level of the system affect other levels (Kozleski & Smith, 2009). As applied to the state level, the SCF illuminates the SEA's dynamic position in the complex and interconnected public education system and how state-level policies influence strategic decisions at the district level and policy implementation at the school level. In the Wisconsin case, the SCF allows for exploration of the engagement between SEAs and school districts with careful attention to how successful collaborations between SEAs, districts, and schools require SEAs to navigate the political and organizational dynamics that complicate policy implementation across the structural layers of the public education system.

Careful attention to organizational dynamics across the interconnected levels of the public education system is particularly crucial to systemic reform efforts because districts are not passive agents in the implementation of education policies. Rather, districts are independent organizations that play a critical role in how policies are implemented at the school level (Kirp & Driver, 1995; Sipple, Killeen, & Monk, 2004; Spillane, 2004). In particular, district administrators use whatever latitude afforded them to reformulate policies in the course of implementation to serve the best interest of their local communities. Districts take a "pro-active approach to policymaking, defining policy problems and developing their own instructional policies" (Spillane, 1996, p. 65). Thus districts may pursue local polices that undermine SEA initiatives. District size, local politics, historical relationships within districts and between districts and their SEA all conspire to create opportunities or barriers to forging powerful change initiatives. Urban school districts deal with a particular constellation of issues that can sometimes overshadow a productive relationship with their SEAs. To further obscure policy implementation, there may be interdistrict variability in how policies are interpreted; meaning different administrators in the same district may interpret the same policy differently (Spillane, 1998). In the next section, we explore how these complexities played out in Wisconsin's efforts to eliminate disproportionality.

## THE FOCUS OF REFORM IN THE WISCONSIN CASE: ELIMINATE DISPROPORTIONALITY

Disproportionality includes both the overrepresentation of minority students in special education and the underrepresentation of minority students in gifted and talented education relative to the proportion of minority students in the overall student population (Artiles & Trent, 1994). Disproportionality is commonly linked to special education, but the problem actually originates in general education when some general educators initiate the special education referral process inappropriately and unwittingly contribute to the disproportionality of minority students in special education (National Education Association, 2007).

The overrepresentation of racially, culturally, and linguistically diverse students in special education has been documented for more than 40 years (Klingner et al., 2005). Since the late 1960s, national surveys by the Office for Civil Rights (OCR) of the U.S. Department of Education (USDOE) have revealed persistent overrepresentation of minority children in certain disability categories (National Research Council, 2002). Several other studies have documented that a child's race and ethnicity are significantly related to the probability that he or she will be inappropriately identified as disabled (Losen & Orfield, 2002; National Research Council, 2002). For decades, African American students have been overrepresented in special education categories, particularly in the categories of cognitive disability and emotional behavioral disability (Artiles, Trent, & Palmer, 2004; Gamm, 2007). American Indian/Alaska Native children have also been overrepresented and are more likely to receive special education services than are the general population (U.S. Department of Education, 2006). In response, the USDOE has issued requirements for all states to examine, monitor, and prevent the inappropriate identification of students for special education (IDEA Partnership, 2007).

There are many deleterious effects associated with the inappropriate identification of students for special education. Once identified, these students tend to remain in special education and often follow a less rigorous curriculum than their general education peers (Klingner et al., 2005). Their teachers often have lower expectations, resulting in fewer academic and postsecondary opportunities (Harry & Klingner, 2006). Finally, disproportionality contributes to racial separation (Losen & Orfield, 2002) where resource rooms and separate school facilities are overpopulated by students of color (Grossman, 1995; Harry, 1992).

Some argue that disproportionality continues to persist because it is a structural problem (Harry & Klingner, 2006) where the presence is so pervasive that it becomes imperceptible in the working lives of many educators (Tatum, 1992). Educators often fail to acknowledge biases in the student identification process and, without awareness of the problems that disproportionality presents, they may even deny that they contribute to disproportionality (Artiles, Kozleski, Trent, Osher, & Ortiz, 2010). Yet these biases remain a key underlying issue that needs to be addressed in order to reverse the impact of disproportionality. In urban school settings many students of color are not only having limited success in general education but are often at greater risk of being misdiagnosed and inappropriately placed in special education programs contributing significantly to disproportionality. "The struggles over special education and achievement in urban school districts are only symptoms of a larger problem with urban districts: the unfinished dream of integration" (Blanchett, Mumford, & Beachum, 2005).

Wisconsin's data are similar to national trends with regard to the disproportionate representation of African American and American Indian students. In this chapter we use a risk ratio calculation to examine the degree to which disproportionality of children who are culturally and linguistically diverse exists in the identification of students for special education. The risk ratio, when applied to a disability category, is the risk of a specific racial/ethnic group for receiving special education and related services for a particular disability as compared with the risk for all other racial/ethnic groups of students combined (Thorius & Stephenson, 2012). In the 2007–2008 school year in Wisconsin, African American students were disproportionately overrepresented in multiple special education categories with the most significant overrepresentation in the categories of Other Health Impairment (risk ratio = 3.55) and Cognitive Disability (risk ratio = 2.38). Also, American Indian students in Wisconsin were overrepresented in multiple categories with the most significant disproportionality in the category of Emotional

Behavioral Disabilities (risk ratio = 3.13) (Wisconsin Department of Public Instruction, 2008b).

Exploration of the underlying dynamics that shape disproportionality within Wisconsin's urban districts revealed a common pattern that starts with inaccurate referrals by some general education teachers who have limited experience teaching or interacting with diverse student populations and who may lack sufficient cultural competency to address the needs of students who are racially, culturally, ethnically, and linguistically diverse. These referrals are often followed by evaluations conducted by assessment staff using tools and practices that are not culturally responsive and could result in the inappropriate identification and placement of a disproportionate number of students who are culturally and linguistically diverse in special education programs (Artiles, Rueda, Salazar, & Higareda, 2005).

With guidance from the Wisconsin Disproportionality Workgroup, one Wisconsin urban district in particular identified the existence of a persistent pattern of bias in their prereferral and identification practices and chose to address disproportionality in special education by focusing on the prereferral process. The prereferral process is a legal requirement to implement and document the accommodations and/or modifications made within the general education program to meet a student's educational needs. Only after these strategies have been considered, documented, and implemented as appropriate, can a student be referred for special education placement (Artiles et al., 2005). Addressing prereferral collaboratively presented a perfect opportunity for the statewide workgroup to mediate connections between research and local practice. By establishing a partnership with this district, the WDPI was able to address a need identified by an urban school district that had far-reaching implications and was a common concern shared by many districts statewide.

WDPI collaborated and supported this project by providing resources and technical assistance in the form of grant funding and the extensive involvement of a consultant from the workgroup. Collaboratively, the Madison Metropolitan School District, WDPI, and researchers from the University of Wisconsin–Oshkosh developed a checklist in 2007 entitled *Culturally Responsive Practices in Schools* to address disproportionality. The checklist (1) guides schools in eliminating the misidentification of RCELD students (racially, culturally, ethnically, and linguistically diverse), in special education and (2) ensures that only students with disabilities (an impairment[s] and a need for special education) are placed into special education programs based upon a comprehensive evaluation process and application of existing eligibility criteria. By building on work with one district, the SEA was able to encourage change in other districts. This shared work helped the statewide workgroup achieve many of its goals around eliminating disproportionality. Perhaps more importantly, the power of developing and sharing transformational tools in partnership with local districts became a mainstream SEA practice.

## SYSTEMIC CHANGE FRAMEWORK (SCF) AT THE STATE LEVEL: LESSONS LEARNED IN WISCONSIN

Chapter 1 outlines the major components of the Systemic Change Framework including the elements of the state level: (1) culture of renewal and improvement; (2) inclusive leadership for equity and accountability; (3) system infrastructure and organizational support; (4) state/community connections and partnerships; (5) inquiry on equity in schooling; and (6) equitable resources development and distribution. In Wisconsin these elements played out in particular ways. In this section we explore how the work of the statewide disproportionality team helped us deepen and expand the state level of the SCF.

### Culture of Renewal and Improvement (Alignment with State Vision)

State administrators can support local change efforts by aligning their work with the broader trends that drive educational policy. This alignment is most productive if state administrators are proactive and make connections as early as possible (Kozleski & Huber, 2012). In the Wisconsin case, the WDPI Disproportionality Workgroup was formed in the 2002–2003 school year right after the passage of No Child Left Behind, without the impetus of legislative action or other agency mandates, and well before federal mandates in later years would require sweeping changes to the administration of special education programs. The initial efforts were sparked by SEA administrators who had taken notice that both the U.S. Department of Education's Office of Special Education Programs (OSEP) and NCLB emphasized the use of data disaggregated by racial categories and that disaggregated data would play a central role in future policies. The workgroup began disaggregating data and developing an action plan to address disproportionality issues before federal mandates required the WDPI to take such action. By linking their efforts to the early adoption of data analysis practices, the workgroup placed itself in a proactive position relative to its constituent districts and seeded several activities early that have served the workgroup and its constituent districts well.

The workgroup also strategically aligned its efforts with federal laws, the state's improvement plan and grant, as well as the New Wisconsin Promise (NWP), the state's promise of a quality education for every child. The alignment to NWP was particularly crucial as it was developed by the state's education superintendent and represented WDPI's commitment to ensuring a quality education for every child. The WDPI also identified guiding prin-ciples for all of the SEA's efforts. In particular, the workgroup's goals and activities were aligned with the NWP's sixth principle, to "Provide effective pupil services, special education, and prevention programs to support learn-ing and development for all students while preventing and reducing barriers to student success" (Wisconsin Department of Public Instruction, 2008a). This alignment helps facilitate continued support from the state superinten-dent and cabinet.

The early start and connection to broader policy trends created several areas of traction that moved the reform agenda forward. The workgroup members had the time to carefully reflect on issues of race and equity as they related to disproportionality, and they enhanced their perspectives on disproportionality with the support of external consultants. They also had a chance to strategize how their efforts could best fit with future policies. The workgroup accomplished these important foundational objectives be-fore taking their work to their constituent districts. The workgroup's early start contrasts with a far more common scenario in education reform where education administrators are forced to "build the plane as they fly it." In a reactive mode, policies are implemented before there is a chance to properly consider the future implications of current actions. This approach creates ambiguity for local school districts and decreases the likelihood that state directives will be implemented beyond superficial compliance.

The workgroup worked within the state agency for first three years before establishing an external partnership with the National Center for Culturally Responsive Educational Systems (NCCRESt). During this time the workgroup also developed and presented its first Summer Institute, a statewide training and professional development opportunity for urban Wisconsin school districts. Over the years, the Summer Institutes would play a critical role in developing and maintaining collaborative relation-ships with urban and rural local school districts. The first Summer Institute, held in August 2005 and entitled "Addressing Disproportionality," included district-level teams from nine of the larger urban districts and represen-tatives from each of the state's cooperative educational service agencies (CESA). District teams were provided technical assistance to review their own disproportionality data, where many administrators were exposed for the first time to the disproportionality rates in their district disaggregated by special education category and race.

The workgroup's goal for the first Summer Institute was to foster the involvement of the early adopter districts that were willing to undertake the additional efforts to go above and beyond the state requirements. This proactive approach served to engage and support districts without the nega-tive perceptions often associated with SEA and district interactions. As with other SEA efforts, the challenge for the disproportionality workgroup was that districts are only willing to accept such a role when they perceive that their involvement meets local interests and they have the capacity to carry out the required tasks (Firestone, 1989). The workgroup's careful attention to align its activities with current state and federal directives along with maintaining consistency between workgroup activities and the policy and legal requirements that would arise in later years rewarded the participation of the early adopter districts while serving as an incentive for status quo districts to accept a more active role. Thus the early adopter districts found the workgroup's proactive efforts as not only credible but worthwhile. As a reward for participating, the early adopter districts then found themselves ahead of the game rather than forced to start from scratch to meet the federal mandates.

## Inclusive Leadership for Equity and Accountability (Supportive Leadership)

The impetus for change can generate from anywhere in an educational organization and many transformative initiatives begin at the bottom and percolate upwards (Fullan, 2003). In these cases, supportive leadership is vital to the survival of these efforts. In Wisconsin the workgroup had the advantage of a supportive administrative leadership team from the beginning. Most of the projects, initiatives, and activities that the workgroup successfully implemented would not have been possible without the support of the SEA leadership. This is especially true in the Wisconsin case because addressing disproportionality can lead to divisive discussions about race and institutionalized racism.

In order to focus improvement efforts on race and equity in a systemic way, the workgroup required the districts identified as having significant disproportionality rates to engage in a minimum number of culturally responsive professional development opportunities. Districts could participate in a number of options for professional learning to build their organizational capacity to acknowledge the role of culture and race in how individuals and systems designed their policies and implemented practices. Of the many types of professional development opportunities, the seminars based on the book *Courageous Conversations About Race* (Singleton & Linton, 2006) were particularly noteworthy because of their explicit focus on race as a correlate to student achievement. The open discussions that developed about the relationship between disproportionality and race would not have been possible without the data analysis that helped focus the district staff on the ways in which racial disproportionality was an unexamined part of their institutional practices.

Race is an inflammatory topic that is often avoided by public officials. Thus, as employees of a state agency, the workgroup members could not have initiated their bold response to disproportionality without the support of a visionary leadership group. On agency leadership, Lusi (1997) differentiates between directors that assume "responsibility for creating the vision and coherence for state reform efforts" and those that "manage implementation" in an effort to remain true to policy designs (p. 156). The former are transformative leaders with the courage to tackle tough issues and the tolerance to take risks.

As part of an interconnected, multilevel system, the workgroup also served in a leadership capacity relative to its constituent districts. The workgroup learned from prior, unsuccessful state-level initiatives that districts had perceived them as another directive handed down by the SEA. The workgroup was careful to maneuver in ways that supported rather than superseded local efforts. The workgroup chose to follow a path that emphasized information, engagement, and support.

This cooperative spirit was behind the workgroup's initial efforts during the Summer Institute when district participation was voluntary. The workgroup supported the "early adopter" districts by choosing policies that continued to move these districts forward so they would continue to be allies in SEA efforts. Sweeping changes in IDEA in 2004 required all states to develop a process and criteria for identifying significant disproportionality. The workgroup was able to implement federal requirements with minimal pushback from districts while sustaining the positive stance created during the first Summer Institute

To implement federal mandates, the WDPI was required to identify those districts with significant disproportionality issues based on criteria that was established by WDPI in collaboration with its external consultants. Districts were identified as having significant disproportionality if the special education identification and placement rates for students of a particular racial or ethnic group were considerably higher than the identification and placement rates for White students. Based on these criteria, 25 districts were identified and required to attend the second Summer Institute where data profiles for each district were developed and presented to district teams.

The WDPI required the identified districts to participate in subsequent Summer Institutes. When SEA officials notified districts that they had been identified as in need of improvement, they expected considerable pushback. Instead, most district special education directors anticipated being on the list and were already reviewing their risk ratio data, identifying their technical assistance needs, and planning to attend the next Summer Institute. This type of positive response was the norm rather than the exception.

Despite the top-down mandate, many school district officials participated in the Summer Institutes with an unexpected spirit of collaboration, and the early adopter districts were integral in forming collaborative relationships with the newly identified districts. Based on their work in the first Summer Institute, the early adopter districts were aware of the coming federal mandates and trained in the analysis of disaggregated data. Their voluntary involvement with the workgroup the previous year had paid off because the new federal mandates did not derail their local efforts. The Summer Institutes allowed WDPI to deliver targeted technical assistance to identified districts while encouraging all districts, especially urban districts, to engage in professional development activities and proactive culturally responsive initiatives in collaboration with the WDPI.

The workgroup's approach runs counter to the command and control strategies that SEAs often use to implement accountability policies, strategies that rely almost exclusively on mandates and sanctions as the primary motivator to drive local reform efforts. The workgroup chose a collaborative stance because more heavy-handed approaches by the state could result in major resistance at the district level and even overt attempts to undermine SEA initiatives. It is essential for SEAs to strike a balance between enforcing legal requirements while at the same time supporting district-led improvement efforts and initiatives. Building relationships by partnering and collaborating with districts on both fronts is how the workgroup was able to successfully accomplish both objectives.

## System Infrastructure and Organizational Support (Cross-Discipline Teams)

SEAs and districts are examples of fragmented centralization (Meyer & Scott, 1983) where funding of individual programs leads to the creation of complex and segmented organizational arrangements. Segmentalism assumes that "problems can be solved when they are carved into pieces and pieces given to specialists who work in isolation" (Kanter, 1983, p. 28). SEAs are organized by specializations that are institutionalized as separate divisions within the agency. These divisions can become entrenched into silos that can operate with little to no meaningful interaction with each other. If left unchecked, this silo structure can result in duplication of effort or issues may receive no attention as they fall between the organizational cracks.

The SCF encourages districts to move toward multidisciplinary teams that address student needs collaboratively. This advice is equally applicable at the state level. By design, the workgroup, along with a broader advisory group that represented all five divisions of the WDPI, all of whom coalesced around the ambitious idea of taking concrete action to address the longstanding issue of disproportionality in school districts statewide. The multiple perspectives and diverse thinking of the workgroup members has allowed the workgroup to examine issues and propose improvement plans that leverage cross-team collaboration for successful implementation.

The workgroup carried its multidisciplinary spirit to the district level. The districts participating in the Summer Institutes were required, at a minimum, to attend the Summer Institutes with a core team consisting of three members (the director of Special Education, director of Curriculum and Instruction, and a school psychologist). Often, in addition to the three required participants, most districts opted to expand their teams and include other members that they identified as playing key roles across the entire district organization in implementing and sustaining their improvement efforts. Many district teams included an average of 6 members but some teams consisted of up to 10 members.

The workgroup, however, has faced an ongoing challenge to sustain the involvement and commitment of ad-hoc workgroup members over time, particularly as the entire SEA has been challenged to meet the NCLB requirements. While the workgroup remains a priority, there are limitations on the part of individuals to commit to collaborations outside of their immediate team/division responsibilities. SEA-level cross-team/cross-division collaborations require support and approval from various administrators who must consider the capacity of individual staff members to fulfill their primary job responsibilities while balancing the need to support cross-team/cross-division collaborations and individual preferences. This tension poses a constant dilemma and requires ongoing communication and flexibility from all involved. The workgroup has addressed this challenge by involving ad-hoc members only to the extent that they are able to commit and only with the approval of their supervisors. Flexibility and positive working relationships have been essential to sustaining cross-team/cross-division collaborations over time.

## State/Community Connections and Partnerships (External Expertise)

Like many state agencies, SEAs operate on limited budgets that increase and decrease in rhythm with state coffers. Often, the expert personnel necessary to accomplish systemic change are not housed within state agencies. State administrators must look outside the agency to the aid of external experts to build capacity and expand the organizational knowledge base. For the workgroup, the enlistment of external experts provided a means to better understand the issues related to disproportionality and brought credibility to the workgroup's agenda. Despite its best efforts, the workgroup would likely have failed without the assistance and guidance of external experts. External partnerships catapulted the workgroup's efforts by forging a path to resources and generating key research.

External expertise in the form of technical assistance from the National Center for Special Education Accountability Monitoring (NCSEAM), the ACCESS Center, and the North Central Regional Resource Center (NCRRC), as well as data analysis and consultation provided by one consultant in particular, Dan Losen, were critical to expanding the capabilities of the SEA. The workgroup entrusted its external experts to represent the agency by asking them to work directly with their school districts, despite the possibility that districts may regard the external experts as outsiders sent to point out faults. In the Wisconsin case, the school districts did not value Losen's contributions until they came to appreciate how the disaggregated data allowed them to understand disproportionality from new vantage points. Losen prepared detailed data profiles that provided not only an overall analysis of the data but a detailed contextual analysis for each district that was enlightening and undeniable. In addition, he skillfully facilitated key discussions and gave the workgroup members, administrators, and district teams a common language and the tools necessary to understand and communicate the implications of the disaggregated data. This approach to understanding also connects with another aspect of the SCF: Inquiry on Equity in Schooling.

There are threats to involving external experts in state agency affairs and, despite the commonsense advice to take advantage of outside expertise, these threats may dissuade some agencies from seeking assistance. First, when seeking external assistance, agencies are placed in a vulnerable position where they must acknowledge their lack of expertise and/ or concede the existence of internal problems. The expert must practice discretion in order to not discredit the agency publicly. Second, the agency and its experts must set boundaries and respect each other's perspectives. For a number of budgetary, logistical, and political reasons, the agency will likely not act on the totality of the expert's advice, and the expert should be considerate of the agency's limitations. These dilemmas are not unlike the experiences of researchers and consultants who find their expertise needed by insider groups.

### Inquiry on Equity in Schooling (Data to Action)

The use of student assessment results in data-driven decision making is a central feature of NCLB. Now, all states have large-scale student assessment data. And, in some cases, states have either constructed or are constructing sophisticated data warehouses that permit stakeholders to query the data in ways that were previously impossible. Data alone, however, are insufficient to influence organizational culture. The Wisconsin case study highlights key requisites for the effective transformation of data into action. State administrators must face tough questions, such as How does one convince districts that they must acknowledge and own their data? How does one convey to districts that a no-excuses approach is the most effective strategy for addressing equity issues?

Due to NCLB, disaggregating data by student subgroups has become common practice in American public schools. The intended purpose of examining data in such detail is to highlight gaps between student subgroups that are masked when analyzing school or district data as a whole. As a fundamental principle, data disaggregated by student subgroup is critical to any effort to address racial inequality. It can keep equity at the core of all transformative agendas. However, interpreting data disaggregated by racial/ethnic group can be conducted absent of any meaningful conversation about the antecedents of racial inequality. For example, much of the NCLB public use literature describes racial categories using the generic term "group." Yet it is the social artifacts of race and equity, not merely membership in a group by itself, that are the roots of the academic achievement gaps between minority and majority students. Thus becoming familiar with the data gaps doesn't necessarily lead educators to examine the structural and institutionalized roots of achievement gaps. And, without careful mediated discourse, data interpretation can become an opportunity to blame students and families.

The subject of how to bridge the disaggregated data analysis with policies and practices that address racial group inequalities, however, has received considerably less attention. Once Wisconsin school districts became familiar with examining data disaggregated by racial subgroup, the workgroup began to expand the discussion about more general issues of race and equity to address the more difficult task of convincing district teams and administrators that some of their practices may actually contribute to racial inequalities. The workgroup took every available opportunity to highlight the implications of racial group identity. In Wisconsin, it started as a whisper, but after the presentation of disaggregated data and related discussions, the attendees could at least say the word *race* without fear of retribution. Over time, the discussion became more direct and attendees began to discuss racial implications more openly and to consider that much of the inappropriate identification and placement of students into the more subjective special education categories may be related to race.

## Equitable Resources Development and Distribution (Resource Acquisition)

Wisconsin was one of the first states to allocate funds specifically for addressing issues of disproportionality in special education. Within the SEA, the allocation of resources to the workgroup's efforts also sent an important message about the importance of their work. Funding is the manifestation of agency priorities; those programs that matter receive funding. For the workgroup, the resource flexibility was a sign that the agency leadership valued its vision enough to provide a tangible commitment to its success.

There are potential drawbacks to resource allocation decisions. For example, those units that are not funded may feel threatened and perceive that they are not valued by the agency leadership. These units may find submissive ways to either impede or undermine the efforts of those they view as the present-day favorites within the agency. In most cases, state employees transcend leadership regimes and these units may wait out the current leadership regime for the chance to make their case anew when another administration arrives. Thus agency leadership should make decisions to allow for their initiatives to sustain over time. Funding should follow priorities, not people. A dynamic few may lead new initiatives but organizational decisions should encourage the sustainability of their key efforts once they leave the agency.

## CONCLUSION

The true measure of success for any major initiative is evidence of change. WDPI officials point to several milestones as a result of the workgroup's efforts. For example, when the workgroup began in 2002, the workgroup was unable to overtly include race or racism on agendas or in discussions without attracting criticism from those who did not believe race was at issue. Now, the SEA includes race and racism on most agendas and in all funding requests with the full support of the Wisconsin state superintendent and his cabinet members. In addition, when the workgroup began, disproportionality was regarded as a special education problem and the agency response was led solely by the special education team. This is no longer the case. Now, the SEA addresses disproportionality as a shared general education and special educational issue. There are cross-team/cross-division workgroups and initiatives focused on closing the achievement gap through coordinated improvement planning initiatives that extend beyond special education.

There is more work to be done to address disproportionality issues for students of color in Wisconsin. Many political issues and challenges must still be addressed and overcome if Wisconsin schools are to improve so all children are able to achieve to their full potential. The workgroup is not disheartened by these hard realities, however, because it knows how far it has come and believes that the best course of action is to continue to support courageous conversations. The workgroup is encouraged that state and district-level teams are having conversations about the importance of race and racism. These organizations have come to realize the inadequacy of analyzing disaggregated data without addressing race, racial inequity, unconscious bias, and racism. The challenging nature of these conversations is no longer viewed as a deterrent, but as a priority.

Those seeking to embark on similarly ambitious reforms at the state level should view this chapter as a roadmap to facilitating dynamic, multilevel systemic change. The workgroup's success in supporting districts with analyzing data, identifying, and implementing interventions to address disproportionality in both urban and rural districts is connected to the elements of the SCF and previous research on SEAs. The challenges and lessons learned by the workgroup's case study are applicable to other states and state-directed initiatives. The first step toward addressing educational inequalities, however, is not scripted. Taking this first step requires the unwavering belief that with a group of committed people anything is possible.

## EPILOGUE

I believe effecting change requires moving beyond our preconceived notions of barriers that may or may not exist. We need to plant seeds without the comfort of knowing whether or not the ground is fertile. First and foremost, I believe those seeking to influence change must be fearless. This is a lesson I've learned over many years as an educator with a passion for addressing issues that impact students of color. I used to believe that systemic change could only occur at the right time with the right players and with the finish line in sight. I no longer hold this belief. The workgroup is an example of systemic change that happened gradually and strategically over time as a result of the commitment of our state agency, that is, individuals within our agency, to stay the course and make it happen. I now realize that true change occurs in baby steps accompanied by occasional fearless leaps of faith.

—Donna Hart-Tervalon

## REFERENCES

Artiles, A. J., Kozleski, E. B., Trent, S., Osher, D., & Ortiz, A. (2010). Justifying and explaining disproportionality, 1968–2008: A critique of underlying views of culture. *Exceptional Children, 76,* 279–299.

Artiles, A. J., Rueda, R., Salazar, J. J., & Higareda, I. (2005). Minority disproportionate representation: English language learners in urban school districts. *Exceptional Children, 71,* 283–300.

Artiles, A. J., & Trent, S. (1994). Overrepresentation of minority students in special education: A continuing debate. *Journal of Special Education, 27,* 410–437.

Artiles, A. J., Trent, S. C., & Palmer, J. D. (2004). Culturally diverse students in special education: Legacies and prospects. In J. A. Banks & C.A.M. Banks (Eds.), *Handbook of research on multicultural education* (2nd ed.). San Francisco, CA: Jossey-Bass.

Blanchett, W. J., Mumford, V., & Beachum, F. (2005). Urban school failure and disproportionality in a post-Brown era: Benign neglect of the constitutional rights of students of color. *Remedial and Special Education, 26*(2), 70–81.

Firestone, W. A. (1989). Using reform: Conceptualizing district initiative. *Educational Evaluation and Policy Analysis, 11*, 151–164.

Fullan, M. (2003). *The moral imperative of school leadership.* Thousand Oaks, CA: Corwin Press.

Gamm, S. (2007). *Disproportionality in special education: Identifying where and why overidentification of minority student occurs.* Bethesda, MD: LRP Publications.

Grossman, H. (1995). *Special education in a diverse society.* Needham Heights, MA: Allyn & Bacon.

Hamann, E. T., & Lane, B. (2004). The roles of state departments of education as policy intermediaries: Two cases. *Educational Policy, 18*, 426–455.

Harry, B. (1992). *Cultural diversity, families and the special education system: Communication and empowerment.* New York, NY: Teachers College Press.

Harry, B., & Klingner, J. (2006). *Why are so many minority students in special education? Understanding race and disability in schools.* New York, NY: Teachers College Press.

IDEA Partnership. (2007). *Dialogue guides for IDEA 2004 Regulations, OSEP Topic Brief.* Retrieved from www.ideapartnership.org/using-tools/topic-briefs/regulatory-provisions/1674-disproportionality-and-overidentification19.html

Kanter, R. (1983). *The change masters.* New York, NY: Simon & Schuster.

Kirp, D. L., & Driver, C. E. (1995). The aspirations of systemic reform meet the realities of localism. *Educational Administration Quarterly, 31*(4), 589–612.

Klingner, J., Artiles, A. J., Kozleski, E. B., Utley, C., Zion, S., Tate, W., . . . Riley, D. (2005). Conceptual framework for addressing the disproportionate representation of culturally and linguistically diverse students in special education. *Educational Policy Analysis Archives, 13*(38), Retrieved from epaa.asu.edu/epaa/v13n38/

Kozleski, E. B., & Huber, J. J. (2012). System-wide leadership for culturally responsive education. In J. Crockett, B. Billingsley, & M. L. Boscardin (Eds.), *Handbook of leadership and administration for special education.* London, United Kingdom: Routledge.

Kozleski, E. B., & Smith, A. (2009). The role of policy and systems change in creating equity for students with disabilities in urban schools. *Urban Education, 44*, 427–451.

Losen, D. J., & Orfield, G. (Eds.). (2002). *Racial inequity in special education.* Boston, MA: Harvard Education Press.

Lusi, S. F. (1997). *The role of state departments of education in complex school reform.* New York, NY: Teachers College Press.

Madison (WI) Metropolitan School District, University of Wisconsin-Oshkosh, & the Wisconsin Department of Public Instruction. (2007). *Culturally responsive practices in schools. The checklist to address disproportionality.* Retrieved from www.uwosh.edu/faculty_staff/chiang/disp-cadse-cklst.doc

Maxcy, B. (2009). New public management and district reform: Managerialism and deflection of local leadership in a Texas school district. *Urban Education, 44*(5), 489–521.

Meyer, J., & Scott, W. (with Rowan, B., & Deal, T.). (1983). *Organizational environments: Ritual and rationality.* Beverly Hills, CA: Sage.

National Education Association. (2007). *Truth in labeling: Disproportionality in special education* (Item No. 2040-5-00-C4, 2007). Washington, DC: Author.

National Research Council. (2002). *Minority students in special and gifted education.* Washington, DC: National Academy Press.

Singleton, G. E., & Linton, C. (2006). *Courageous conversations about race: A field guide for achieving equity in schools.* Thousand Oaks, CA: Corwin Press.

Sipple, J. W., Killeen, K., & Monk, D. H. (2004). Adoption and adaptation: School district responses to state imposed learning and graduation requirements. *Educational Evaluation and Policy Analysis, 26*(2), 143–168.

Spillane, J. P. (1996). School districts matter: Local educational authorities and state instructional policy. *Educational Policy, 10*, 63–87.

Spillane, J. P. (1998). State policy and the non-monolithic nature of the local school district: Organizational and professional considerations. *American Education Research Journal, 35*(1), 33–63.

Spillane, J. P. (2004). *Standards deviation: How schools misunderstand education policy.* Boston, MA: Harvard University Press.

Sunderman, G. L., & Orfield, G. (2006). Domesticating a revolution: No Child Left Behind reforms and state administrative response. *Harvard Educational Review, 76*, 526–556.

Tatum, B. (1992). Talking about race, learning about racism: The applications of racial identity development theory. *Harvard Educational Review, 62*, 1–24.

Thorius, K.A.K., & Stephenson, J. (2012). Racial and ethnic disproportionality in special education. In A. L. Noltemeyer & C. McLoughlin (Eds.), *Disproportionality in education and special education: A guide to creating more equitable learning environments.* Springfield, IL: Charles C. Thomas.

United States Department of Education. (2006). *Twenty-sixth annual report to Congress on the implementation of the Individuals with Disabilities Education Act.* Washington, DC: Author.

Wisconsin Department of Public Instruction. (2008a). *Coordinated early intervening services (CEIS).* Retrieved from sped.dpi.wi.gov/sped_ceis

Wisconsin Department of Public Instruction. (2008b). *State of Wisconsin state performance plan.* Retrieved from sped.dpi.wi.gov/sped_spp-disp

# CHAPTER 10

# Making Policy Sticky

## Distributed Networks of Reform

*Elizabeth B. Kozleski and Kathleen King Thorius*

One of the fascinations with successful urban schools is how they have found paths around, under, and over policies that seem to block progress in a variety of ways (Geier et al., 2008; Scheurich, McKenzie, & Skrla, 2011). Yet, while highly personalized, idiosyncratic, locally driven learning spaces have emerged from a complex policy landscape, the features of such spaces seem to travel poorly (Fuller, 2009). In other cases, equity-driven attempts to reform U.S. urban public schools through federal (i.e., macro) and state (i.e., meso) policy development and implementation have been unsuccessful at scaling reform across large numbers of schools or districts (Lipman, 2011). Policy intended to destabilize historically embedded practices that result in uneven, inequitable educational outcomes such as special education overidentification seems particularly vulnerable to failure. Implementation appears to fail to account for the ways in which local histories, politics, knowledge frameworks, and practices temper policy intentions (Thorius & Maxcy, 2012).

This is the problem of what we call "stickiness" in this chapter. Policy has to be transportable into locally viable implementation strategies. The rationale for why a policy is important, how it benefits students and the institutions that support them, and the connections between implementation and context are often not developed. Policy created without conscious attention to the challenges of localized implementation lacks stickiness. In such cases, even though policy is enacted, the tendency of the educational system to maintain stasis constrains such policy from becoming part of the local culture. For example, resistance to policy is readily exemplified by the ways in which No Child Left Behind (NCLB) was modified, critiqued, and negotiated at state and local levels. By the summer of 2012, more than half of all the states in the United States had received waivers from many of its provisions (U.S. Department of Education, 2012). While NCLB was a deeply flawed educational policy, its failure offers many lessons about understanding the strength of local context including history, culture, de-

217

mographics, politics, and economics. Sticky policy lasts over time, sustains human interaction and activity, and becomes part of the way that things are. In this chapter, we explore the role of policy in the promotion of equitable student opportunities and outcomes in urban schools and the importance of its development in light of local translations that will afford and constrain policy's stickiness (Gladwell, 2000), or ability to take hold and remain active in local contexts.

What follows is an introduction to the notion of stickiness and its applicability to policy development, including features of policy that leads to successful student outcomes and emerges from a developmental, reciprocal, and contextual process in its design, launch, and exploration including the conditions we argue are necessary for such policy to remain active over time, or in other words, stick. Throughout all of the previously noted discussions, we critique the roles of power and privilege in driving urban educational policy, including who has (or assumes) authority to write policy for whom and for what purpose.

Finally, we offer consideration of a set of tools that, consciously engaged, have the potential to move a distal policy set at the federal level into local spaces with respect for their contexts and to spur development of local policy that engages all stakeholders while being mindful for what and who may be oppressed in these systems.

## TALES FROM AN URBAN CORRIDOR DISTRICT

Koyama and Varenne (2012) describe policy as *play* that has consequential effects for those who put it in motion (e.g., the superintendent whose job may be on the line) as well as for those whose actions it is intended to regulate. They take the notion of play further to suggest that once policy is put into play as one might throw a ball into the field, it is dependent on actors' using it in very specific ways to achieve its outcomes. And what a playing field it is! Participants who enact policy are busy constructing and interpreting what the policy is, how it might affect their work, what effects might be achieved, and how it matches with their own conceptions of what is worth working on and how things should be accomplished. To illustrate, we open with a vignette from our work that foregrounds ways in which a district's politically charged culture shapes how and what policy decisions are made and by whom, as a window into ways macro and local policy intersects and unfolds in urban schools.

> The essential missing link in our district is a culture that believes that our kids can and will achieve. The district pretests given under duress in November were within 5 points of predicting our state test scores

in April. The only way to ignore the data is to say, "See I told you, our kids can't do it," rather than saying, "Wow, there are 5 kids who are really close. Let's see if we can get them there." We need to shake up the culture here in a very dramatic way. I don't think we will be able to do that. The culture of this place is really very sick.
—(Email to author from senior leader in a U.S. urban school district)

Cut to a later board meeting. The superintendent (not the email author) came into the meeting 20 minutes late. She held her phone in her hand, frequently checking texts, and asked to interrupt the discussion to make a few "important points." She was quite upset about "leaks" that had come out of the cabinet and/or executive sessions with the board and reminded us firmly that confidentiality was important in these meetings. It wasn't clear who was being targeted with these comments. Checking with other members of the meeting afterwards, it appeared that the author of the email and one other cabinet member were being viewed suspiciously. Part of the problem was that cabinet members weren't sure what was confidential. When pressed for specifics, it became clear that emails and personal communications should not contain information or commentary about the cabinet and executive sessions. It was hard to know how to move forward without using information from those meetings to inform action. It was difficult to know what should happen once an idea was presented. The process for serious consideration, how decision would be arrived at and by whom continued to vacillate over the course of 2 years of these meetings. Two specific incidents point out the incongruities.

The first cabinet discussion had to do with the upcoming textbook adoptions. The finances for funding the adoption had not yet been worked out, in spite of a decision having been made in the associate superintendent's office to adopt a particular series. There was a long discussion about where the money was going to come from and how the board and teachers' association would view it. The conversation about financing was braided with a lengthy discussion about how not to make the mistake made a few years ago with the math textbook adopted but never used by teachers. The associate superintendent explained that the possibility teachers would not use what the district had adopted had been addressed through a process of "consensus building." When pressed for what consensus building looked like, she explained that one teacher representative from each building had agreed to a particular series. The superintendent countered with information from her own sources that suggested consensus was not there. A little more than half (54%) of the faculty had voted for adoption. The previous math adoption had gone forward with a vote of 52%. Neither the superintendent nor her associate engaged a discussion of what consensus might look like. They merely gave one another conflicting data without addressing the conflict. Observers described a pervasive gap in communication between the two leaders as a chasm. The textbook adoption went forward without clear understanding of the consequences on the budget or the degree of adoption and potential use by the district's faculty.

In a second cabinet meeting the group conversed about an institute attended by teams from each building along with the associate superintendent and staff from his office. The discussion included contributions from everyone at the meeting. It was the first time such an inclusive pattern was observed. The communications officer offered to write something about it for the district newspaper. The chief operating officer and his budget managers followed the conversation and asked questions and the associate superintendent suggested restructuring around the chief educational functions of the district. Examples about how these structure frames might alter even position postings, using current job announcements, were discussed. The superintendent declared interest in changing the title of the associate superintendent to Chief Academic Officer for Teaching and Learning. This discussion also allowed some internal tensions to bubble up around the role of the learning coordinators in elementary schools, a role that had been created the previous year. It was reported that teachers wanted management and discipline support, not academic intervention. As a result, they paid little heed to the instructional coaching and mentoring they were receiving. The conversation produced several potential solutions from creating positions to handle behavior problems to looking at the balance between the principal and instructional coach with regard to instructional leadership and management skills. In the end, no follow-up was identified. At the next cabinet meeting, the superintendent announced changes that would be made to the learning coordinator job description, abandoning its coaching function and returning the position to a student discipline function. The associate superintendent looked surprised. (Compiled from fieldnotes by authors)

In both meetings, discussions by the superintendent's cabinet raised important issues around curriculum and improving learning environments, but decisions were made in ways, at times, and in places that were not clear to district educators, students, and families. The "culture" referred to in the initial email was illustrated throughout the district in the ways policy issues were determined by the most senior administrators, without transparency or articulation of the goals toward which policies were meant to drive change. Thus the capacity of the district to make sustained improvements in its practice was thwarted by the ways in which policy issues were determined internally. These discontinuities fractured the power of state and federal policies to leverage change within the district; after 12 years of heavy accountability pressure on the district, student scores remained far below the state average with the majority of students scoring below proficient in math, reading, and writing at all grade levels tested.

## MAKING SENSE OF POLICY AT THE LOCAL LEVEL

This vignette makes the point that macrolevel policy never lands in neutral territory. It depicts a district situated at the intersection of federal neoliberal policies focused on standardization, privatization, and gentrification, resulting in local school district rules and regulations designed to ensure compliance and increase monitoring. To wit, current assumptions embedded within U.S. Race to the Top policy's funding agenda are that the unit of analysis for improving student outcomes is the state educational agency (SEA). Thus Race to the Top policy-related incentives have focused on a number of fronts aimed at state leadership, leading to SEA enactment of structural reforms around (1) the assessment of student and teacher performance, (2) the use of charter schools as a device to improve all schools, and (3) the design of data systems that ease access to data. Yet these approaches have little evidence to support their impact on improved student outcomes, particularly for underserved students in urban schools, and particularly students identified with disabilities in these settings. None of them come close to addressing the kinds of issues revealed in the vignette.

Good (2011) asserts that much of the work of macrolevel policymakers seems to be organized around the assumption that the design and implementation of robust learning environments and relationships are simple and, therefore, easy to fix. Teachers need better and more complete educations. Teachers need more content knowledge so that they can better understand and organize the curriculum. Teachers need more structure in how they organize and set up the curriculum. And, the list of fixes continues to expand. Teachers work in schools; therefore, schools need to be fixed. Schools are organized into districts and are regulated by state education agencies; that process needs fixing. These simple cause/effect equations are attractive. They signal specific kinds of policy needs. But, because they don't examine the underlying causes, the nuanced ways that problems play out in specific contexts, and the connections and boundaries between classrooms, schools, district, and states, simple policies lack the substance to make a difference.

Perhaps even more relevant to consider in how macro (i.e., federal) and meso (i.e., state) policy intersect with local urban educational contexts, however, is that by focusing on structural contexts such as state education agencies, macro policymakers are working at the periphery of the activity system (Spillane, Gomez, & Mesler, 2009). That is, district administrators, educators, students, and families are the cultural mediators for how policy enters the playing field of districts, schools, and classrooms. Without seeing educators as cultural mediators of policy as it enters a system, policymakers continue to miss the fundamental opportunities that policymaking offers to create processes and supports for implementation to bolster the potential of policy to be appropriated locally in ways that contribute to reform.

Defining the arena of concern as the urban *district* as a grounding principle of NUISI's work was in response to our experience that many times, large urban districts have more power than SEAs. Of the 100 largest school districts in the United States, the vast majority are urban (National Center for Education Statistics, 2011); they are so large that they envelope the SEA, which simply does not have the capacity to make sure how and whether policy is carried out in the complex and powerful bureaucracies of urban systems. Within these bureaucracies, local agendas and local players even collude to actively resist federal policy, and because of their critical mass, as well as social and political capital, they are able to do so. Accordingly, attention to these agendas and players in urban districts is central to examining the ways in which policy is engaged in within them.

## Local Agendas

To illustrate, the development of policy to monitor and eliminate racial disproportionality in special education appeared, at least superficially, to have potential to do just that. The Individuals with Disabilities Education Act in 2004 included prioritization of regulations first introduced in IDEA 1997 that required states and local educational agencies (LEAs) to address the disproportionate representation of racial/ethnic groups in special education. The strengthened regulations required that SEAs have in place policies and procedures designed to prevent inappropriate overidentification or disproportionate representation in special education by race and ethnicity. Specifically, five regulatory requirements regarding disproportionality appeared in the IDEA, one of which required that states have policies and procedures in place that prevent disproportionate representation of racial and ethnic minority students. One requirement is that SEAs monitor district disproportionality, "to the extent the representation is the result of inappropriate identification" (IDEA, 2004).

Yet consider urban educational contexts where such policy collides with local agendas and players' concerns with federal accountability policy. Why examine whether disproportionality is related to policies and practices that marginalize minority students, rather than assume disability in light of poor performance, when local conditions incentivize placement in more restrictive settings where their test scores are less likely to impact schools' overall adequate yearly progress (AYP)? Urban schools and school systems serve talented, capable students. At the same time, National Institute for Urban School Improvement (NIUSI) partner districts like the District of Columbia, New Orleans, Memphis, and Chicago have unique histories and sets of circumstances that conspire to maintain poor outcomes (e.g., school achievement, dropout and graduation rates, the school to prison pipeline) for large percentages of students from the 1980s until now despite federal policies aimed at their elimination. In these urban districts where disproportionality has ranged from 2:1 to a soaring 30:1 ratio of students of color versus White students being placed in special education (Artiles, Kozleski, Trent, Osher, & Ortiz, 2010; Dyson & Kozleski, 2008), the determination of extent to which disproportionality is a result of inappropriate identification as the regulation requires is indeed not a simple matter of policy implementation. It is an issue of how local conditions, agendas, goals, and players' concerns collide in light of such policy.

## Local Players

By examining local cultures at the nexus of steps in policy development processes—framing problems, proposing solutions, and building political consensus—it is possible to deepen strategic and tactical decision making throughout the policy development phase. It means that policymakers must consider historical artifacts embedded within notions of how schools and school systems operate. In 2009 Kozleski and Smith reported on the different conceptions of the role of the principals in southern schools, particularly those held by some of the African American principals they studied over time. At that time, many comprehensive school reform efforts were anchored by views of the principal as an instructional leader (Rowan, Correnti, Miller, & Camburn, 2009). This view of the principalship had been adopted and widely discussed in the school districts where NIUSI had an official reform role. School principals in those districts voiced solidarity with the idea in their district meetings but what some principals practiced in their buildings was very different from the role being promoted at district headquarters and in district meetings with principals. On their own campuses, on their own turfs, some principals took on a community care role that was analogous to that of a local church minister. The needs and cares of families, teachers, and students took precedence over instructional design and delivery. The agency of the principal and the expectations of faculty and families mediated the degree to which notions of the principal's role in forming federal policy, as well as the stated policy of the district, was implemented at individual buildings (Kozleski & Smith, 2009). This example—one of many from the NIUSI years—helps explain how policy that does not account for the ways in which roles and responsibilities are constructed in situ limits its own stickiness.

The previous discussion illustrates how concerns and efforts to support macro to meso to local policy *implementation* reflect the same problematic cause/effect equation that characterizes many current policies themselves. That is, they position local players as containers into which policy is deposited and ignore the crucial role of local playing fields in shaping the ways in which policy is understood, interpreted, and enacted. Rather, analysis and mediation of policy trajectories across the institutional sites of SEAs, LEAs, schools, and classrooms must center accounts for local actors' negotiation of policy meaning as situated within and across these contexts (Artiles, Thorius, et al., 2011). Central to such matters is how local actors selectively attend to policies that do not align with those already existing in that environment, such that some policies are less likely to be enacted, and more likely to be adapted (Thorius & Maxcy, 2012). In other words, local policy players (Koyama & Varenne, 2012) put into motion new versions of policy contingent upon their individual interests, contextual circumstances, and goals, as well as larger institutional and historical forces, all of which converge in day-to-day practice (Levinson, Sutton, & Winstead, 2009). We turn now toward applying the preceding discussion to an examination of how these considerations played out in the urban corridor district.

## POLICY PLAY IN THE URBAN CORRIDOR DISTRICT

Reflecting back on the vignette, such conditions (e.g., concerns with student test scores and local constructions of leaders' roles) emerged in the local district to mediate the ways in which the intersection of macro, meso, and local policies were enacted. We present these in the form of questions that emerged during our work with the urban corridor district on the basis of our interactions and observations during the partnership, but suggest their relevance to examining policy in other large urban systems like this one.

### What Does It Really Mean to Build Consensus?

As the vignette depicted, even in light of what was represented by administration as an attempt to glean input from educators across schools in the decision to change textbooks, it is apparent that this process was flawed from the start. Relatedly, the decision to change the function and title of the associate superintendent's role to that of a chief academic officer was discussed with a number of stakeholders, but the decision played out in a way that appeared to neglect any conversation having happened. In sum, both the careful consideration of the possible impact of policy changes, and of how information about proposed changes would or should be shared with those it stood to affect were missing from the process of policy change in this district. Without deliberation on these and other implementation issues, policy changes proposed and/or required by system administrators across macro, meso, and local levels stand to be resisted or ignored, or else simply performed as an act of compliance by local stakeholders (Thorius & Maxcy, 2012), eventually fizzling out or appropriated in ways that maintain stasis, rather than spur any lasting change.

The chapter vignette provides an example. The lack of a deliberate, authentic consensus-building process led to resistance, compliance-driven adoption, and weak implementation. Despite poor outcomes from a past adoption of a math text with a very narrow majority of staff backing the decision and, relatedly, marginal use in classrooms, the district decided to move forward in adopting new texts in other subject areas with similar lackluster support.

## When Did Being a Technocrat Become the Primary Identity of District Leaders?

Through interaction and interpretation, people within organizations appropriate and translate policy, often creating new tools and frames that then are instantiated into new policies. Many policies codify technical work in states, school districts, and, depending on the state, in schools themselves, identifying what is to be done, by whom, and how. While the intent may be to smooth the efficiency of work, technical policies that prescribe what is to be done also run the risk of creating friction with local conceptions of what work should look like and why it should be done. And by defining the technical aspects of the work, the identities of the practitioners (e.g., teachers, school psychologists, related service providers like social workers, speech/language therapists, and others) are also shifted to technocrats, commissioned to perform particular tasks in specific patterns and sequences. Relatedly, a primary concern of leaders in local educational systems becomes the management of educators' rights and responsibilities. The vignette provides an excellent example of this process. Changing the job title of an associate superintendent with one plucked from the corporate world signaled that management and decision making about teachers' responsibilities were inherent to the role.

## How Are Players' Communicative Rights and Responsibilities Defined?

The culture of secrecy and guardedness about communications with outsiders pulsed through the district, as depicted in the superintendent's concerns with leaks and staff confusion about what district challenges were fair game for open discussion. Furthermore, the vignette provides several examples that how decisions were made and by whom were opaque, as evidenced when "the associate superintendent looked surprised," at the superintendent's policy announcement. Policy decisions happened at the top and were implemented without preparation or analysis of impact on educator practice and student outcomes. Because the key players in the district—the teachers—were notably absent in many discussions around policy, their potential to contribute to decision making had been effectively stifled. Shared governance and decision making are crucial in educational reform; without representation of the multiple perspectives including those who have been historically marginalized in urban schools, power and privilege imbalances are reproduced and certain outcomes continue to evade the most historically underserved (Kozleski & Smith, 2009).

## What Is the Function and Purpose of Student Performance Data?

As the email from the senior district administrator to one of the authors indicated, she believed the primary function of student assessment data should be to identify and target for intervention students who were almost meeting the performance benchmarks to "see if we can get them there." We contend that when the chief utility of student assessment data is to make diagnostic decisions, as is endemic within current accountability concerns, educators' roles shift from making sure every child learns toward intervening with those who will get schools better ratings and rankings within state and federal accountability systems. Of course, this is also an issue of self-preservation as data on poor student performance are often used to push educators out of the profession (Lipman, 2011).

## What Is the Tolerance for Change Over Time?

The superintendent decided to change the entire focus of the learning coordinator role based on a preliminary report during a brief discussion that some educators had voiced different priorities. Rather than any exploration of whom these concerns were coming from, or problem solving around the processes of coaching or how to support educators making use of the coaching they were receiving, for example, and despite the creation of these positions only a year earlier, the notion that things were not "working" quickly (i.e., technically sound and efficient) signaled a need to shift direction. These types of rapid vacillations without exploration of the ways in which policy shifts have actually been carried out in assessments that such policy is ineffective make it almost impossible for innovations to take hold and have the potential to create conditions for fatigue and wariness toward new policies in the future (Joseph, 2001).

## WHAT MAKES POLICY STICK?

As we hope to have illustrated above, history, time, and space contribute to contexts within which policies are embedded and inform and influence how policy is derived and sustained locally (Kozleski & Artiles, in press). The vignette at the beginning of this chapter sharpens the point that culture is at the heart of policy transportability: Notably, we suggest that almost all reforms beneficial to student learning and social outcomes have not been sticky enough to transcend the stasis of local systems that already exists. Here, we explore the notion of policy's stickiness, including how it evolves and helps sustain transformational change, particularly in relationship to increasing equity in urban school communities and outcomes. We also note that in other circumstances, as is currently the case within the neoliberal macrolevel policy agenda, sticky policies have lasting impact because they resonate with multiple dimensions of the dominant culture, simultaneously. But it is also important to notice that stickiness may resonate only in some communities. Stickiness is neither the sole mark of robust policy nor does it necessarily signal soundness since sticky policy can also potentially have deleterious effects. We illustrate below with public health and education policy scenarios.

The shift from breast feeding to formula as the common and preferred method of feeding infants from the 1930s through the 1970s in the United States is an example of a sticky idea, now being reversed (Stevens, Patrick, & Pickler, 2009). Promoted by the medical establishment and regulated by the U.S. Food and Drug Administration, recommendations for infant formula feeding became part of regular discourse patterns between pediatricians and mothers in the mid-20th century. A variety of factors, including prevailing assumptions about how women, and particularly mothers, should behave, notions of the science of childrearing, emerging business interests, and other contextual factors contributed to the use of formula for children in the growing middle class in the United States. While this came to be the assumed practice of choice, a variety of mothers from nondominant cultural groups never adopted formula feeding. Economic, social, cultural, and religious factors influenced their practice. There are many examples of sticky policies that have lasting impact because they resonate with multiple dimensions of the dominant culture, simultaneously. But it is also important to notice that stickiness may resonate only in some communities.

The organization of schools into *middle schools* has demonstrated stickiness for different reasons. Since 1970, school districts have increasingly configured grades 5, 6, 7, and 8, or some subset of these four grades, into middle schools, reducing their reliance on junior high schools that historically served grades 7 and 8 or 7th through 9th grades. By the 2000–2001 academic year, there were 11,200 middle schools as compared to 3,600 junior highs. In 1970, the converse was true: 7,800 junior highs and 2,100 middle schools were in service. While middle schools are increasingly critiqued, they remain the dominant configuration for middle grades in the United States (National Center for Education Statistics, 2011). The middle school movement differentiated itself from the design of junior highs based on a set of cultural assumptions about the nature of puberty, the needs of children transitioning from childhood into adolescence, and how schools might be best organized to serve students in that process. While little acknowledgment was given to the cultural nature of the assumptions about the passage out of childhood, nevertheless, the notion of middle schools was very much in line with what Rowan, Correnti, Miller, and Camburn (2009) term "cultural control." Accordingly, the organization of middle schools was designed to build professional teams of educators across disciplinary content areas who would work together to educate a cohort of students each year (National Middle School Association, 2003). Middle school teams were typically organized around language arts, math, science, and social studies. Teams of four teachers each skilled in one of the core areas worked as a team to design, develop, and implement social and academic content. The idea was that students would have a set of adults who would develop relationships with students, be able to identify students with challenges quickly, institute preventative tactics designed to support their needs, and bolster their transitional issues with a peer group that kept together throughout the school day. Junior highs, in contrast, required students to move through a set of classes each day in which students were drawn from across the entire population of students at that grade level (George, Stevenson, Thomason, & Beane, 1992). It was possible for a student to have distinctly different peer groups in each class. Further, since the departments were organized by discipline, teachers rarely shared their observations about students within departments because their teacher cohort did not share these students. This push to change from junior high to middle schools meant changing the professional identities and behaviors of middle school teachers, reframing the lenses that school leaders used to gauge the effectiveness of their school models and thus, their instructional leadership, and persuading students and families that the new model offered advantages over the historical configuration of junior high schools. This switch represented a major structural change that has had stickiness over time.

As we discussed briefly above, some policies entering local systems have been shown to be less efficient, practical, healthy, and/or beneficial to the individuals who carry out or experience the activities, yet the practice remains deeply embedded within the culture of the educational setting. Other equity-driven polices and/or practices may have merit, yet they do not flourish over time. Their inception is met with disinterest or resistance, and they fail to grab the attention needed to become part of everyday life. Or policies are initially heralded only to be discarded quickly before they have opportunities to become embedded in practice. Urban schools have certainly experienced these phenomena repeatedly in the multiple waves of reform that come and go with local administrations. In the Washington, DC, schools, for instance, a total of six superintendents in 10 years (from 2001 to 2011) offered strong leadership and established policies to improve student outcomes but emphasized different approaches to accomplish those ends. They appeared to draw on different sets of assumptions about the goals of reform, the challenges that existed, the locus of improvement, and the processes of change. Over time, student performance outcomes, as measured by standardized assessments, suggest that the majority of students continued to receive inadequate opportunities to learn and succeed. Concurrently over the same decade, federal reform efforts like the reauthorizations of the Elementary and Secondary Act (renamed No Child Left Behind) and the Individuals with Disabilities Educational Act (IDEA) were developed, implemented, and monitored by the SEA. The combination of federal and local reform efforts bolstered by fiscal incentives to shift local practices through policy realignment appeared to make few shifts in outcome measures of educational success in the district's public schools (Office of the State Superintendent of Education, 2012).

To the extent that much of the federal policy agenda is focused on structural contexts as we've discussed above, the notion of policy's stickiness has application for seeing beyond these milieus as the only relevant focus for policy dissemination. By situating discussion of local urban contexts first, rather than approach our examination of policy as moving from macro to micro settings, we emphasize a need for anticipation and exploration of the factors and features that intersect in local educational settings as important to creation of conditions that make it more likely that equity-driven policies will stick in such places. We draw from Gladwell's notion of stickiness to suggest that as policy traverses macro to local scales, it is better positioned to stick when it is attractive to a critical mass already existing in a context and when its entrance into local contexts relies on three types of key players in educational contexts. These "mavens," "connectors," and "salesmen" are trusted locally to cull information relevant for the community, have the power to pass this information along within the complex social networks of the setting, and sell the policy locally, respectively. Drawing from these ideas, we suggest three areas for consideration in bolstering policy stickiness in urban educational settings, particularly as related to the development of sticky policy that is focused on improving equity in access, participation, and outcomes for historically marginalized students and their families, as is the focus of this volume.

## Centering Marginalized Perspectives

Examining policy and critiquing its purposes with some nuance requires understanding that such policies are the product of multiple agendas and discourse communities (Ball & Exley, 2010). Yet whose agendas remain untapped, neglected, or marginalized, particularly in urban schools? Relatedly, the exercise of power and privilege is part of the political process that undergirds policymaking and implementation. In response, development of educational policy must account for the access, participation, and sustained feedback of individuals and groups that represent multiple perspectives and ways of knowing (Kozleski & Smith, 2009). This kind of diverse constituency development as policy is proposed augurs well for building the political will to implement and sustain change over time.

Politics, which according to Laswell (1936) concerns "who gets what, when, and how?", is a critical dimension of how emergent solutions that are expansive and inclusive of diverse perspectives can be initiated (Opfer, 2009). Through politics, dominant views about things such as where students with significant disabilities are best educated (i.e., in self-contained classrooms) can be mediated by alternative perspectives to the degree to which individuals and groups gain access to informing and designing new policy. Once at the table, those who have not been served by educational systems and the policies that drive them may challenge the presiding policy agenda by poking at its vulnerabilities and providing solutions to those vulnerabilities through storytelling about the ways things are and ought to be from *their* perspectives. These stories set up a counternarrative that shakes faith in current initiatives and also proposes a new vision for how things ought to be (McDonnell, 2009).

## Emancipatory Intent

Given the current contexts of standardization and accountability that we discussed above, we suggest that macrolevel policies such as Common Core learning standards are being used to constrain and contain local actors' daily practice, which is counter to policy use in ways that promote inclusive educational systems. Current neoliberal concerns have created contexts where the individual has become the policy target (making teachers better, looking at parts of the whole), and the roles of families and neighborhoods in creating the fabric of local communities are diminished (Lipman, 2011).

Rather, just as we suggest the utility of macrolevel policy in opening the playing field to new (i.e., historically marginalized) players, this also means this local field must be open with new roles and opportunities as a result of engaging in policy enactment. This is consistent with a view of policy as an emancipatory agent (Apple, 1994; Habermas, 1981) which engages and encourages policy audiences by offering opportunities to "eliminate the causes of unwarranted alienation and domination and thereby enhance the opportunities for realizing human potential" (Stahl, 2008, p. 163). Toward this end, youth, businesses, and civic organizations, along with religious groups, government agencies, health and education agencies, social services, and local government all have a vested interest in what education is and should become. Their role in forging transformation is critical to this process. In one of our sites, a popular superintendent remained so because of the work that she did over time with community members to excavate historical legacies of racism in the city and district and their connections to students' learning opportunities. In a focus group of local political, religious, and community service leaders, the police chief noted:

> But if you really want to look at one thing, like if you want us to start going backwards, just remove the superintendent. It's the one factor that has moved us from a community that first became aware, to a community that started talking about it quietly, very quietly behind the scenes, almost whispering, and we didn't quite know how to get beyond that because of the great ethical moral difficulty with the root cause of the problem, if the root cause of the problem is racism and all these kids are coming from the north end of the city and they're all Black there and it's all White here, well, who put them there? And nobody really deals with that question, how'd they get there? How did it get like this? Well, it must be our fault because we're White. Why didn't you do something about it? You know, I mean, those real basic questions never get addressed so people go around not knowing how to address them and therefore they stay away from them, so, the conversations on race I think helped. Other kinds of dialogue in mentoring, training classes, discussions about literacy, I think the literacy push in the school has had a big impact because it's given a lot of kids at the elementary level little bits of kind of incremental success and they take that success and run with it and that again changes expectations of them by their teachers and again it just helps with that community mentality as well.

Emancipatory policy and practice, then, start with excavation. That is, they require deep unearthing and analysis of oppression and disempowerment patterns and histories in any system.

## Transparency in Installation and Impact

Central to the ways in which policy is developed and traverses multiple levels of educational systems, and more specifically, central to the beneficial and deleterious effects of policy that is meaningful, disseminated, and talked-up enough to stick, is the notion of power. In particular, the multiple people and groups who sponsor and drive policies from conception to installation are often invisible to the publics that receive and are impacted by particular sets of policies. We contend that transparency in the process of installation also contributes to the degree to which any policy becomes sticky and sustains influence over how organizations and individuals behave. Relatedly, information about the impact of any policy on practice and outcomes also contributes to its vigor and sustainability; McDonnell (2009) characterizes this as the feedback from public attitudes and actions that inform future policy direction. In the vignette at the beginning of this chapter, district leaders developed policies in private spaces where the calculus that drove their choices was not apparent to those who were required to carry it out: "The finances for funding the adoption had not yet been worked out, in spite of a decision having been taken in the associate superintendent's office to adopt a particular series." The public rationales used to explain new policy initiatives sometimes tell only part of the history behind any given decision. Each policy comes with a particular mix of fiscal resources, political gain, organizational merit, opportunity for improved outcomes for students, and community satisfaction. The degree to which it satisfies the individuals involved on all these dimensions contributes to its impact upon launching, the consequential nature of that impact, and the degree to which the policy creates lasting shifts in the work and experiences of the people and organizations it impacts.

As policies move closer to everyday action arenas in schools and classrooms, decisions tend to rest in a smaller and smaller group of individuals. A school board may only have seven to eleven members setting policy. A superintendent's cabinet may have as few as two or three individuals or as many as 10 to 15, depending on the size of the district. These individuals and the constituencies they represent negotiate policies together within the constraints of school financing arrangements. What they decide has immediate impact on the lives and livelihood of teachers and students in schools. Schools are closed, bus routes cancelled, teachers let go, contracts for school maintenance issued and retracted. Repercussions of these policies can change career trajectories but they also have lasting effects on the capacity of systems to make sustained progress over time. Each time administrations shift, whatever accumulated capital was created in service of a change mission begins to crumble. New coalitions are created when new leadership is constituted, but it rarely is able to capitalize on what has already been built and disassembled; new leadership builds its own coalitions and social capital working on different targets. These targets are shaped by the new coalitions, emerging agendas within external change organizations (nongovernment agencies, advocacy organizations, universities, and technical assistance arms of the state or federal government), and state and federal mandates. Understanding who and what benefits from the leadership fragmentation in public education is an important key to sustaining a change trajectory over time.

Further, the agency that teachers exercise in their own classrooms reminds us that the politics of policy initiatives cannot afford to disregard the individual decisions and actions of those within them, from their unique positions of power and privilege. This idea is illustrated by teachers' assumptions about what matters in terms of student behavior, language, social interactions, and academic behavior that undergird many of the decisions they make to recognize, support, and challenge their students. While teachers are undoubtedly constrained by prescriptive curricula, increasing administrative record-keeping burdens that sap time and energy, and pernicious evaluation procedures, they still retain a significant amount of decision-making authority in their classroom. Many of the decisions they make have long-lasting impact on how children understand themselves, the institutional practices of schools, and their notions of what it means to learn and innovate.

## TOOLS TO ADVANCE STICKY EQUITY POLICY

Opportunities to engage together, in person, around tough issues surfaced again and again in our work in NIUSI. People need opportunities to talk together. And out of these opportunities, which can be contentious and difficult, comes understanding when tools for discourse and questioning are used to modulate different interaction styles and needs (Barrera & Corso, 2002). Tools mediate, or facilitate, the work people do in joint activity toward goals (Engeström, 1999). Tools that seem to advance the work of stickiness and equity encourage discourse that brings different points of view into a commons where people can listen and begin to understand different and contradictory viewpoints.

Tool development, we contend, requires specialized expertise about how to develop and facilitate people's use of tools. Given the multiple demands placed on those working within urban districts and the related resources available to them in doing so, we suggest it may be unrealistic to expect districts to have the time or money to invest in tool building. However, the U.S. Department of Education's funding of technical assistance and dissemination centers like NIUSI, within which tool development was a central aspect of the center's work, provides myriad potential resources for urban education stakeholders in the thick of policy development processes.

Accordingly, tools should facilitate stakeholders in their critical reflection on areas we contend are necessary in considering policy's function, purpose, and sustainability in urban education settings as related to how policy affords and constrains the following: (1) their roles in the educational system, (2) their day-to-day practice, (3) outcomes for students and families, and (4) the consideration of data that informs the preceding points. Each of these areas is informed by the contextual factors that emerged during our NIUSI work in the urban district detailed throughout this chapter which mediated the ways in which the intersection of macro, meso, and local policies were enacted in that setting (i.e., building critical mass for policy implementation, definition of leadership roles, communication strategies and directionality, function and purpose of student performance data, and tolerance for change over time). While there are certainly additional factors to contend with, we offer this as a preliminary (i.e., not exhaustive) set.

To illustrate, what follows are details about a suite of tools with origins in the SCF and related NIUSI work, that was developed into its current state within a technical assistance and dissemination center led by K. K. Thorius and colleagues. Flexible enough to center local context as participants utilize them, the tools are grounded also in six assertions about equity-focused policies that transcend context:

1. *Create access:* Policies should afford all staff and students equal opportunity to maintain or improve well-being.
2. *Educate:* A rationale for the policy is made explicit, communicated in ways that make sense within the local context, and includes guidance with examples to facilitate decision making.
3. *Liberate:* Policies should provide opportunities and suitable constraints to allow for decision making that is most appropriate for specific situations and contexts.
4. *Rely on research:* Policies should be supported by research, including local data and/or evidence.
5. *Center those on the margins:* Policies enumerate specific student groups in order to be responsive to students who have been historically marginalized in school settings.
6. *Provide accountability measures:* Equity-focused policies specify steps for action by school officials in order to comply with the policies (Kozleski & Skelton, 2007; Maxcy, Thorius, & Skelton, 2012, p. 7; McLaughlin & Mongeon, 2012).

The first tool serves as a facilitation guide as teams examine the ways in which current school policy supports equitable practice. In preparation for the review, teams consider policy intent and social constructions the policy relies upon, who benefits/does not benefit from the way things are (Freire, 1998), and what actions are required to redress the inequities (Kozleski & Waitoller, 2010). More specifically, the guide provides a set of questions under six analytical domains to support the examination of regulatory documents (e.g., policies and standard operating procedures) with a particular focus on educational equity. The questions, meant to facilitate critical examination and reflection on policies that shape and inform daily practice, critique policy's legality, research-base, responsiveness to current contexts, efficiency, educative features, and accountability structures. For example, within the responsiveness to current context, teams are asked to consider the extent to which the policy addresses disparities in treatment between and among student groups (e.g., disproportionality in participation and/or outcomes). The review guide is complemented by two additional tools: a brief written for practitioners and a podcast. Here is a short excerpt from the brief:

> As the number of state and national policy mandates in the educational realm continues to multiply, teachers, students, and administrators may feel increasingly overwhelmed as they are required to understand and respond to multiple, sometimes contradictory, policies created by individuals who may or may not share their familiarity with the local context (Braun, Maguire, & Ball, 2010). But, at the local level, the school itself, community members have the opportunity to engage in a democratic process to interpret policy mandates, develop responses, and determine local policy (Heimans, 2012). This brief describes a process by which school communities can engage in critical examination of and reflection on the policies that shape and inform their daily practices and thereby ensure that local policy and practice are consistent with the larger goals of the community, including a focus on social justice. (Macey, Thorius, & Skelton, 2012, p. 2)

The podcast allows listeners to follow a school/community team enact the processes described in the brief and policy review guide as they engage in a review of zero-tolerance discipline policy that has been utilized with disparate negative impact on students of color and with disabilities in urban schools (Great Lakes Equity Center, 2013).

As the vignette illustrates, one of the challenges with reform decisions is inadequate examination of the current conditions prior to planning for action. NIUSI's tool allows stakeholders within an urban district (e.g., students, family members, administrative staff, and so on) to engage in assessment of the degree to which existing policies and practices support an inclusive educational system, and identify specific goals for the coming school year. In other words, the tool facilitates the use of multiple forms of data to inform continuous improvement and reform efforts. Crucial to this process is the composition of teams that represent the diverse constituency of the district, along with the strategic use of critical questioning strategies, in order to create the conditions for centering marginalized perspectives and consensus building that we have discussed throughout the chapter as necessary for equity-minded policy to stick. Specifically, the tool creates space for dialogue on the key functions across levels of the school system (i.e., district, school, and practitioner), the ways in which decisions are made, and how roles and responsibilities are defined.

Grounded in the systemic change framework and vignettes developed through work in NIUSI's network of urban schools, these rubrics facilitate discussion and assessment of a number of policy and practice arenas. For example, stakeholders consider to what extent existing policies help schools make the best use of all the resources in a particular building. Once teams assess their current status, they consider the following questions: (1) How robust are efforts at all levels of your system? (2) Is there a particular level that seems noticeably stronger than others? (3) Are there areas that seem critical to continued growth? (4) What kinds of assets currently exist? and (5) What assets will you need to improve? (National Institute for Urban School Improvement [NIUSI], 2006, p. 11).

While the types of questions noted above are important in preparation for local reform decisions, adding to a process developed in the person-centered planning movement for individuals with disabilities (O'Brien, O'Brien, & Mount, 1997), the next step for using this tool is explicitly geared toward fostering discussion of emancipatory intent for reform. Person-centered planning emphasizes "five essential outcomes or accomplishments" (O'Brien, 1987, p. 178)—community presence, community participation, positive relationships, respect, and competence—and assessment of outcomes requires operational definition, designing strategies to assess change, and collecting data (Holburn, Jacobson, & Vietze, 2000).

One methodology for person-centered planning called the "PATH" process, as it is commonly abbreviated (i.e., Planning Alternative Tomorrows with Hope; Pearpoint, O'Brien, & Forest, 1993), uses backward planning (i.e., starting with the end in mind; Covey, 1989; Wiggins & McTighe, 1998) to determine desired outcomes for reform, the people and resources needed to enact it, and a timeline for doing so. Here is an excerpt of the tool's questions geared toward facilitation: "(1) Where are you and where do you want to be? (2) Who benefits from the way things are? (3) Who is disadvantaged by the way things are? Who should be present as you make plans for the future? (4) Where do you want to be by this time next year? (5) Who do you need to enlist?" (NIUSI, 2006, p. 13). Drawing from Gladwell's stickiness notion, we suggest that mavens, connectors, and salespeople are crucial in the creation of district teams who will use the rubric, as well as in identifying people necessary in the PATH process.

## CONCLUSION

Making policy sticky means acknowledging the extent to which culture is central to how people make sense of the world around them. Policy is a way of disturbing everyday life, rebalancing it in effect to adjust course, redress inequities, propel and fuel specific kinds of innovation, and build particular kinds of collective capital—social, intellectual, creative, and material. Disturbances (like policies) that emerge either from within a group or outside a given group but with the conferred authority (conferred within a hierarchy or established through the constitution of a governing body) can mediate the work of a group initially, but to do so over time means that the policy provides a benefit to the group to continue to refashion its cultural habits and daily work. The Systemic Change Framework that was introduced in Chapter 1 and served as the organizing strategy for this book, offers a way of conceptualizing the constraining and supporting roles of different levels of the educational system in the United States. However, the notion of activity systems nested within one another does not capture the ways in which policy can travel across systems rather than seep through them. Further, the work that policies seek to inform, shift, and ultimately transform cannot be done without understanding that implementation happens locally and therefore is dependent on the particular constellations of circumstances within those local systems. Attention to the people connected within systems and connected across multiple levels offers an important insight into the ways that some policies are accommodated with differential rigor at different levels. Moreover, the degree to which policies acknowledge and account for the kinds of everyday work at different levels of the system might predict the degree to which intended changes produce intended and unintended results that have consequential implications for the success of further policy development.

## REFERENCES

Apple, M. W. (1994). Texts and contexts. The state and gender in educational policy. *Curriculum Inquiry, 24*, 349–359.

Artiles, A. J., Kozleski, E. B., Trent, S., Osher, D., & Ortiz, A. (2010). Justifying and explaining disproportionality, 1968–2008: A critique of underlying views of culture. *Exceptional Children, 76*, 279–299.

Artiles, A. J., Kozleski, E. B., Waitoller, F., & Lukinbeal, C. (2011). Inclusive education and the interlocking of ability and race in the U.S.: Notes for an educational equity research program. In A. J. Artiles, E. B. Kozleski, & F. Waitoller (Eds.), *Inclusive education: Examining equity on five continents* (pp. 45–68). Cambridge, MA: Harvard Education Press.

Artiles, A. J., Thorius, K. A. K., Bal, A., Waitoller, F., Neal, R., & Hernandez-Saca, D. (2011). Beyond culture as group traits: Future learning disabilities ontology, epistemology, and research knowledge use. *Learning Disabilities Quarterly, 34,* 167–179.

Ball, S. J., & Exley, S. (2010). Making policy with "good ideas": Policy networks and the intellectuals of New Labour. *Journal of Education Policy, 25,* 151–169.

Barrera, I., & Corso, R. M. (2002). Cultural competency as skilled dialogue. *Topics in Early Childhood Special Education, 22,* 103–113.

Braun, A., Maguire, M., & Ball, S. J. (2010). Policy enactments in the UK secondary school: Examining policy, practice and school positioning. *Journal of Education Policy, 25,* 547–60.

Covey, S. R. (1989). *The 7 habits of highly effective people: Powerful lessons in personal change.* New York, NY: Free Press.

Dyson, A., & Kozleski, E. B. (2008). Disproportionality in special education: A transatlantic phenomenon. In L. Florian & M. McLaughlin (Eds.), *Dilemmas and alternatives in the classification of children with disabilities: New perspectives* (pp. 170–190). Thousand Oaks, CA: Corwin Press.

Engeström, Y. (1999). Activity theory and individual and social transformation. In Y. Engeström, R. Miettinen, & R.-L. Punamaki (Eds.), *Perspectives on activity theory* (pp. 19–38). Cambridge, United Kingdom: Cambridge University Press.

Freire, P. (1998). *Pedagogy of freedom: Ethics, democracy, and civic courage* (P. Clarke, Trans.). Lanham, MD: Rowman & Littlefield.

Fuller, B. (2009). Policy and place: Learning from decentralized reforms. In G. Sykes, B. Schneider, & D. N. Plank (Eds.), *The handbook of education policy research* (pp. 855–876). New York, NY: Routledge.

Geier, R., Blumenfeld, P. C., Marx, R. W., Krajcik, F. S., Fishman, B., Soloway, E., & Clay-Chambers, J. (2008). Standardized test outcomes for students engaged in inquiry-based science curricula in the context of urban reform. *Journal of Research in Science Teaching, 45*(8), 922–939.

George, P. S., Stevenson, C., Thomason, J., & Beane, J. (1992). *The middle school— and beyond.* Alexandria, VA: ASCD.

Gladwell, M. (2000). *The tipping point: How little things can make a big difference.* Boston, MA: Little, Brown.

Good, T. L. (2011). Reflections on editing the Elementary School Journal in an era of constant reform. *The Elementary School Journal, 112,* 1–15.

Great Lakes Equity Center. (2013). *Critical reflections on policy.* [Audio podcast] Indianapolis, IN: Author. Retrieved from glec.education.iupui.edu/podcasts/

Habermas, J. (1981). New social movements. *Telos, 49,* 33–37.

Heimans, S. (2012). Education policy, practice, and power. *Educational Policy, 26*(3), 369–393.

Holburn, S., Jacobson, J. W., & Vietze, P. M. (2000). Quantifying the process and outcomes of person-centered planning. *American Journal on Mental Retardation, 5,* 402–417.

Individuals With Disabilities Education Act, 20 U.S.C. § 1400 (2004).

Joseph, L. B. (Ed). (2001). *Education policy for the 21st century: Challenges and opportunities in standards-based reform.* Chicago, IL: University of Chicago.

Koyama, J., & Varenne, H. (2012). Assembling and dissembling: Policy as productive play. *Educational Researcher, 41,* 157–162.

Kozleski, E. B., & Artiles, A. J. (in press). Mediating systemic change in educational systems through sociocultural methods. In P. Smeyers, K. U. Leuven, D. Bridges, N. Burbules, & M.Griffiths (Eds.), *International handbook of interpretation in educational research methods.* New York, NY: Springer.

Kozleski, E. B., & Skelton, S. (April, 2007). *Culturally responsive educational leadership.* Louisville, KY: Council for Exceptional Children Annual Meeting.

Kozleski, E. B., & Smith, A. (2009). The role of policy and systems change in creating equity for students with disabilities in urban schools. *Urban Education, 44,* 427–451.

Kozleski, E. B., & Waitoller, F. R. (2010). Teacher learning for inclusive education: Understanding teaching as a cultural and political practice. *International Journal of Inclusive Education, 14,* 655–666.

Laswell, H. (1936). *Who gets what, when and how.* New York, NY: Whittlesey House.

Levinson, B., Sutton, M., & Winstead, T. (2009). Education policy as a practice of power: Theoretical tools, ethnographic methods, democratic options. *Educational Policy, 23,* 767–795.

Lipman, P. (2011). *The new political economy of urban education: Neoliberalism, race, and the right to the city.* Florence, KY: Routledge, Taylor & Francis Group.

Macey, E., Thorius, K.A.K., & Skelton, S. M. (2012). *Engaging school communities in critical reflections on policy,* Equity by Design,Indianapolis, IN: Great Lakes Equity Center. Retrieved from glec.education.iupui.edu/Images/site%20photos/ Critical%20Reflection%20on%20Policy.pdf

McDonnell, L. (2009). A political science perspective on education policy analysis. In G. Sykes, B. Schneider, & D. N. Plank (Eds.), *The handbook of education policy research* (pp. 57–70). New York, NY: Routledge.

McLaughlin, I., & Mongeon, D. J. (2012). *Eight essential elements for strong public health policies* [PowerPoint slides]. Oakland, CA: Public Health Law & Policy. Retrieved from changelabsolutions.org/sites/phlpnet.org/files/Eight_Essential_ Elements_for_Strong_Public_Health_20120113.pdf

National Center for Education Statistics. (2011). *The nation's report card: Trial urban district assessment mathematics 2011* (NCES 2012-452). Washington, DC: U.S. Department of Education, Institute of Education Sciences, National Center for Education Statistics.

National Institute for Urban School Improvement (NIUSI). (2006). *Systemic change framework rubrics assessment handbook.* Tempe, AZ: Author.

National Middle School Association. (2003). *This we believe: Successful schools for young adolescents.* Westerville, OH: Author.

O'Brien, J. (1987). A guide to life-style planning: Using the Activities Catalogue to integrate services and natural support systems. In G. T. Bellamy & B. Wilcox (Eds.), *A comprehensive guide to the Activities Catalogue: An alternative curriculum for youth and adults with severe disabilities* (pp. 175–189). Baltimore, MD: Brookes.

O'Brien, J., O'Brien, L., & Mount, B. (1997). Person-centered planning has arrived . . . or has it? *Mental Retardation, 35,* 480–488.

Office of the State Superintendent of Education. (2012). *Historic AYP report: DC Public Schools*. Washington, DC: Author.

Opfer, V. D. (2009). Commentary: Getting "critically real" about the state of education politics and policy process research. In G. Sykes, B. Schneider, & D. N. Plank (Eds.), *The handbook of education policy research* (pp. 402–406). New York, NY: Routledge.

Pearpoint, J., O'Brien, J., & Forest, M. (1993). *PATH: A workbook for planning positive possible futures and planning alternative tomorrows with hope for schools, organizations, businesses, and families* (2nd ed.). Toronto, Canada: Inclusion Press.

Rowan, B., Correnti, R., Miller, R. J., & Camburn, E. (2009). School improvement by design: Lessons from a study of comprehensive school reform programs. In G. Sykes, B. Schneider, & D. N. Plank (Eds.), *The handbook of education policy research* (pp. 637–651). New York, NY: Routledge.

Scheurich, J. J., McKenzie, K. B., & Skrla, L. (2011). The equity road: Five examples of successful reform in urban schools and districts. *Journal of Education for Students Placed at Risk, 16*(2), 65–66.

Spillane, J. P., Gomez, L. M., & Mesler, L. (2009). Notes on reframing the role of organizations in policy implementation: Resource for practice, in practice. In G. Sykes, B. Schneider, & D. N. Plank (Eds.), *The handbook of education policy research* (pp. 409–425). New York, NY: Routledge.

Stahl, B. C. (2008). Empowerment through ICT: A critical discourse analysis of the Egyptian ICT policy. In C. Avgerou, M. L. Smith, & P. Van den Besselaar (Eds.), *Social dimensions of information and communication technology policy* (pp. 161–177). New York, NY: Springer.

Stevens, E. E., Patrick, T. E., & Pickler, R. ( 2009). A history of infant feeding. *Journal of Perinatal Education: Advancing Normal Birth, 18*, 32–39.

Thorius, K.A.K., & Maxcy, B. D. (2012, April). *A critical practice framework for examination of special education policy appropriation*. Paper presented at the annual meeting of the American Educational Research Association. Vancouver, Canada.

United States Department of Education. (2012). *Obama administration approves two more states for NCLB flexibility–More than half of the country now approved for waivers, more to follow* [Press release]. Washington, DC: Author.

Wiggins, G., & McTighe, J. (1998). *Understanding by design*. Alexandria, VA: ASCD.

# Epilogue

## And the Quest Continues

*Kathleen King Thorius and Elizabeth B. Kozleksi*

Perhaps you picked up this book because you are a teacher like Kris, the vignette protagonist in Chapter 3, with a strong commitment to carrying out your career in urban settings. Maybe you are a community organizer like Chapter 4 coauthor Sandra Vazquez who leads an educational advocacy organization focused on empowering immigrant parents in special education processes. Or maybe you are a "faceless bureaucrat," pondering "special education, disability, and White privilege" (Smith, 2001, p. 180) like National Institute for Urban School Improvement (NIUSI) project officer and Chapter 1 coauthor, Anne Smith, who considers, as well, ways in which "social interaction and physical proximity conspire to blur the boundaries of *us*, *them*, and *the other* through shared experience and increased understanding of shared humanity" (p. 181). There's nowhere like our urban centers—and indeed our urban schools—to examine and build our understandings of human diversity and shared experience. In these urban schools, we've seen communities engaged in activities toward this end, resulting in a renewed commitment for some and a new pledge by others that the creation of inclusive schools is an equity imperative (Kozleski, Sullivan, & King 2009).

Whoever you are, and whatever your stake in urban education reform, we hope that you have seen yourself and others like you in this book; it is written for you and by people who also have worked on the project of transforming schools to more just, safer, and intellectually challenging spaces. As the discussion of power, privilege, and oppression woven throughout the volume underscores, the voices and decision-making authority at the urban reform table need to be inclusive enough so that we all share in leading the decisions made around it. This takes conscious work on all of our parts, through which we learn from each other and from critical reflection on the mistakes, tragedies, and triumphs of our collective and individual pasts and current contexts (i.e., cultural historical analysis).

As Ladson-Billings (2012) says, "the children who walk through the doors of the nation's schools are the best Black, Brown, Yellow, Red, and

White children we have and until we truly recognize and embrace that reality we will continue to look through a glass darkly" (p. 120). There are also students labeled with disabilities in urban educational systems, those from minority and majority religious, as well as atheist traditions, those who identify as lesbian, gay, bisexual, transgender, questioning, queer, or intersex (LGBTQI), those from immigrant and other world language backgrounds. Together, these children are ours and they are the very best. We embrace them with our hopes and dreams but also with leadership from them and us for the future. If you are an urban school student, you are at the core of the education system: the reason we are who we are and do what we do. Yet every day many like you are disenfranchised, disrespected, and neglected. Every day many like you are challenged, fired up, and inspired by what you are learning about yourself, your communities, and your world. As Zion and Petty remind us in Chapter 2, urban reform that actually transforms the system so that all students are fired up about learning must rely on *you* to define the problems to be addressed by school change efforts. What's unjust, boring, incorrect, or out of touch about school leaders, teachers, curriculum, instruction, classrooms, policies and rules, expectations, and buildings? How and what should school personnel learn about you and your families and communities? And what roles need to be rethought, created, or eliminated in order for you to take your place at the head of the reform table? In other words, beyond just being asked to critique what's wrong, how are you provided with opportunities to design solutions and act upon them? Further, consistent with how Kozleski and Artiles expand our notions of what learning is and how to support it in Chapter 3, what about your school culture provides learning affordances (e.g., cool learning spaces, latest technologies), and to what extent is learning something you do with your peers, socially and in conversation about the things that get under your skin, make you tick, and keep you up at night? The answers to all these questions should drive our efforts to make urban schools as great as the students like you whom they serve.

Not only are families students' first teachers, they are their most persistent teachers, as it is through your ways of knowing, being, and sharing your histories with your children throughout their lives that they come to see their possible place and potential in the world. As Chapter 4 contemplates, however, not only are there times when you are made to feel unwelcome in urban schools, but sometimes you are treated as inferior and incapable of making the best educational decisions for your children. That can hurt, anger, and incite, all at once. Through Santamaría Graff and Vazquez's depiction of Beatriz's conscious and conscientious resistance to the institutional structures and the individual treatment she received from some educators and special education service providers, dominant narratives of your apathy and ignorance are excavated and countered, and replaced with the truth: You are capable, you care, and you are resourced.

If you are a pre- or inservice urban teacher, regardless of your content area or status as a veteran or novice, or special or general educator, Gonzalez and Mulligan (Chapter 5) define your charge to design your classroom as your most crucial activity in urban education reform. It is through careful and critical reflection and planning that you set up expectations for how students are to engage and interact with the curriculum, you, and each other and create a space in which every student matters, leads, experiences success, and grows in her or his empowerment to impact the multiple formal and informal learning environments they will encounter throughout their lives. Chapters 3 and 5 provide you with examples of your colleagues dedicated to these practices in their daily praxis. And Chapter 6, which provides a framework for urban teacher learning, emphasizes that we educators who are serious about urban education reform are concerned not only in building our capacity to serve urban students, families, and communities, but to critique our collective and individual role in marginalizing, essentializing, and oppressing those we serve and have served. Whether our positionality aligns us with historically minoritized or dominant groups—or both—this is difficult and emotional work, but crucial to transforming urban systems. We thank you for the millions of hours and tireless efforts you give to doing this work, often in spite of discouraging conditions, poor resources, and constraining political environments, as we witnessed over the life of the NIUSI project.

Chapter 7 depicts two principals who define their roles around disrupting inequitable educational practices that had crystallized over time. If you are a building leader—a principal, dean of students, vice/assistant principal, teacher coach—you know that many times such work is unwelcome, as disturbing the way things are makes those who benefit from them uncomfortable, even angry. You may have had significant ratios of personnel ask for a transfer after you entered a new building eager to lead by building coalitions with communities and educators, only to find resistance, particularly as has been the experience of many leaders of color responsible for schools composed of mostly White educators who hold deficit-grounded assumptions about urban students, families, and communities—your students, families, and communities—as rationale for why the change you propose is doomed for failure. However, this chapter also gives hope in illustrating the kinds of shifts in school culture that are possible when leaders build trust with their school communities, are transparent and distributive in their leadership and decision making, and center inquiry into equity concerns in their leadership plans and activities.

As Sullivan, Abplanalp, and Jorgensen drive home in Chapter 8, successful urban district leaders are not technocrats, as appeared to be the primary role of the superintendent in Chapter 10's vignette. Rather, they work concurrently in technical, contextual, and critical arenas of policy and practice. The decision to work with NIUSI in order to restructure a "categorical, label-driven" special education program "model into one that today is recognized as highly inclusive and collaborative" required consideration of policy and practice not only focused on technical issues such as scheduling, coplanning time, and building facilities, but also addressing beliefs that some students were better off educated separately from their nondisabled peers and examining underlying assumptions that fueled such beliefs. The Madison District leaders asked not only how and why the inclusiveness of their system needed to be improved, but also focused on retooling the school and classroom environments into which students with disabilities were to be included.

Hart-Tervalon and Garcia's Chapter 9 presents the efforts engaged and the tensions experienced by state education agents trying to reform raced outcomes such as special education overrepresentation in districts across their states. Given the ways that federal education policy positions SEAs as emphasized in Chapter 10, it is particularly notable that the Wisconsin Department of Public Instruction was able to expand and in some ways resist their role definition as compliance monitors.

Our discussion in Chapter 10 unpacks a theory behind and key features of policy like those developed by the WDPI that sticks in local contexts: It centers marginalized perspectives, it intends to emancipate rather than constrain, and it is transparent in installation and impact. Even if the tools we described in Chapter 10 are not immediately useful to you, we hope the design principles that governed creation of these and many tools developed over the course of NIUSI's 12-year existence are valuable to you in searching for the holy grail of urban education reform. While we haven't found it yet, we are bolstered by what we've witnessed in our partnerships with federal bureaucrats, state education agents, district administrators, building leaders, educators, students, family members, and community activists along the way. We do believe it is out there.

## REFERENCES

Kozleski, E. B., Sullivan, A. L., & King, K. A. (February, 2009). *How early intervening transforms practice: Equity as an education imperative.* Paper presented at the annual convention of the National Association of School Psychologists, Boston, MA.

Ladson-Billings, G. (2012). Through a glass darkly: The persistence of race in education research and scholarship. *Educational Researcher, 41,* 115–120.

Smith, A. (2001). A faceless bureaucrat ponders special education, disability, and White privilege. *Research and Practice for Persons with Severe Disabilities, 26,* 180–188.

# About the Editors and Contributors

*Elizabeth B. Kozleski* is the chair of the Special Education Department at the University of Kansas. Her work theorizing systems change for equity, inclusive education, and professional learning for urban schools regularly appears in national and international publications. She works with colleagues to advance systems transformation in schools, districts, teacher education, and state education agencies. She was awarded the UNESCO Chair in Inclusive International Research in 2005, received the 2011 TED-Merrill award for her leadership in special education teacher education, and was honored by the University of Northern Colorado with the 2013 Century of Scholars award. Her research interests include analyzing models of systems change in urban and large school systems, examining how teachers learn in practice in complex and diverse school settings, researching multicultural educational practices in the classroom to improve student learning, and examining the impact of professional learning schools on student and teacher learning. She recently coauthored *Inclusive Education: Examining Equity on Five Continents* (2011, Harvard Education Press). She has been the principal investigator of four technical assistance centers (NCCRESt, NIUSI, NIUSI-LeadScape, Region IX Equity Assistance Center) focused on reform and equity issues, statewide improvement grants, a number of personnel preparation projects, and research grants from private foundations as well as the U.S. Department of Education. Kozleski has been an advisor to the Council for Exceptional Children, the Teacher Education Division, the American Association of Colleges of Teacher Education, the Colorado Partnership for Educational Renewal, the National Center for Educational Outcomes, the American Institutes for Research, the National Board for Professional Teaching Standards, National Institutes for Health, TASH, and a variety of state and local education agencies.

*Kathleen King Thorius* serves as an assistant professor of urban special education in Indiana University's School of Education at Indiana University–Purdue University Indianapolis (IUPUI). She was recently named by IUPUI's chancellor as the university's Diversity Scholar of the Year and is

Principal Investigator for the Great Lakes Equity Center, a Regional Equity Assistance Center funded by the U.S. Department of Education. Thorius's work examines policy and practice related to eliminating racial and linguistic disproportionality in special education, including response to multitiered intervention frameworks, and educators' equity-focused professional learning. Previously Thorius was a codirector at the Equity Alliance at Arizona State University, which was the Region IV Equity Assistance Center, and served as the professional learning coordinator for two U.S. Department of Education national technical assistance and dissemination centers: the National Center for Culturally Responsive Educational Systems (NCCRESt) and the National Institute for Urban School Improvement (NIUSI). Thorius has a strong record of facilitating partnerships with state departments of education and school districts to create inclusive, culturally responsive educational systems. She also has extensive experience developing professional development resources and providing equity-oriented professional development to states, districts, institutes of higher education, and professional organizations.

**Susan L. Abplanalp** is the deputy superintendent and chief learning officer of the Madison Metropolitan School District in Madison, Wisconsin. She has been part of the district for 23 years. She is a nationally recognized speaker, consultant, and coach whose professional life has been dedicated to addressing equity and creating opportunities for children who are marginalized and oppressed by the education system. Author of the 2007 book *Breaking the Low-Achieving Mindset: A Journey of Purposeful Change*, her leadership and advocacy are admired and respected.

**Cynthia Alexander** is currently the instruction leadership director for the Shelby County Schools, a newly redistricted school system comprised of schools in Memphis, Tennessee and its surrounding suburban areas. Her previous positions include teacher, assistant principal, district staff development coordinator, and principal. As a lifelong learner, she is also a candidate for a doctoral degree in curriculum and instructional leadership with an emphasis in urban education at the University of Memphis. She truly believes that the success of an organization, department, or individual school is accomplished through the collective efforts of families, teachers, coaches, staff, and administrators.

**Alfredo J. Artiles** is the Ryan Harris Memorial Endowed Professor at Arizona State University. His scholarly interests include education policy and cultural analysis of disability and other sociocultural differences. He is a Spencer Foundation/National Academy of Education postdoctoral fellow and a resident fellow at Stanford University's Center for Advanced Study in the Behavioral Sciences. Artiles coedits the *International Multilingual Research Journal* and Teachers College Press's book series *Disability, Culture, and Equity*. He is a former vice president and a fellow of the American Educational Research Association. His most recent (coauthored) book is *Inclusive Education: Examining Equity on Five Continents* (Harvard Education Press).

**David R. Garcia** is an associate professor in the Mary Lou Fulton Teachers College at Arizona State University. Prior to ASU, he served as the Associate Superintendent of Public Instruction for the state of Arizona. His academic publications focus on school choice, accountability, and the factors that facilitate or distort policy implementation in public education. Garcia received a bachelor of arts degree and honors diploma from Arizona State University. He holds master of arts and doctor of philosophy degrees from the University of Chicago in education policy, research, and institutional studies.

**Dorothy Garrison-Wade**, PhD, is an associate professor and associate dean for Faculty Affairs in the School of Education and Human Development at the University of Colorado-Denver. She has served in public and private schools as a secondary school principal, counselor, secondary and postsecondary teacher, and researcher. These experiences spur her research agenda on inclusive leadership, which explores access to equitable and fair educational opportunities for individuals, regardless of race, disability, gender, or social status. Garrison-Wade's numerous publications and presentations aspire to transform the field of educational leadership by advocating change in oppressive social structures and institutions.

**JoEtta Gonzales** has spent the last 25 years as a teacher, principal, national Equity Assistance Center director, and district administrator who is passionate about equity in public education. While in these roles she introduced and implemented multiple initiatives related to educational equity and systemic school reform. She earned her doctorate in educational leadership and policy development from Arizona State University with a focus on leading diverse school communities. In addition to her work in K–12 education, she also taught university courses in bilingual and multicultural special education. She currently lives in Reno, Nevada, where she works as an area school superintendent.

**Taucia Gonzalez** is a doctoral student in Arizona State University's Mary Lou Fulton Teachers College. Her research focuses on using students' out-of-school literacy practices to inform in-school literacy instruction for students living at the intersection of language, ethnicity, and ability differences. Her experience working as an educator in an urban dual-language school taught her that students enter school with knowledge and tools; they just need opportunities to learn how to use them in new ways and new contexts. She believes that educational reform does not mean fixing students, but rather fixing the systems they enter.

**Donna Hart-Tervalon** has more than 35 years of combined experience in the field of education/special education that includes cross-categorical teaching (pre-K–16), early childhood and special education consulting, grant writing, and developing, implementing, and evaluating programs for public and private educational agencies. Hart-Tervalon has taught undergraduate- and graduate-level courses and provided professional development to educators on issues of equity, diversity, cultural awareness, and culturally responsive practices. Her current educational reform focus is on promoting, supporting, and advancing racial equity initiatives and projects. She is the recipient of several awards and honors for her work in addressing issues of racial disproportionality and advancing racial equity for all students and families.

**Jack Jorgensen** has served as associate dean for Partnerships and Outreach Services at the University of Wisconsin–Madison School of Education since 2008. Prior to this appointment, Jack was employed for 22 years with the Madison Metropolitan School District, the last 10 as executive director for the Department of Educational Services. During this period of time he led major district reform and improvement efforts in special education that received national recognition. Jack received his PhD in special education from the University of Wisconsin–Madison. He has presented at numerous national and state conferences on topics related to inclusive education, creating collaborative and culturally responsive schools, and addressing the disproportionate representation of students of color in special education.

**Elaine Mulligan** has been the project director of the National Dissemination Center for Children with Disabilities (NICHCY) since March of 2011. In this position, she develops dissemination resources, provides technical assistance in dissemination planning, monitors emerging technologies to identify new dissemination strategies and outlets, and oversees social media and other web-based technology applications for dissemination. Prior to joining NICHCY, Elaine was the assistant director of the NIUSI-LeadScape principal leadership academy initiative. She's an experienced special educator who is committed to the well-being of individuals with disabilities and those who care for and about them.

**Sheryl Petty** has worked in educational systems change and organizational development for nearly 20 years. She has been a consultant to districts, nonprofits, foundations, and schools, and is a principal associate at the Annenberg Institute for School Reform, and an associate consultant with Movement Strategy Center (Oakland, California) and Management Assistance Group (Washington, DC). She was a fellow at Stanford University's Center for Opportunity Policy in Education; executive director of California Tomorrow; and program manager at the Stupski Foundation. Petty is lead designer for the Transforming Education Systems Alliance, focused on promoting aligned approaches to democratic education. She holds an EdD in educational leadership and change. Her expertise includes equity-driven change process facilitation, visioning, analysis, and coaching.

**Cristina Santamaría Graff** is an assistant professor in special education at Central Washington University in Ellensburg, Washington. Her background is in bilingual special education and her research interests include immigrant families of children with disabilities, the intersecting space of dis/ability and cultural and/or language difference, participatory action research, and authentic collaboration of stakeholders within special education. She believes that inclusion extends to all stakeholders involved in the education and learning of all students, with or without disabilities. Consequently, social equity, compassion, mutual respect, and understanding are at the heart of transformational educational reform.

**Samantha Paredes Scribner**'s research and teaching focus on the organizational and political dynamics within and around urban K–12 schools, the policy contexts of these dynamics, and the consequences of leadership practices within and around such schools for various constituents of urban school communities. She is currently investigating the ways in which schools (and leaders) in urban settings, serving high percentages of ethnolinguistically and racially diverse students and families, navigate current reform context, and the implications on educational equity and social justice. Her recent work focuses on Latino immigrant school–family engagement and urban principal professional identity.

**Anne Smith** worked as an education research analyst at the U.S. Department of Education Office of Special Education Programs from 1989 to 2011 to improve policy, practice, and research efforts to increase the inclusion of children with special needs into systemic education improvement initiatives. Her efforts, focused on creating equitable partnerships to improve teaching and learning, emphasized the importance of families and communities in school improvement. Following this Sisyphean effort, Anne retired and left the Baltimore–Washington area for life as an old crone in idyllic Ithaca, New York.

*Amanda L. Sullivan* is an assistant professor at the University of Minnesota. Sullivan received her doctorate in school psychology from Arizona State University. Her research examines education and health disparities affecting diverse learners with special needs. She is particularly interested in understanding the ecological and interpersonal factors that place children and youth at risk for educational disabilities and mental health problems, the treatment of diverse learners in education, and professional issues related to providing evidence-based school psychological services for diverse learners.

*Sandra L. Vazquez* is a first-generation immigrant from Mexico. She is the mother of two children, the youngest having been born medically fragile and with severe cerebral palsy. She has been a parent/peer advocate with Pilot Parents of Southern Arizona for 22 years. Having to overcome the barriers of language and culture, she has dedicated herself to making the journey of newly diagnosed children and their parents easier by providing information on community resources for the equalization of opportunities. This equalization is the process through which resources are distributed so that every individual, including those with disabilities, have an equal opportunity to participate in society.

*Shelley Zion* works in the School of Education at the University of Colorado, Denver. She teaches and conducts research on topics related to student voice, school reform, and social justice. Her work is situated within a framework of sociopolitical development, informed by a range of critical theoretical perspectives, and advanced by an understanding of the nature of both individual and systemic change. To do this work is to disrupt dominant ideologies by creating spaces in which people begin to develop a critical understanding of the cultural, political, economic, and other institutional forces that perpetuate systems of privilege and oppression.

# Index

Laswell, H., 230
Latinos
  access to higher education and
    employment, 64
  family resistance and, 80–82, 85, 87,
    88–89, 92–99, 242–243
  special education referrals, 25, 199–214,
    222–223
  as urban school principals, 153–161,
    163–174
  in urban schools, 13
Lave, J., 96, 138
Leachman, G., 43
Leadscape (National Institute for Urban
  School Improvement), 143
Learning affordances, 69–70
Learning communities, 23
  classroom culture and, 6, 110–113, 115,
    127–131, 132
  teacher communities of practice, 138–
    139, 141–142
Lee, Carol D., 13, 14, 111–112
Lee, L., 39
Leithwood, K. A., 162–163, 166
Lemke, J., 14
Leonardo, Z., 12, 22
Leont'ev, Aleksei, 14
Levin, B., 36, 46, 56
Levine, P., 176
Levinson, B., 224
Lewin, K., 14
Lewis, A. E., 145–146
Lewis, G., 100
Lieberman, A., 135, 137
Lincoln, Y., 35–36
Lindsey, R., 47–48
Lin, P., 142
Linton, C., 117, 207
Lipman, P., 13, 22, 217, 226, 231
LISTEN, Inc., 51, 52–53
Liston, D., 145
Little, J. W., 139, 140
Livingston, S., 74–75
Lopez, E. J., 82
Losen, Dan J., 25, 202, 203, 211
Louis, K. S., 139
Lucas, T., 84
Luppescu, S., 139
Lusi, S. F., 201, 208
Lyter, D. M., 145

Macedo, D., 119, 121
Mace, D. P., 135, 137
Macey, E., 234, 235
Madeline (teacher), 72–73, 75–76
Madison Metropolitan School District
  (MMSD), 8, 174–195, 244
Maguire, M., 235
Maguire, P., 92
Marginalization
  engaging student voice, 42–43
  of historically underserved families,
    81–83, 86–87, 89, 100
  power sharing and, 42–43
  school culture and, 125
  student learning and, 5, 18–19, 64–65,
    72–73
Marx, R. W., 217
Mauer, R., 89–90
Maxcy, B. D., 200, 217, 224, 225
McDonnell, L., 230, 232
McGregor, G., 157
McIntosh, P., 161
McKenzie, K. B., 83, 217
McLaren, P., 7, 142
McLaughlin, I., 234
McLaughlin, J., 35–36
McLaughlin, M. W., 76, 140
McMahon, A., 139
McTighe, J., 125, 236–237
Meagher, C., 183
Menchaca-Lopez, E., 82
Mental maps, 68
Mesler, L., 222
MetLife Foundation, 37
Metzger, D., 39
Meyer, J., 49, 209
Microaggressions, 19
Middle schools, 228–229
Middleton High School (pseudonym), 134–
  135, 140–141, 143–144, 145, 146–147
Miller, R. J., 223, 228
Milner, H. R., 141, 145, 146
Miramontes, O., 43
Moje, E. B., 90–91
Moll, L. C., 5, 86
Mongeon, D. J., 234
Monk, D. H., 201
Monzó, L. D., 89
Moral skills, 46–47, 48
Morocco, C. C., 135